Marx and Lincoln:
An Unfinished Revolution

Marx and Lincoln:
An Unfinished Revolution

Robin Blackburn

VERSO

London • New York

First published by Verso 2011
© the collection Verso 2011
Introduction © Robin Blackburn 2011

1 3 5 7 9 10 8 6 4 2

Verso
UK: 6 Meard Street, London W1F 0EG
US: 20 Jay Street, Suite 1010, Brooklyn, NY 11201
www.versobooks.com

Verso is the imprint of New Left Books

ISBN-13: 978-1-84467-722-1

British Library Cataloguing in Publication Data
A catalogue record for this book is available from the British Library

Library of Congress Cataloging-in-Publication Data
A catalog record for this book is available from the Library of Congress

Typeset by MJ Gavan, Truro, Cornwall
Printed in the US by Maple Vail

Contents

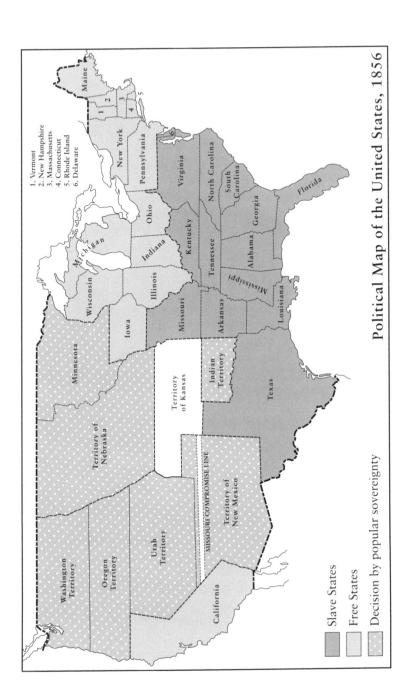

Political Map of the United States, 1856

- 1. Vermont
- 2. New Hampshire
- 3. Massachusetts
- 4. Connecticut
- 5. Rhode Island
- 6. Delaware

Slave States

Free States

Decision by popular sovereignty

Karl Marx and Abraham Lincoln: An Unfinished Revolution

In photographs Karl Marx and Abraham Lincoln both look the part of the respectable Victorian gentleman. But they were almost diametrically opposed in their attitude toward what was called at the time the social question. Lincoln happily represented railroad corporations as a lawyer. As a politician he was a champion of free wage labor. Karl Marx, on the other hand, was a declared foe of capitalism who insisted that wage labor was in fact wage slavery, since the worker was compelled by economic necessity to sell his defining human attribute—his labor power—because if he did not, his family would soon face hunger and homelessness.

Of course Marx's critique of capitalism did not deny that it had progressive features, and Lincoln's championing of the world of business did not extend to those whose profits stemmed directly from slaveholding. Each man placed a concept of unrewarded labor at the center of his political philosophy, and both opposed slavery on the grounds that it was intensively exploitative. Lincoln believed it to be his duty to defend the Union, which he saw as the momentous American experiment in representative democracy, by whatever means should prove necessary. Marx saw the democratic republic as the political form that would allow the working class to develop its capacity to lead society as a whole. He regarded US political institutions as a flawed early version of the republican ideal. With their "corruption" and "humbug," US political institutions did not offer a faithful representation of US society. Indeed, too often they supplied a popular veneer to the rule of the wealthy—with a bonus for slaveholders. But Marx's conclusion was that they should become more democratic, broadening the scope of freedom of association, removing all forms of privilege, and extending free public education.[1]

As a young man Marx had seriously considered moving to the United States, perhaps to Texas. He went so far as to write to the mayor of Trier, the town where he had been born, to request an *Auswanderungschein*, or emigration certificate. In the following year he wrote an article considering the ideas of the "American National Reformers," whose comparatively modest original aims—the distribution of 160 acres of public land to anyone willing to cultivate it—he recognized as justified and promising: "We know that this movement strives for a result that, to be sure, would further the industrialism of modern bourgeois society, but that ... as an attack on land ownership ... especially under the existing conditions ... must drive it towards communism."[2] (The idea of distributing public land in this way did indeed have explosive implications, as we will see, and the new smallholders did often lack the resources needed to flourish, as Marx predicted, but his idea that they would therefore embrace "communism" was more than a stretch.) In 1849, writing as editor of Germany's leading revolutionary democratic journal, the *Neue Rheinische Zeitung*, Marx praised the frugal budget and republican institutions of the United States in comparison with the bloated bureaucracy and unaccountability of the Prussian monarchy. [3]

Subsequently Marx remained fascinated by events in the US, and for ten years—1852 to 1861—he became the London correspondent of one of its leading newspapers, the *New York Daily Tribune*. The invitation to write for the *Tribune* came from Charles Dana, its editor, who had met Marx in Cologne in 1848 when Marx was in charge of the *Neue Rheinische Zeitung*. Marx accepted Dana's

---

1   August Nimtz, *Marx and Engels: Their Contribution to the Democratic Breakthrough*, Albany 2000.
2   Karl Marx, "American Soil and Communism," in *Karl Marx on America and the Civil War*, Saul Padover, ed., New York 1971, pp. 3–6.
3   Karl Marx, "The American Budget and the Christian-German One," in *Karl Marx on America and the Civil War*, pp. 9–12. For Marx's emigration plans, see Padover's Introduction.

invitation, and for a decade this was his only paid employment. He contributed over 400 articles, 84 of which were published without a byline, as editorials. Although initially happy with the arrangement, Marx complained of the pay ($5 an article, later raised to $10), of the fact that he was not paid for pieces that were not published, and of the editorial mangling of what he had written. In one moment of particular vexation—he had received no fees for months—he confided to his friend Frederick Engels that the whole arrangement was one of pure exploitation:

> It is truly nauseating that one should be condemned to count it a blessing when taken aboard a blotting paper vendor such as this. To crush up bones, grind them and make them into a soup like [that given] to paupers in a workhouse—that is the political work to which one is constrained in such large measure in a concern like this ...[4]

On other occasions Marx expressed himself as pleased to find an outlet for his views and the results of his research into British social conditions. He wrote about the everyday problems of British workers, about the Indian mutiny, the Crimean War, Italian unification, French financial scandals, and Britain's disgraceful Opium Wars.[5]

For obvious reasons, the one topic Marx did not cover was events in the United States. In February 1861 the *Tribune* responded to the crisis by dropping all its foreign correspondents except Marx. However, the paper, finding room for few of his dispatches, soon ceased paying him. He accordingly found another outlet for his journalism, the Viennese paper *Die Presse*, which, unlike the *Tribune*, expected him to write about the extraordinary conflict unfolding in North America; most of the longer articles reprinted in this book first appeared in *Die Presse*.

Abraham Lincoln had a rather more unalloyed experience of exploitation as a young man, since he worked for no pay on his

---

4   These remarks are quoted in the introduction to an interesting selection of the articles, James Ledbetter's *Dispatches for the New York Tribune: Selected Journalism of Karl Marx*, London 2006, p. 8.
5   British military expeditions that forced China to open its ports to British suppliers of the drug, which was produced in dismal circumstances by exploited Indians.

father's farm until the age of twenty-one. Indeed, the elder Lincoln would hire out Abraham's services to other farmers, without handing over any payment to his son. In later life his relations with his father were cool and distant.[6] Marx obtained a doctorate from one of Germany's leading universities; Lincoln had only one year of formal education. Acquiring a license to practice law required no academic credential, but simply a judge willing to swear in the candidate and vouch that he was of good character. Working for a law firm was itself an education, one that evidently allowed Lincoln to hone his skills as a reasoner and advocate. His legal business prospered, and he came to embody the social mobility that was linked to the celebration of "free labor." As he was first a Whig and later a Republican, it is likely that he read quite a few of the articles Marx wrote for the *Tribune*, signed or otherwise, since this paper was favored by those interested in reform and the fate of the Republican Party. Marx was probably unaware of Lincoln, a one-term representative from Illinois, until the later 1850s, when Lincoln shot to prominence because of his debates with Stephen Douglas, as the two men contended to become senator for Illinois. Lincoln was nine years older than Marx; even so, it is still a little strange to read Marx's affectionate references to him as the "old man" in the mid-1860s.

Marx and Lincoln both saw slavery as a menace to the spirit of republican institutions. But Lincoln believed that the genius of the Constitution could cage and contain the unfortunate slaveholders until such time as it might be possible to wind up slavery in some gradual and compensated manner. Marx saw the progressive potential of the republic in a different light. Its institutions, however flawed, as least allowed the partisans of revolutionary change openly to canvass the need for organization against capitalism and expropriation of the slaveholders.

In this introduction I explore why two men who occupied very different worlds and held contrary views nevertheless coincided on an issue of historic importance and even brought those worlds into fleeting contact with one another, and how the Civil War and

---

6   Eric Foner, *The Fiery Trail: Abraham Lincoln and American Slavery*, New York 2010.

Reconstruction—which Eric Foner has called America's unfinished revolution[7]—offered great opportunities and challenges to Marx and to the supporters of the International in the United States. Furthermore, I will urge that the Civil War and its sequel had a larger impact on Marx than is often realized—and, likewise, that the ideas of Marx and Engels had a greater impact on the United States, a country famous for its imperviousness to socialism, than is usually allowed.

It is, of course, well known that Karl Marx was an enthusiastic supporter of the Union in the US Civil War and that on behalf of the International Workingmen's Association he drafted an address to Abraham Lincoln congratulating the president on his reelection in 1864. The US ambassador in London conveyed a friendly but brief response from the president. However, the antecedents and implications of this little exchange are rarely considered.

By the close of 1864 many European liberals and radicals were coming round to supporting the North, but Marx had done so from the outset. To begin with, the cause of the South had a definite appeal to liberals and radicals, partly because many of them distrusted strong states and championed the right of small nations to self-determination. Lincoln himself insisted in 1861 that the North was fighting to defend the Union, not to free the slaves. Many European liberals were impressed by the fact that the secessions had been carried out by reasonably representative assemblies. The slaves had had no say in the matter, but then very few blacks in the loyal states had a vote, either, and hundreds of thousands remained slaves.

If the Civil War was not about the defense of slavery, as many claimed, then the pure argument for Unionism was a weak one. Progressive opinion in Europe was supportive of a right to self-determination and in 1830 had not been at all disturbed when

---

7   Eric Foner, *Reconstruction: America's Unfinished Revolution*, New York, 1989. For further discussion of whether these events amounted to a revolution, finished or otherwise, see Philip Shaw Paludan, "What Did the Winners Win?" in *Writing the Civil War: the Quest to Understand*, James McPherson and William Cooper, eds., Columbia, SC, 1998, pp. 174–200. However, Foner's conclusions concerning the winners seem to me closer to the mark than Paludan's, as I will explain below.

Belgium separated from the Netherlands, nor would it be in 1905 when Norway split from Sweden. Had the Netherlands or Sweden resorted to war to defend these unions, they would have been widely condemned. Consider, also, that Garibaldi began his career as a freedom fighter in the late 1830s as a partisan of the Republic of Rio Grande do Sul, a breakaway from the Empire of Brazil. Marx himself denounced Britain's dominion over Ireland. In December 1860, Horace Greeley, who had just replaced Dana as editor of the New York *Tribune*, wrote an editorial arguing that though the Secession was very wrong, it should not be resisted by military means. There were also minority currents in the European labor and socialist movement who preferred Southern agrarianism to the commercial society of the North.

The attitude toward the war of many outside North America greatly depended on whether or not slavery was seen as a crucial stake in the conflict. Some members of the British government were inclined to recognize the Confederacy, and if they had done so this would have been a major boost to the South. But ever since 1807, when Britain abolished its Atlantic slave trade, the British government had made suppression of Atlantic slave trafficking central to the Pax Britannica. When Lord Palmerston, as foreign secretary, negotiated a free trade agreement with an Atlantic state, he invariably accompanied it with a treaty banning slave trading. During the Opium Wars, British war ships were sent by Palmerston to demand that China should allow the drug traffic to continue in the name of free trade and pay compensation to British merchants whose stock they had seized.[8] Marx found the hypocrisy of "Pam" and the British breathtaking:

> Their first main grievance is that the present American war is "not one for the abolition of slavery" and that, therefore, the high-minded Britisher, used to undertake wars of his own and interest himself in other people's wars only on the basis of 'broad humanitarian principles," cannot be expected to feel any sympathy for his Northern cousins.[9]

8   Jasper Ridely, *Lord Palmerston*, London 1970; see especially pp. 329–30, 346–7, 375–6, 403–4.
9   Karl Marx, "The American Question in England," *New York Daily Tribune*, October 11, 1861.

Withering as he was about the British government's humbug, he was well aware that large sections of the British people, including much of the working class, were genuinely hostile to slavery. The slaves in the British colonies had been emancipated during 1834–8, following a slave uprising in Jamaica and sustained, large-scale popular mobilizations in Britain itself. Public opinion was sensitized to the issue and uncomfortably aware of the country's dependence on slave-grown cotton. If it became apparent that the secessionists really were fighting simply to defend slavery, it would be extraordinarily difficult for the London government to recognize the Confederacy.

MARX REJECTS ECONOMIC EXPLANATIONS OF THE WAR

From the beginning, Marx was intensely scornful of those who supported what he saw as basically a slaveholders' revolt. He insisted that it was quite erroneous to claim, as some did, that this was a quarrel about economic policy. Summarizing what he saw as the wrongheaded view espoused by influential British voices, he wrote:

> The war between North and South [they claim] is a mere tariff war, a war between a tariff system and a free trade system, and England naturally stands on the side of free trade. It was reserved to the *Times* [of London] to make this brilliant discovery…The *Economist* expounded the theme further…Yes [they argued] it would be different if the war was waged for the abolition of slavery! The question of slavery, however, [they claim] has absolutely nothing to do with this war. Then as now, the *Economist* was a tireless advocate of the "free market."

Marx's unhesitating support for the North did not mean that he was unaware of its grave defects as a champion of free labor. He openly attacked the timidity of its generals and the venality of many of its public servants. Nevertheless he saw the Civil War as a decisive turning point in nineteenth-century history. A victory for the North would set the scene for slave emancipation and be a great step forward for the workers' cause on both sides of the

Atlantic. Support for the North was a touchstone issue, he believed, and it became central to his efforts to build the International Workingmen's Association.

Marx's political choice stemmed from an early analysis of the roots of the war in which he refused to define the struggle in the terms first adopted by the belligerents themselves. Marx's well-known conviction that politics is rooted in antagonistic social relations led him to focus on the structural features of the two sections, and the emergence therein of contradictory interests and forms of social life. Marx and Engels were quite well informed about US developments. Many of their friends and comrades had emigrated to the United States during the years of reaction that followed the failure of the European revolutions of 1848. With few exceptions those émigrés had gone to the North, especially the Northwest, rather than to the South. Marx and Engels corresponded with the émigrés and wrote for, and read, their newspapers.

Marx and Engels were well aware of the privileged position of slaveholders in the structure of the American state, but believed that this privilege was menaced by the growth of the North and Northwest. Lincoln's election was a threat to the Southern stranglehold on the republic's central institutions, as embodied in Supreme Court rulings, cross-sectional party alignments, and fugitive slave legislations. In July 1861 Marx writes to Engels:

> I have come to the conclusion that the conflict between the South and the North—for 50 years the latter has been climbing down, making one concession after another—has at last been brought to a head...by the weight which the extraordinary development of the Northwestern states has thrown into the scales. The population there, with its rich admixture of newly arrived Germans and Englishmen and, moreover, largely made up self-working farmers, did not, of course, lend itself so readily to intimidation as the gentlemen of Wall Street and the Quakers of Boston.[10]

One might wish this expressed a little more delicately and appreciatively—the Quakers had played a courageous role in resisting

---

10   Marx to Engels, July 1, 1861, from Karl Marx and Frederick Engels's *Collected Works*, Volume 41, *Marx and Engels 1860–64*, London 1985, p. 114.

the slaveholders—but it is quite true that many of the Germans and English who sought refuge in the United States after 1848 brought with them a secular radicalism that changed and strengthened the antislavery cause in the United States by broadening its base of support. Before considering the nature of what might be called the German corrective it will be helpful to look at the evolution of Marx's analysis.

The clear premise of Marx's argument is that the North was expanding at a faster pace than the South—as indeed it was. But Marx contends that it is the South that is consumed by the need to expand territorially. The expansion of the North and Northwest, as Marx well knew, was even more rapid, a reflection of a momentous industrial growth and far-reaching commercialization of farming. The North and the Northwest, with a combined population of 20 million, were now linked by an extensive network of railroads and canals. The South might talk about King Cotton, but the truth was that economic growth in the South was not at all as broadly based as that in the North. Cotton exports were growing, but little else. In 1800 the South had the same population as the North; by 1860, it was only a little more than half as large, 11 million persons, about 7.5 million being Southern whites and 3.5 million slaves.

In Marx's view, the South had three motives for territorial expansion. First, its agriculture exhausted the soil, and so planters were constantly in quest of new land. Second, the slave states needed to maintain their veto power in the Senate, and for this purpose needed to mint new slave states just as fast as new "free" states were recognized. Third, there was in the South a numerous class of restive young white men anxious to make their fortune, and the leaders of Southern society were persuaded that an external outlet must be found for them if they were not to become disruptive domestically.[11]

By itself the argument that there was a shortage of land in the

---

11 Karl Marx, "The North American Civil War," *Die Presse*, October 25, 1861. This text is reproduced in full in the present volume. However there is no space here to print all Marx's writings on the United States and the Civil War. These are to be found either in the *Collected Works*, or in the already-cited collection edited by Saul Padover, or in Karl Marx and Frederick Engels, *The Civil War in the United States*, third ed., New York 1961, pp. 57–71.

South has limited validity. Expansion of the railroads could have brought more lands into cultivation. Additionally, the planters could have made better use of fertilizers, as did planters in Cuba. If there was a shortage, it was a shortage of slaves, relative to the boom in the cotton plantation economy of the 1850s.

Combined with the third point—the mass of restless filibusters[12]—the shortage argument gained more purchase. There was no absolute shortage of land and slaves, but planters could offer only so much support to their children. Southern whites had large families, and there was a surplus of younger sons who wished to make their way in the world. In the 1850s these young men—with what Marx called their "turbulent longings"—had been attracted to "filibustering" expeditions aimed at Cuba and Nicaragua—just as similar adventurers had sought glory and fortune in Texas and Mexico. Their parents might not always approve of freelance methods, but did see the attraction of acquiring new lands.

Undoubtedly Marx's clinching argument was that which referred to political factors:

> In order to maintain its influence in the Senate, and through the Senate its hegemony over the United States, the South therefore requires a continual formation of new slave states. This, however, was only possible through conquest of foreign lands, as in the case of Texas, and through the transformation of the territories belonging to the United States first into slave territories and then into slave states.[13]

---

12 During this period the term *filibuster* meant an irregular military adventurer, particularly one from the United States who hoped to seize land abroad, especially in Latin America.

13 Marx, "The North American Civil War." Marx's stress on the centrality of political issues can be compared with the brilliant analysis offered by Barrington Moore Jr., in *The Social Origins of Dictatorship and Democracy* (New York 1969, pp. 111–58). Moore writes: "The fundamental issue became more and more whether the machinery of the Federal government should be used to support one society or the other" (p. 136). Although Moore's analysis stands up very well, it does not sufficiently register three vital aspects to which I will be paying particular attention: the rise of nationalism, the role of African American resistance, and the awakening of the working classes. Directly or indirectly, Marx's articles and letters do address these issues. For other accounts that were influenced by Marx, see Eric Foner, "The Causes of the American

He concluded:

> The whole movement was and is based, as one sees, on the *slave question*. Not in the sense of whether the slaves in the existing slave states should be emancipated or not, but whether twenty million free men of the North should subordinate themselves any longer to an oligarchy of three hundred thousand slaveholders.[14]

As social science and as journalism this was impressive, but it did not bring Marx to the political conclusion at which he aimed. The political subordination of Northerners—scarcely the equivalent of slavery—would be ended by Southern secession. Marx was focused on the possibility of destroying true chattel slavery, which he knew to be a critical component of the reigning capitalist order. He further insisted that it was folly to imagine that the slaveholders, aroused and on the warpath, would be satisfied by Northern recognition of the Confederacy. Rather, it would open the way to an aggressive South that would strive to incorporate the border states and extend slaveholder hegemony throughout North America. He reminded his readers that it was under Southern leadership that the Union had sought to introduce "the armed propaganda of slavery in Mexico, Central and South America."[15] Spanish Cuba, with its flourishing slave system, had already been singled out as the slave power's next prey.

Marx's argument and belief was that the real confrontation was between two social regimes, one based on slavery and the other on free labor: "The struggle has broken out because the two systems can no longer live peaceably side by side on the North American continent. It can only be ended by the victory of one system or the other." In this mortal struggle the North, however moderate its initial inclinations, would eventually be driven to revolutionary measures.

Civil War," in Foner's *Politics and Ideology in the Age of the Civil War* (Oxford 1980, pp. 15–33) and John Ashworth, *Slavery, Capitalism and Politics in the Antebellum Republic*, Vol. 2, *The Coming of the Civil War*, Cambridge 2007.
14   "The North American Civil War," p. 71.
15   "The North American Civil War," p. 71. Marx's argument was on target. See Robert May, *The Southern Dream of Caribbean Empire*, London 2002.

Marx believed that the polity favored by the Southern slave-owners was very different from the republic aspired to by Northerners. He did not spell out all his reasons, but he was essentially right about this. Southern slaveholders wished to see a Federal state that would uphold slave property; that would return and deter slave runaways, as laid down in the Fugitive Slave Act of 1850; and that would allow slaveholding Southerners access to Federal territories. The planters were happy that the antebellum state was modest in size and competence, since this meant low taxes and little or no inter-ference with their "peculiar institution."[16] They did not favor either high tariffs or expensive internal improvements. But this restricted view of the state was accompanied by provisions that affected the lives of Northerners in quite intimate ways. The fugitive slave law of 1850 required all citizens to cooperate with the Federal mar-shals in apprehending runaways. In the Southern view, slaveholders should be free to bring slaves to Federal territories, an importation seen as an unwelcome and unfair intrusion by migrants from the Northern states, whether they were antislavery or simply antiblack. Southerners had favored censorship of the Federal mail, to prevent its use for abolitionist literature. They supported a foreign policy that pursued future acquisitions suitable for plantation development. But they did not want a state that had the power to intervene in the special internal arrangements of the slave states themselves. For them, a Republican president with the power to appoint thousands of Federal officials in the Southern states and with no intention of suppressing radical abolitionists spelled great danger.

Marx did not support the North because he believed that its vic-tory would directly lead to socialism. Rather, he saw in South and North two species of capitalism—one allowing slavery, the other not. The then existing regime of American society and economy embraced the enslavement of four million people whose enforced toil produced the republic's most valuable export, cotton, as well as much tobacco, sugar, rice, and turpentine. Defeating the slave power was going to be difficult. The wealth and pride of the 300,000 sla-veholders (there were actually 395,000 slave owners, according to the 1860 Census, but at the time Marx was writing this had not yet

16   Robin Einhorn, *American Slavery, American Taxation*, Berkeley 2008.

been published) was at stake. These slaveholders were able to corrupt or intimidate many of the poor Southern whites, and they had rich and influential supporters among the merchants, bankers and textile manufacturers of New York, London and Paris. Defeating the slave power and freeing the slaves would not destroy capitalism, but it would create conditions far more favorable to organizing and elevating labor, whether white or black. Marx portrayed the wealthy slave owners as akin to Europe's aristocrats, and their removal as a task for the sort of democratic revolution he had advocated in the *Communist Manifesto* as the immediate aim for German revolutionaries.

LINCOLN ON MOB VIOLENCE AND THE RIGHT OF REVOLUTION

Lincoln, as a Whig brought up in Kentucky and southern Illinois, was quite familiar with the tensions created by slavery in the borderlands between South and North. His wife's close relatives were slaveholders; one of his great uncles owned forty slaves. As a moderate Whig and, later, moderate Republican, Lincoln was ready to uphold the legal and constitutional rights of slaveholders. But he worried about the nation's coherence and integrity. The earliest statement of his political philosophy, his speech "On the Perpetuation of Our Political Institutions," delivered at the Young Men's Lyceum in Springfield in 1838, gives expression to his pride in US political institutions. But it also expresses deep dismay at the growing streak of lawlessness he sees in American life. He was alarmed at rising antagonism stemming from race, slavery and abolition, citing the summary execution of blacks believed to be plotting rebellion; the wanton killing of a mulatto; and attacks on law-abiding abolitionists by violent mobs, leading to the death of Elijah Lovejoy, editor of an antislavery paper. These events violated the rule of law that should be every citizen's "political religion."[17] As he will have

---

17   Lincoln, "The Perpetuation of Our Political Institutions," in *Abraham Lincoln: His Speeches and Writings*, Roy Basler, ed., New York 1946, pp. 76–84, 81. See also Eric Foner, *The Fiery Trial: Abraham Lincoln and American Slavery*, New York 2010, pp. 26–30.

been aware, such mob actions were orchestrated by self-described "men of property and standing," the supposedly patriotic allies of Southern politicians—at this point all parties were cross-sectional in their support. The rioters portrayed the Abolitionists as the pawns of a foreign—specifically British—plot against America.[18] Here were disturbing signs that the republic's institutions were infected by an uncontrollable and deep-seated malady. Lincoln feared for a future in which some aspiring tyrant would establish his personal rule "at the expense of emancipating slaves or enslaving free men."[19] The lawless threat might come either from slaveholders or from abolitionists.

Lincoln's stress on the republic of laws and due process was accompanied by a defense of the need for a National Bank to collect and disburse the public revenues and by his consequent hostility to Van Buren's proposal that revenues should instead be entrusted to local "sub-treasuries." In a major speech he gave as a member of the Illinois state legislature Lincoln attacked this scheme. In Lincoln's view the Bank, run as a privately-owned public corporation, had two decisive advantages. Firstly, it put the money deposited with it to work, earning interest and furnishing credit, where the unspent revenue would simply rust away in the network of sub-treasury lock boxes. Secondly the National Bank better served align the "duty" and the "interest" of Bank officials than would a dispersed chain of sub-treasuries. As a permanent corporation the Bank knew that it would only continue to be entrusted with the public revenues if it proved a faithful custodian. The shifting personnel of a scattered network of sub-treasury officials in each state would be far more vulnerable to individual frailty or fecklessness (leading to the wry comment: "it may not be improper here to add, that Judas carried the bag, was the Sub-Treasurer of the Savior and his disciples"[20]).

---

18 Leonard Richards, *Gentlemen of Property and Standing: Anti-Abolition Mobs in Jacksonian America*, New York 1971. See also David Grimstead, *American Mobbing, 1828–61: Towards Civil War*, Oxford 1998, pp. 11–2. Several of the riots were directed at the lecture tour of George Thompson, a British abolitionist.
19 "The Perpetuation of Our Political Institutions", p. 83.
20 Lincoln, "The Sub-Treasury," 26 December 1839, in Basler, *Abraham Lincoln: His Speeches and Writings*, pp. 90–112, 98.

Already at this comparatively early period, Lincoln saw corporate capital and credit as a fructifying force, idealizing corporate ownership and distrusting public initiatives in the realm of finance.

When elected to the House of Representatives in Washington, Lincoln's first act (in January 1848) was to denounce the victorious and almost concluded war with Mexico as unnecessary, unconstitutional, and the result of presidential mendacity and aggression.[21] While not pinning the blame for the war on slavery, as some did, and while accepting its result as a *fait accompli*, Lincoln backed David Wilmot's motion, which stipulated that slavery should be entirely excluded from any newly acquired land. Slavery had been abolished in Mexico in 1829, during the administration of Vicente Guerrero, and there was a real prospect that the self-proclaimed champions of "Anglo-Saxon freedom" would reestablish slavery in lands where it had already been eliminated.[22]

In the course of his speech attacking the way the Mexican war had been launched, Lincoln delivered the following judgment:

> Any people anywhere being inclined and having the power, have the right to rise up and shake off the existing government, and form a new one that suits them better. This is a most valuable, a most sacred right—a right which, we hope and believe, is to liberate the world. Nor is this right confined to cases in which the whole people of an existing government may choose to exercise it. Any portion of such a people that *can, may* revolutionize, and make their *own* so much of the territory as they inhabit. More than this, a *majority* of any portion of such a people may revolutionize, putting down a *minority*, intermingled with or near about them, who may oppose their movements. Such a minority was precisely the case of

---

21 "The War with Mexico," in Basler, *Abraham Lincoln: His Speeches and Writings*, pp. 202–16.

22 Theodore Vincent, *The Legacy of Vicente Guerrero*, Gainesville 2001, pp. 195–9. For the significance of the black and mulatto population of Mexico, see Gonzalo Aguirre Beltrán, *La población negra de México, 1519–1810*, Mexico City 1946, pp. 223–45. For the racial rhetoric of "Anglo-Saxonism" at this time in the US see Roger Horsman, *Race and Manifest Destiny: the Origins of American Racial Anglo-Saxonism*, Cambridge, MA, 1981, pp. 249–71. Even opponents of the war sometimes appealed to the supposed superiority of the Anglo-Saxons, but Lincoln did not.

the Tories in our own Revolution. It is a quality of revolutions not
to go by *old lines*, or *old laws*.[23]

This blunt and brusque version of the "self-determination" principle
was offered as the right way to look at Mexico's "revolution" against
Spain and Texas's "revolution" against Mexico. Its terms might easily
endorse "settler sovereignty," but Lincoln was later to enter a crucial
caveat on this point (to be considered below).

Lincoln set out his views on slavery in a series of major speeches
that defined him as a politician. These included one in Peoria in
1854 that dwelled on the implications of the Kansas-Nebraska Act
and offered a sketch of the republic's successive attempts to compromise over slavery; the "House Divided" speech in 1858, delivered to
a Republican convention; several speeches he gave as a Republican
senatorial candidate in debate with Stephen Douglas (including
one devoted to the Dred Scott ruling); and a speech at the Cooper
Union in New York, in 1860. Put together, they make a weighty
tome, and no other Republican leader devoted such sustained attention to the topic. The speeches often lasted two or three hours, were
each heard by audiences of several thousand, and were reprinted
verbatim in sympathetic newspapers. Southern leaders and opinion
formers became familiar with their contents. Characteristically, they
are quite unrelenting about the wrongs of slavery, but also moderate in their conclusions. Once he became a presidential candidate,
Lincoln reiterated his respect for the compromises embodied in the
US Constitution and the compromise acts of 1820 and 1850, but
he opposed any further concessions. He favored an end to slavery
in the Federal district in Washington because such a move was not
excluded by those agreements. Likewise he opposes the Dred Scott

---

23 Basler, *Abraham Lincoln: His Speeches and Writings*, p. 209. Lincoln was
at this time involved in a group that called itself the Young Indians. He was
hugely impressed by a speech against the Mexican War delivered by Alexander
Stephens of Georgia, another member of the group, in which he attacked hos-
tilities that were "aggressive and degrading," since they involved "waging a war
against a neighboring people to compel them to sell their country." Stephens
insisted that facing such a prospect he would himself prefer to perish on "the
funeral pyre of liberty" rather than sell "the land of my home." Stephens, who
remained friendly to Lincoln, was, of course, to become vice president of the
Confederacy. The quoted excerpts are from Basler, p. 214.

ruling allowing slaves to be brought into Federal territory. But he was prepared to recognize and implement established law, including that relating to fugitives. For the long term Lincoln believed that means should be found gradually to emancipate the slaves, for example by freeing the children born to slave mothers once the children reached the age of 25, or some other alternative that gave compensation to their owners and allowed the former slaves to be settled in Africa. Abolitionists like William Lloyd Garrison had long attacked the latter idea. It was associated with Whig slaveholders, notably Henry Clay, a man much admired by Lincoln, who supported what was known as the colonization of African Americans, treating them as aliens in the land where most of them had been born and inviting them to "return" to the land of their ancestors.

Lincoln's support for colonization separated him from the main currents of abolitionism, but his concern for the integrity of the Federal state, his early disapproval of the lawlessness of the defenders of slavery, and his distaste for the slaveholders' demand for special treatment all signal themes that characterized the Republican Party of the 1850s. Unlike the Radicals, he did not fulminate against the "slave power," but he did attack the exorbitant representation of Southern white men in the House of Representatives and electoral college, which came about because the slave population of each state was counted when apportioning delegates, with each slave deemed equivalent to three-fifths of a free man. He sought a new and more demanding ideal of the nation and the republic. Whereas antebellum US national feeling characteristically deferred to the slaveholders, the Republicans sponsored a new vision of the nation that challenged the South's claim to special consideration. In the Republican view, if slaves could be brought into Federal territories then the incoming slaveholders would be able to grab the best land and develop it more rapidly than free farmers. The Republicans also favored public improvements and free education. The Republican vision had great appeal in the regions characterized by cheap and rapid transportation, the growth of manufacturing, and the spread of the "market revolution."[24] This surge of growth spread wealth

24 See Charles Sellers, *The Market Revolution: Jacksonian America, 1815–1846*, Oxford 1991, pp. 125–30, 271–8, 396–427, and Melvyn Stokes and

quite broadly among farmers, artisans, and small businessmen, in contrast to the South, where the cotton boom enriched a narrower circle of slave owners and their hangers-on.[25] Lincoln believed that the broad prosperity of the North and the Northwest was rooted in its free labor system, a view shared by Marx. Republican pride in the progress of the free states repelled the Southern mainstream. Lincoln won 40 percent of the popular vote in 1860, but all of these votes came from the free states.

That Lincoln detested slavery was clear from his speeches and writings, and it is not surprising that he sketched half a dozen different key arguments on the topic in his notebooks.[26] He was also willing to talk about complex and gradual schemes of compensated emancipation. But as a national leader, what he offered was not an attack on slavery but implacable resistance to its territorial expansion. The puzzle here can only be resolved by identifying what else it was about his outlook and deepest convictions that restrained his evidently sincere opposition to slavery. The answer is probably his profound attachment to the Constitution and his awareness that within that Constitution it would be extraordinarily difficult to change the historic compromise the document represented between North and South, slavery and freedom. Lincoln's patriotism was even stronger than his dislike of slavery and obliged him, he believed, to accommodate to the latter out of due regard for a nation established by, and catering to, Southern slaveholders.

RIVAL NATIONALISMS?

The Republican Party was founded to defend the rights of "free labor" and to fight for a ban on slavery in Federal territories. The Republicans also adopted the "agrarian" stakeholder view, a semi-socialist idea that any man wishing to become a farmer should be given land for a homestead in the Federal territories, a proposal

---

Stephen Conway, eds., *The Market Revolution in America: Social, Political and Religious Expressions*, Charlottesville 1996.

25 Gavin Wright, *Slavery and American Economic Development*, London 2004.

26 For example, those in *Abraham Lincoln: His Speeches and Writings*, Basler, pp. 278–9, 427, 477–8, and 513.

that was to be translated into legislation in 1862. Lincoln had worked hard, educated himself, and become a prominent attorney and political figure. This background reinforced his belief that the free labor system allowed a man to make his way in the world. The Republicans also supported a system of public education for all and the foundation of a chain of "land grant" colleges, namely colleges endowed with revenue from the sale of public land. Lincoln believed that the pacts that had made the United States must be respected, but he also held that in the long run the nation could not remain half slave and half free.

Marx did not directly compare the claims of North and South as competing nationalisms. Instead he questioned whether the South was a nation, writing, "'The South,' however, is neither a territory strictly detached from the North geographically, nor a moral unity. It is not a country at all, but a battle slogan." Many who were much closer to the situation than Marx entered the same judgment in the years before 1861, yet soon had to acknowledge that the Confederacy did rapidly acquire many of the ideological trappings of a nation, complete with a claimed "moral unity" based on exaltation of the racial conceits and values of a slave society and of the conviction that white Southerners were the true Americans. Their values were a strange mixture of traditional patriotism and paternalism and— for whites alone—libertarianism. Hundreds of thousands of white Southerners who owned no slaves nevertheless fought and died for the rebellion, seeing the Confederacy as the embodiment of their racial privileges and rural civilization. The rebels were fighting for a cause that embodied a way of life, one that embraced minimal taxation and extensive "states' rights." The mass of slaveless whites not only had the vote but also enjoyed the "freedom of the range," which is to say that they could graze their animals on vast tracts of public land and on uncultivated private land. They also enjoyed significant hunting rights. Such privileges allowed them to live, as they put it, "high on the hog." Engels pointed out to Marx that the secession movement had backing from the generality of whites in the more developed and populous parts of the South.[27]

27   Engels to Marx, July 3, 1861, from Marx and Engels, *The Civil War in the United States*, p. 326.

Southern nationalism itself responded to, and stimulated, Unionist or Yankee nationalism.[28] Whereas patriotism was about the past, the new nationalist idea, a reflection of modernity, was about the future. Even at a time when truly industrial methods only affected a few branches of society, "print capitalism" and the "market revolution" were already transforming public space and time. The new steam presses poured out a torrent of newspapers, magazines, and novels, all of them summoning up rival "imagined communities."[29] Rail and cable further accelerated the dynamics of agreement and contradiction. Harriet Beecher Stowe's *Uncle Tom's Cabin* appeared first as serial installments in a newspaper, then as a book. It moved the Northern reader to tears, but seemed a grotesque libel to Southerners. The North's imagined community could not embrace the slaveholder, let alone the degraded slave traders, and the South's drew the line at the abolitionist and the radical newspaper editor. That incompatible national imaginings played a part in precipitating the conflict by no means takes away from the underlying discrepancy between the two social formations.

That the Civil War was an "irrepressible conflict," that its roots lay in the different labor regimes of the two sections, and that these differences crystallized in opposing images of the good society are not novel propositions. Different versions of them have been entertained by, among many others, such notable historians as David Potter, Don Fehrenbacker, Eric Foner, Eugene Genovese, John Ashworth and Bruce Levine.[30] The idea that rival nationalisms

---

28   Many historians reject out of hand, as Marx did, the idea that there was a Southern nationalism. Often they do so because they do not wish in any way to endorse the Confederacy or the later cult of Dixie. This is understandable, but wrong, as Drew Gilpin Faust has argued in an important study of the topic. Nationalism can be flawed and self-destructive, and it can change for better or worse. See Faust's *The Creation of Confederate Nationalism: Ideology and Identity in the Civil War South*, Baton Rouge 1989. See also Manisha Sinha's *The Counter-Revolution of Slavery*, Chapel Hill 2000, pp. 63–94. For the general argument, see Tom Nairn, *Faces of Nationalism*, London 1995.

29   The classic study is, of course, Benedict Anderson, *Imagined Communities*, second ed., London 1993.

30   David Potter, *The Impending Conflict*, Don Fehrenbacker, ed., New York 1976; Eugene Genovese, *The Political Economy of Slavery*, New York 1967; Eric Foner, *Free Soil, Free Labor, Free Men*, New York 1970 and Foner, "Causes of

played their part is an extension of such views, but Daniel Crofts points to the difficulty of pinpointing the exact moment of their birth:

> It is tempting to project back onto the prewar months the fiercely aroused nationalisms that appeared in mid-April [1861]. To do so would not be entirely in error, but it invites distortion. The irreconcilably antagonistic North and South described by historians such as Foner and Genovese were much easier to detect after April 15. Then and only then could Northerners start to think in terms of a conflict urged on behalf of "the general interests of self-government" and the hopes of humanity and the interests of freedom among all peoples and for ages to come.[31]

But this account gives too much to Unionist rhetoric. The Union's war aim was quite simply the preservation of the Union, and the frustration of "the interests of self-government" as understood by the majority of Southern whites. Both nationalisms had a markedly expansive character, but the Union's was purely continental at this stage, whereas the Confederacy's looked toward South America (notably to Cuba) as well as to the west. The clash was thus one of rival empires as well as competing nations.

It was the election of Abraham Lincoln that precipitated Secession. Lincoln's positions on slavery, as we have seen, were moderate—he took his stand only against any *expansion of slavery*, as he carefully explained in his exchanges with Stephen Douglas in the 1850s. But he represented a dangerous figure for Southern slaveholders nonetheless, because he attacked slavery as a wrong and because he concentrated on this issue to the virtual exclusion of any other. If Marx was right about the inherently expansionist character of Southern slavery, then Lincoln's modest but firm stance against it was enough to provoke them to the desperate expedient of secession. As I have already noted, there was no real space constraint—and if there had been, Kansas was not the right place

---

the Civil War" in *Politics and Ideology*; John Ashworth, *Slavery, Capitalism and Politics in the Antebellum Republic*, 2 vols., Cambridge 1998 and 2007; Bruce Levine, *Half Slave and Half Free: the Roots of Civil War*, New York 1992.

31   Daniel Crofts, "And the War Came," in *A Companion to the Civil War and Reconstruction*, Lacy Ford, ed., Oxford 2005, pp. 183–200; p. 197.

for cotton plantations—but Lincoln's presidency rankled for other reasons.

The vehement speeches that defined Lincoln's emergence as a Republican challenger were insulting as well as alarming to Southern ears. He was not more radical than other Republicans in his conclusions—rather the reverse—but he was more consistent and unwavering in his focus, and that was very unsettling.[32] How could his appointees be trusted? How would he and they respond to any future John Brown–style adventure? Many leading Southerners, though exercised by such dangers, nevertheless still at first opposed secession (Alexander Stephens, the future Confederate vice president, being a case in point), on the grounds that it was fraught with even worse danger—revolutions invariably destroy those who start them. But the more moderate Southerners were at the mercy of the more extreme. The departure of one slave state, let alone five or more, would decisively weaken the remaining Southern states' position in Washington. Such a conclusion belongs to the realm of rational calculation, but at a certain point, the clash of two incompatible nationalisms—and the sense of rightfulness and justification they entail—is needed to explain the willingness to engage in a life-and-death struggle.

Marx had scorn for national one-sidedness and self-satisfaction, but he did see a sequence of national revolutions as necessary to the war against aristocracy and monarchy. He may not have been fully aware of the extent to which he saw both German nationalism and North American nationalism as progressive forces. In 1861 his options stemmed from a conviction that the Civil War had a good prospect of destroying the world's major bastion of chattel slavery and racial oppression. But he was also aware that ideas produced by the German national revolution were helping to redefine the Union.

---

32 Lincoln's steady focus on slavery after 1854 emerges clearly in Foner's *The Fiery Trial*.

THE GERMAN AMERICANS

This brings us to the too often neglected contribution of the German Americans. Bruce Levine's study *The Spirit of 1848* shows the transformative impact of the huge German immigration around the midcentury.[33] At this time the level of immigration was rising to new heights, and Germans comprised between a third and a half of all newcomers. In the single year 1853, over a quarter of a million German immigrants arrived. The German Americans soon became naturalized and formed an important pool of votes for those who knew how to woo them. To begin with, Democratic rhetoric had some impact on them, but by the mid-1850s many German Americans were attracted to the Republicans, and they in turn helped to make Republicanism and the antislavery position more broadly attractive.

Protestant evangelicalism strongly influenced US abolitionism. The evangelical repudiation of slavery was very welcome, but eventually too close an association between the two served to limit antislavery's base. The evangelicals twinned antislavery with temperance and Protestantism, and this diminished the appeal of abolitionism in the eyes of many Catholics and not a few freethinkers. Already in the 1830s William Lloyd Garrison and William Channing were seeking to root the antislavery critique in more rationalist varieties of Protestant Christianity. There was also a current of radical English immigration that inclined to antislavery and the secular politics of Tom Paine.[34] But the large-scale German influx greatly strengthened the secular culture of antislavery. With their breweries, beer gardens, musical concerts, and *turnverein* (exercise clubs), the German radicals furnished a strong secular current in the antislavery movement, and even the German Protestants had concerns which differentiated them from the US Methodists and Baptists.

The temperance cause loomed large for evangelicals but had no charm for German and Nordic immigrants. The more radical German Americans supported women's rights and female suffrage;

---

33   Bruce Levine, *The Spirit of 1848: German Immigrants, Labor Conflict, and the Coming of the Civil War*, Urbana, IL, 1992.
34   The overrepresentation of British immigrants among antislavery activists in the 1830s is noted in Richards, *Gentlemen of Property and Standing*.

Mathilda Anneke published a German-language women's paper. Margarete Schurz was influential in the introduction of public kindergartens. Sometimes Marx's German American followers are portrayed as deferring to the prejudices of white, male trade unionists, but this is unfair. When Joseph Wedemeyer, Marx's longtime friend and comrade, helped to found the American Workers League (*Amerikanische Arbeitersbund*) in Chicago in 1853, its founding statement of principles declared that "all workers who live in the United States without distinction of occupation, language, color, or sex can become members."[35] Today such a formula sounds entirely conventional, but in 1853 it was very fresh. Indeed, this may have been the first occasion on which a workers' organization adopted it. The revolutionary German Americans did not invent this stance all by themselves, but they did readily adopt a critique of racial and gender exclusion pioneered by radical abolitionists. Like other exiles, the German Americans quarreled with one another, some inclining to the Republicans and others opting for purely labor-oriented groups, and Marx's followers shared this division. Many saw the founding of a labor party as the long-term goal, but even some of those closest to Marx, like Wedemeyer, also saw a tactical need to strengthen the Republicans and attack the slave power. Indeed, August Nimtz concludes that "the Marx party, specifically through Wedemeyer...played an important role in winning the German émigré community to the Republican cause."[36]

The mass of German Americans were naturally hostile to the

---

35 Levine, *The Spirit of 1848*, p. 125. In later decades some German Americans did indeed soft-pedal women's rights when seeking to recruit Irish American trade unionists, but while this should be duly noted, it is far from characterizing all German Americans, whether followers of Marx or not. For an interesting study that sometimes veers towards caricature, see Timothy Messer-Kruse, *The Yankee International, 1848–76: Marxism and the American Reform Tradition*, Chapel Hill 1998. This author has a justifiable pride in the native American radical tradition and some valid criticisms of some of the positions adopted by German American "Marxists," but he is so obsessed with pitting the two ethnic political cultures against one another that he fails to notice how effectively they often combined, especially in the years 1850–70. See Paul Buhle, *Marxism in the United States*, New York 1983, for a more balanced assessment.

36 Nimtz, *Marx and Engels*, p. 170.

nativist chauvinism of the Know Nothings (or American Party). The Republican Party only emerged as the dominant force in the North in the 1850s by defeating the Know Nothings and repudiating its own nativist temptation. While some Republican leaders flirted with nativist prejudice, the party itself attacked—even demonized—"the Slave Power" and not the immigrants. The presence of hundreds of thousands of German American voters helped to ensure this orientation.[37]

As the Civil War unfolded, German Americans and their overseas friends furnished vital support to the Northern cause. At the outbreak of the war, a German American militia in St. Louis played a key role in preventing Missouri's governor from delivering the state—and the city's huge arsenal—into Confederate hands. Wedemeyer became a colonel, served as a staff officer in St. Louis for General John Frémont, and was put in charge of the city's defenses. Eventually 200,000 Germans fought for the Union, with 36,000 fighting in German-speaking units. Carl Schurz became a major general, and later a senator. Franz Sigel and Alexander Schimmelfennig became generals. Two other members of the Communist League who also became Unionist officers were August Willich and Fritz Anneke. Indeed, the correspondence of Marx and Engels is studded with references to the military progress of these friends and acquaintants. The imperative to rally against the "Slave Power" also alleviated the sometimes bitter differences of émigré politics.

The military resources represented by the wider German-American enrollment were very significant, but the same could be said of the Irish American contingents, which grew to be just as large. The German Americans brought with them an openness to the antislavery idea that was to promote a new sense of the character of the war and the way it should be fought. Reviewing a recent collection of hundreds of letters written by German American volunteers, Kenneth Barkin writes: "the major reason for volunteering

---

37   For the role of antislavery in swinging German Americans to the Republican Party in upstate New York, see Hendrik Booraem, *The Formation of the Republican Party in New York: Politics and Conscience in the Antebellum North*, New York 1983, pp. 204–5.

[for the Union army] was to bring slavery to an end."[38] This new research very much vindicates Levine's argument in *The Spirit of 1848*.

The veterans of 1848 saw themselves as social revolutionaries but also as exponents of a national idea and movement. Whatever their ambivalence—and it was considerable—they were aware of the lessons of the Napoleonic epoch and of the nationalist renewal that it had provoked in Germany. One of the most striking expressions of this movement had been the doctrines of Carl von Clausewitz— his contention that war was the continuation of politics by other means, his attention to moral factors, and his insistence on the priority of destroying the enemy's social basis rather than capturing territory or capital cities. Clausewitz's magnum opus, *On War*, had been published in 1832, and its ideas had currency among the 1848 veterans. Unionist military strategy at first ignored the Clausewitzian imperatives and instead preferred the doctrine of Antoine Jomini, a Swiss military theorist who had sympathized with the French Revolution.[39] With few exceptions, Northern commanders were determined to avoid resorting to revolutionary measures, fearing that this would lead to race war. Instead, they relied implicitly on a strategy of blockade and cordons to exhaust the Confederacy and on the capture of Richmond (a strategy that Marx questioned in his article for the March 27, 1862, issue of *Die Presse*).

At a different level, Francis Lieber, a teacher at Columbia College and a German American of pre-1848 vintage, helped to shape the Union response to the war. The War Department looked to him when devising its rules of military conduct. Lieber played an important role in the Loyal Publication Society. He had been a strong exponent of the need for a party system in the antebellum period, but thought a new approach was needed once fighting began. His pamphlet *No Party Now But All for Our Country* stressed the wartime need to suppress party conflict and devote all energies to defeating the rebellion. His program for a more thoroughgoing

38   Kenneth Barkin, "Ordinary Germans, Slavery and the US Civil War," *Journal of African American History*, March 2007, pp. 70–9.
39   Gary Gallagher, "Blueprint for Victory," in *Writing the Civil War*, James McPherson and William Cooper, eds., Charlottesville 1998, pp. 60–79.

and single-minded mobilization for the war effort was welcomed by the Union Leagues.[40]

The German American mobilization for the Union was disinterested in that it did not ask for anything for itself in return for its support, though it did sometimes urge recognition for the workingman.[41] (Northern Protestant churches gave strong support to the Union, but some of their leaders urged that the time had come for Protestantism to be recognized as the country's official religion.)[42]

The national imagination pitted producers against parasites, or plain folk against snobs. Both Marx and Lincoln used a class-like language in evaluating the conflict. Marx stressed that secession was, above all, the work of aristocratic slaveholders, implicitly absolving the plain folk of the South from responsibility. There were clear majorities for secession in the representatives' gatherings that agreed to the setting up of the Confederacy, with the issue of secession decided by special conventions in ten cases and by the legislature in one other. Scrutiny of these decisions—and the contrary decisions taken by one special convention and three legislatures—shows that the participants were nearly all slaveholders and considerably better off than the average free citizen (only about a third of the heads of Southern households owned slaves). The supporters of immediate secession were considerably richer than those who were lukewarm or opposed. Put another way, those with more slaves—the main form of wealth—were keenest on secession.[43]

---

40   Mark Neeley, *The Union Divided*, Cambridge, MA, 2002, pp. 9–12.

41   Lincoln made a friendly response to an address delivered to him by a torchlight procession of German Americans at Cincinnati, Ohio, on February 12, 1861, in which he observes, "I agree with you that the workingmen are the basis of all governments, for the plain reason that they are the more numerous" but adds that "citizens of other callings than those of the mechanic" also warranted attention. See "Address to Germans at Cincinnati, 12 February 1861," in Basler, *Abraham Lincoln: His Speeches and Writings*, pp. 572–3.

42   George Frederickson, "The Coming of the Lord: The Northern Protestant Clergy and the Civil War Crisis," in *Religion and the American Civil War*, Randall Miller, Harry Stout, and Charles Reagan Wilson, eds., New York 1998, pp. 110–130.

43   Ralph Wooster, *The Secession Conventions of the South*, Princeton 1962, pp. 256–66.

Lincoln claimed to find a similar pattern in Washington in the first days of the war as many deserted their posts:

> It is worthy of note that while in this the government's hour of trial large numbers of those in the Army and Navy, who have been favored with offices, [have] proved false to the hand that had pampered them, not one common soldier, or common sailor, is known to have deserted his flag. The most important fact of all is the unanimous firmness of the common soldiers and common sailors...This is the patriotic instinct of the plain people. They understand, without an argument, that destroying the government which was made by Washington means no good to them.[44]

Though certainly invoking class-like qualities, at the same time Lincoln is certainly appealing to national sentiment, just as on the Confederate side there was also, very emphatically, an appeal to the spirit of George Washington (and Thomas Jefferson) and a claim that the common (white) folk were the heart of the nation and that it was they who filled the fighting ranks of the rebel army. (This was true, though by the end of the extraordinarily grueling conflict, Southern desertion rates were to be higher.)

THE NORTH DECIDES TO FIGHT

Lincoln was to spell out an important qualification to the sweeping endorsement of the right of revolution in his Mexican War speech, one that had a direct bearing on the South's right to self-determination. He declared: "The doctrine of self-government is right—absolutely and eternally right—but it has no just application, as here attempted. Or perhaps I should rather say that whether it has such just application depends upon whether a negro is not or is a man. If he is not a man, why in that case, he who is a man may, as a matter of self-government, do just as he pleases with him. But if the negro is a man, is it not to that extent a total destruction of self-government to say that he, too, shall not govern himself?

---

44 Quoted by William Lee Miller in *President Lincoln: the Duty of a Statesman*, New York 2008, p. 106.

When the white man governs himself that is self-government, but when he governs himself and also governs another man, that is more than self-government—that is despotism. If the negro is a man, why then my ancient faith teaches me that 'all men are created equal' and that there can be no moral right in connection with one man's making a slave of another."[45]

Lincoln uttered these words in Peoria in 1854 responding to the debate over the Kansas-Nebraska Act and the dispute over the right of communities in the Federal territories to establish themselves as newly formed states, with or without slaves. The principle outlined in the above passage ruled out what Marx called "settler sovereignty." However attractive and compelling Lincoln's argument might be, it could only be urged in favor of Unionist resistance to secession if the Union had itself repudiated slavery. But Lincoln and the majority of Republicans expressly condoned the survival of slavery in the Union and only opposed its extension to the Federal territories.

Once elected, Lincoln's main concern was to court the slaveholding border states and make sure as few of them as possible backed the rebellion. His success in this became the source of his caution in moving against slavery. Amending the Constitution in order to outlaw slavery was anyway out of the question—it would have needed large qualified majorities to pass in Congress and be endorsed by the states. Lincoln also held that the wrong of slavery was a national and not personal affair, and therefore slaveholders should be compensated for their loss of property. Given that the slaves of the South were worth more than all the machines, factories, wharves, railroads, and farm buildings of the North put together, any program of emancipation was going to be very gradual. In his first inaugural address Lincoln declares that the only major difference

---

45   Abraham Lincoln, speech in Peoria (Illinois) on October 16, 1854. Available in Basler, *Abraham Lincoln: His Speeches and Writings*, pp. 283–325. The quote from the Declaration of Independence strikes a patriotic note, though some might conclude that the speech also queried the break of 1776, given the prominence of slavery in several North American slave colonies. No doubt Lincoln would have insisted that the objection was not available to George III and his governments, since they were massively implicated in slavery, and that at least the Founding Fathers were uneasy about the institution.

between the sections was with reference not to slavery as such but to its expansion.

Many US historians treat the Northern decision to go to war in a fatalistic way, echoing Lincoln's own later phrase: "And the war came."[46] The Unionist cause—US or American nationalism—is simply taken for granted as an absolute value needing no further explanation or justification. However, Sean Wilentz adopts a bolder line, taking his cue from the Lincoln's first inaugural address:

> Above and beyond the slavery issue, Lincoln unflinchingly defended certain basic ideals of freedom and democratic self-government, which he asserted he had been elected to vindicate. There was, he said, a single "substantial dispute" in the sectional crisis: "one section of our country believes that slavery is right and ought to be extended, while the other believes it is wrong and ought not to be extended." There could be no doubt about where Lincoln stood, and where his administration would stand, on that fundamental moral question.[47]

---

46   The phrase "And the war came" occurs in Lincoln's second inaugural address (reprinted in this volume). It has been adopted for many valuable accounts, but its implicit denial of Northern agency fails to acknowledge the emergence of a new nationalism or to pinpoint the Union's legitimacy deficit in 1861–2 and hence a vital factor impelling the president to remedy it. See Kenneth Stampp, *And the War Came*, Baton Rouge 1970; Daniel Crofts,"And the War Came," in *A Companion to the Civil War and Reconstruction*, Lacy Ford, ed., pp. 183–200; James McPherson, "And the War Came," in *This Mighty Scourge: Perspectives on the Civil War*, Oxford 2007, pp. 3–20, 17. The legitimacy deficit was the more damaging in that abolitionists and Radicals, who might have been the warmest supporters of the administration, felt it keenly. It was alleviated by the Emancipation Proclamation but not fully dispelled until 1865, as we will see.

47   Sean Wilentz, *The Rise of American Democracy*, New York 2005, p. 783. Wilentz proceeds from these remarks to this conclusion: "The only just and legitimate way to settle the matter [the difference over slavery extension], Lincoln insisted…was through a deliberate democratic decision made by the citizenry" (p. 763). A riposte to this is suggested by Louis Menand's observation: "The Civil War was a vindication, as Lincoln had hoped it would be, of the American experiment. Except for one thing, which is that people who live in democratic societies are not supposed to settle their disagreements by killing one another." Louis Menand, *The Metaphysical Club: A Story of Ideas in America*, New York 2001, p. x. This important book, together with Drew Gilpin Faust's *The Republic of Suffering*, New York 2007, prompts the thought that the massive

But Lincoln's formula was deliberately circumscribed to allow agreement to disagree, and not to challenge slavery as such. If slavery really was a moral outrage—and if it disqualified sovereign right, as Lincoln himself had declared in Peoria in 1854—then he should have said that slavery was "wrong and ought to be abolished." In the absence of any action against slavery—even something very gradual like a "Free Womb" law—the war policy of the Union, measured against Lincoln's own statements, suffered a yawning legitimacy deficit. As to whether there could be doubt about where Lincoln stood, it is a simple fact that many of his contemporaries, especially the Radicals and abolitionists, did indeed doubt him and his administration. Marx, for his part, was aware of the problem, and troubled by it, but prepared to place a wager that the North would be forced to take revolutionary antislavery measures.

During the secession crisis Lincoln refused to compromise an iota of his stand against any expansion of slavery, something that could not be said of other Republican leaders once thought to be more radical than Lincoln (notably Seward). But he was prepared indefinitely to extend or perpetuate the compromise that he had made. He supported a proposed new amendment—it would have been the Thirteenth—to declare the future of slavery in the various states to be wholly the concern of those states forevermore, and no business of the Federal authorities. In February and March the proposed amendment received the necessary qualified majority in Congress and the approval of several Northern states, as well as Lincoln's approval. But it was then overtaken by the logic of secession and the firing on Fort Sumter.[48]

If the new president could not come out more clearly against slavery, then he could not challenge the South's "right to revolution." Lincoln declared himself satisfied that the Union cause and his oath of office were fully self-sufficient and amply justified resistance to rebellion. To underline that secession was rebellion,

---

bloodletting of the war weakened the justifications offered for it. Of course, those who went to war on both sides made poor guesses as to its duration, and this ignorance was itself a very significant cause of the war.

48 William Freehling, *The South Vs. the South: How Anti-Confederate Southerners Shaped the Course of the Civil War*, Oxford 2001, p. 39; and Michael Vorenberg, *Final Freedom*, Cambridge 2001, pp. 18–22.

he waited until a Federal installation had been attacked before ordering military action. While there was certainly room for doubt concerning Lincoln's exact position on slavery, it is also very possible that he was himself aware that the Union cause *with* slavery was very much weaker that it would be *without* slavery. The gains of an emancipation policy were later explained in terms of weakening the Confederate economy or strengthening the Union Army, but, important as these considerations were, there was another just as important: the imperative to remedy the North's legitimacy deficit, for the sake of the morale of the Union's keenest supporters. At some level Lincoln was probably aware of this, but in 1861 he was beset by an immediate and elemental challenge to which he had to respond. In his statement concerning the right to revolution there was a half-stated implication that such a right only existed where it was realistic. For a while opposition to secession could be offered in terms of realpolitik—the South was too weak to sustain it and its rebellion was destroying international respect for the republic and what it stood for.

William Seward, shortly to become Lincoln's secretary of state, broadly hinted at the international situation and the damage that secession would do to the projection of US power. Speaking in the Senate in January 1861 he declared:

> The American man-of-war is a noble spectacle. I have seen it enter an ancient port in the Mediterranean. All the world wondered at it and talked about it. Salvos of artillery, from forts and shipping in the harbor, saluted its flag. Princes and princesses and merchants paid it homage, and all the people blessed it as a harbinger of hope for their own ultimate freedom…I imagine now the same noble vessel entering the same haven. The flag of thirty-three stars and thirteen stripes has been drawn down, and in its place a signal is run up, which flaunts the device of a lone star or a palmetto tree. Men ask, "Who is the stranger that thus steals into our waters?" The answer, contemptuously given, is: "She comes from one of the obscure republics of North America. Let her pass on."[49]

---

49   Quoted in a perceptive study by Richard Franklin Bensel, *Yankee Leviathan: the Origins of Central State Authority in America, 1859–1877*, Cambridge 1990, p. 18. That rival expansionist impulses in both sections provoked sectional hostility was clear enough by the 1850s. See Michael Morrison, *Slavery and the*

The secession of a limited number of rural states would, in this view, drastically diminish US power. It would hand over control of the Mississippi to the rebels and put in question free access to Southern markets. Even worse, it would spell the end of the "empire of liberty," harming both sections, since, separated, they would no longer count. Seward was speaking in the Senate and addressing his remarks as much to moderate Southerners, who could be deterred from joining the secession movement, as to Northerners. All concerned were aware that the European powers were already jostling to take advantage of Washington's distraction. (A French military expedition had landed in Mexico and was about to install a puppet regime, that of the "Emperor Maximilian.") If there had been a sectional compromise, and some sort of nominal union had been salvaged, we can be pretty sure that it would have been sealed by territorial expansion—most likely the seizure of Cuba.

The Confederate president, Jefferson Davis, sought to play down the defense of slavery as the motive for the conflict and instead dwelt on the Northern threat to states' rights and on the affronts that had been offered to Southern honor. He stressed continuity between the ideals of the American Revolution and their latter-day embodiment in the Confederacy. The Confederate Constitution was closely modeled on that of 1787. Davis's vice president, Alexander Stephens, was not so careful—he described slavery as the "cornerstone" of the Confederacy. The nature of the conflict itself would steadily highlight Southern dependence on slavery. The slaveholders' aversion to taxation led the Confederate authorities to try to finance the war simply by printing money, with paralyzing consequences.

Of course dissidents in the North claimed that Lincoln rode roughshod over republican liberties. But this was in the service of a Unionist nationalism to which many Democrats as well as Republicans also subscribed. As the conflict proceeded, the salience of slavery in Southern society itself became of decisive importance, creating severe problems for the Confederacy and becoming a target of Unionist strategy. The Confederacy's very belated attempt

---

American West: the Eclipse of Manifest Destiny and the Coming of the Civil War, Chapel Hill 1997.

to free a few hundred slaves and enroll them in a colored regiment came much too late to have any impact and still rested on a racial compact. But implicitly it conceded that the South had built on a faulty foundation.[50]

Let us return to the sources of the conflict and the nature of the Republican threat. The Civil War crisis was, of course, precipitated by the growth of the Republican party and the election of a Republican president. Lincoln would be able to make a host of appointments, including many in the Southern states themselves. He would be able to veto legislation and give orders to the executive apparatus. Moreover, civil society in the North had become tolerant of provocations escalating from *Uncle Tom's Cabin* and its more militant sequel (*Dred: A Tale of the Great Dismal Swamp*, 1856) to John Brown's attack on Harper's Ferry. Brown was an out-and-out revolutionary yet broad sections of Northern opinion were inclined to excuse—or even endorse—his bloody escapades. Southern leaders abominated religious abolitionism, but they were even more alarmed at the growth of a secular Republican politics that could win Northern majorities and use these to dominate the state. Southern fear of Republicanism and radical abolitionism imbued secession with a pre-emptive counter-revolutionary purpose and vocation, something easily perceived by Marx. Yet while the South's counter-revolution speedily carved out a new state, the Northern revolution proved weak and laggard.

CONTRABANDS AND EMANCIPATION: CIVIL WAR STRATEGY AND POLITICS

Lincoln had gone to great lengths to promote the widest possible alliance in defense of the Union, accommodating moderates and making concessions to slaveholders in the border states. But by the summer of 1862, lack of progress, heavy casualties, and the cautious and defensive conduct of the war were inspiring mounting criticism and a greater willingness to listen to abolitionists and Radical

---

50 Bruce Levine, *Confederate Emancipation: Southern Plans to Free and Arm Slaves During the Civil War*, Oxford 2006.

Republicans, who argued for a bolder strategy, both militarily and politically.

The more Marx learned about militant abolitionism, the more impressed he became. In an article for *Die Presse* of August 9, 1862, he wrote of the growing attention paid in the North to Abolitionist orators, and in particular to Wendell Philips, who "for thirty years... has without intermission and at the risk of his life proclaimed the emancipation of the slaves as his battle cry." He paraphrases at length a speech by Phillips "of the highest importance" in which the veteran abolitionist indicts Lincoln's conservative and cowardly policy:

> The government [of Lincoln] fights for the maintenance of slavery and therefore it fights in vain ... He [Lincoln] waits ... for the nation to take him in hand and sweep away slavery through him ... If the war is continued in this fashion it is a useless squandering of blood and gold ... Dissolve this Union in God's name and put another in its place, on the cornerstone of which is written: "Political equality for all the citizens in the world" ... Let us hope that the war lasts long enough to transform us into men, and then we shall quickly triumph. God has put the thunderbolt of emancipation into our hands in order to crush the rebellion.[51]

Lincoln's willingness to adopt an emancipation policy was somewhat greater than his abolitionist and Republican critics allowed. Even compensated emancipation was still keenly opposed by the loyal border states, and by many Democrats who declared they would fight for the Union but not for the Negro. Lincoln believed that maintenance of the broadest Unionist coalition was essential to victory. He also greatly preferred an emancipation accompanied by compensation, and allowing due process to the property-holders. Democrats and moderate Republicans long hoped to persuade the Confederacy to come to terms, and to this end, they opposed measures that would irrevocably alienate the South. But while abolitionists and radical Republicans railed against Lincoln's studied moderation, it was the actions of a few thousand slave rebels

---

51 "Abolitionist Demonstrations in North America," Marx and Engels, *The Civil War in the US*, pp. 202–6.

outside the political system—the "contrabands"—which helped the Radicals in Washington eventually to win the argument.

The arrival of fugitive slaves in Union encampments surrounding the Confederacy made slavery and its role in the conflict impossible to ignore. Some Union commanders tried to return the fugitives to their masters. Others found this a perverse and impractical response. General Benjamin Butler—stationed in Virginia—became the first Union commander to obtain Washington's backing for a policy of refusing to return escaping slaves; instead, he put them to work as civilian auxiliaries. The legal term *contraband* was adopted to explain and justify this practice, though the term awkwardly implied that the (ex)-slaves were confiscated rebel property. A Confiscation Act passed by Congress and "reluctantly" endorsed by the president declared that slaves working for the rebel forces would be subject to confiscation and would be put to good use as support workers by the Union Army. In August, General Frémont, commanding in Missouri, declared martial law and announced that rebels were liable to summary execution and that their slaves were free. There was an outcry; Frémont refused to modify his order and was dismissed.

Lincoln allowed the pragmatic use of "contrabands" but not advocacy of an emancipationist military policy. Frémont had acted impulsively and in hope of political advancement. But the deeds and words of two field commanders—David Hunter in South Carolina and John Phelps in Louisiana—showed that military emancipation had an operational logic. General Phelps, commanding a Vermont regiment, urged, "The government should abolish slavery as the French destroyed the ancien régime."[52] His men enrolled all slaves who presented themselves, and forbade planters to use the whip. Similar proposals came from General Hunter, who was advancing along the South Carolina coast and islands. Both men would be removed from their commands. General Butler, who had welcomed the contrabands, at first declined to form black regiments, but by mid-1862 he had dropped his opposition. (Refusing to accept colored soldiers in Louisiana was particularly absurd, as they had

---

52 "The Destruction of Slavery," in *Slaves No More!*, Ira Berlin et al., Cambridge 1993, pp. 1–76; 36. The full text of Phelps's proclamation is given in *Freedom: a Documentary History of Emancipation*, Ira Berlin et al., Cambridge 1985.

always existed in this state and had even been recognized by the Confederacy.) Thanks to his political connections, Butler managed to recruit black units without getting immediately dismissed. Meanwhile the growing number of "contrabands" showed the folly of making no open attempt to deprive the rebels of slave labor and of not urging Union commanders to enroll as many former slaves as possible by offering them their freedom.[53]

By the summer of 1862 the Union's failure to make military progress led many to listen to the abolitionists and radical Republicans who were making the case for an immediate emancipation policy. Speaking tours by Wendell Phillips, Anne Dickinson, and Frederick Douglass attracted huge and enthusiastic crowds. Lincoln became increasingly eager to break what seemed like a military stalemate. The Confederacy was able to send more white soldiers to the front because slaves were still toiling to produce the supplies needed by the Confederate armies. The Confederates also used slaves in their military camps to carry out service and support roles. A second Confiscation Act in July allowed Union commanders to commandeer rebel property, and put "contrabands" to work, with fewer formalities. But in Lincoln's view neither Congress nor the military had the authority to determine the future fate of the "contrabands" who, in law, had become the property of the state, not free citizens.

The president still worried about the reaction of the border states—their representatives in Congress ensured that—but by June 1862 their key centers were securely held by Union troops. More worrying was the military impasse and a discouraging international reaction, with the British considering diplomatic recognition of the rebels. Lincoln believed that his "war powers" as president and commander-in-chief fully entitled him to free the slaves of rebels and to arm freedmen if he deemed it a military necessity. But he had to frame his use of these powers in such a way as to minimize the risk of a challenge from Congress or the Supreme Court (where there was still a Democratic majority). He also felt the need to justify emancipation in such a way as to avoid giving the impression

---

53   Kate Masur, " 'A Rare Phenomenon of Philological Vegetation': the Word 'Contraband' and the Meanings of Emancipation in the United States," *Journal of American History*, 93:4, March 2007, pp. 1050–84.

that he wanted slaves to slaughter their masters and mistresses in their beds. Cabinet colleagues urged him to wait until there was good news, so that the emancipation would not seem like an act of desperation. In September 1862, following the battle of Antietam, he issued the preliminary proclamation, giving the rebels time to abandon the insurrection, failing which the proclamation would come into force on January 1, 1863.

Marx and Engels had from the outset insisted on the war's anti-slavery logic, but the first eighteen months of the conflict tested their conviction. Engels was particularly distressed by the passivity and defensiveness of the Union commanders, and beyond that what he called "the slackness and obtuseness" that appeared throughout the North, the lack of popular zeal for the republic, contrasting it with the daring and energy of the rebels. On August 7, 1862 Marx urged his friend not to be overinfluenced by the "military aspect" of matters. On October 29, following the announcement of the Emancipation Proclamation, Marx was powerfully reassured. He wrote:

> The fury with which the Southerners have received Lincoln's [Emancipation] Acts proves their importance. All Lincoln's Acts appear like the pettifogging conditions which one lawyer puts to his opposing lawyer. But this does not alter their historic content. Indeed it amuses me when I compare them with the drapery in which the Frenchman envelops even the most unimportant point.[54]

Thereafter Marx and Engels had growing confidence in Lincoln, even if they continued to complain about the quality of the Union's military leadership and the need for a thoroughgoing shake-up in the republic's ruling institutions.

The Emancipation Proclamation brought new legitimacy and—at least in principle—new opportunities to deepen the struggle. However, it did not entirely sever the Union from support of slavery. Its terms respected the slave property rights of loyal slaveholders in the border states and in areas occupied by the Union Army. Emancipation applied to the roughly three million slaves beyond

---

54 Marx and Engels, *The Civil War in the US*, p. 258.

Union control, since they were the property of slaveholders still in rebellion. These freed people were enjoined "to abstain from all violence, unless in necessary self-defense" and to be willing to work at "reasonable wages." The Proclamation includes a clause permitting freedmen to be enrolled for garrison duty. The Proclamation went further than the Confiscation Acts in allowing former slaves to be organized in fighting units though for some time many were kept in menial support roles. Those who were enlisted as soldiers were placed under white officers and, to begin with, given a lower rate of pay. Eventually the thirst for manpower in a hugely destructive war led to the enrollment of 180,000 African Americans in the Union Army and over 10,000 in the Navy. (By the end of the conflict, however, only about a hundred African Americans had been commissioned as officers of the colored units, most of these being chaplains or doctors). Many "contrabands" did not become soldiers but were put to work digging trenches or graves, or in other support roles. Most Union commanders remained cautious in their use of black troops and their appeals to the black population, shunning the sort of autonomous mobilization thought entirely appropriate for German American or Irish American troops.

The Emancipation policy exacerbated Confederate problems in areas near the fighting, but it remained unclear whether the proclamation's message was reaching much further or whether the slaves could respond even if it was. Militia, patrols, and military police roamed the Southern countryside looking for slave fugitives and Confederate deserters. The number of slave fugitives grew to as many as 400,000 or 500,000 by the end of the war, a total that includes many who fled their masters in Kentucky, the border states, and the other Union-occupied areas that had been excluded from the Emancipation Proclamation. Although there are some signs of slave desertion or noncooperation in rebel-held areas, the patrols, militia, and military police were still a strong deterrent for those deep in Confederate territory, and only those close to the front could escape. A few could hide out in swamps and forests, but it was Union advances—from Vicksburg in July 1863 to Atlanta in September 1864—that eventually made it possible for slaves to desert the plantations en masse. This having been said, the war placed the slave order under great strain, with many white men of military age away and their wives managing as best they could. Anxious about their economic fate, planters ordered cotton to be grown and neglected the cultivation of foodstuffs. The war still made for very uneasy relations between slaves and overseers or mistresses. Peter Kolchin writes:

> Slaves took advantage of wartime disruption in numerous ways: they obeyed orders with less alacrity, they challenged weakened authority more readily, they followed the progress of Yankee forces and aided that progress in a variety of ways, from providing valuable military intelligence to enlisting in the Union army, and they fled in increasing numbers, especially when Federal troops neared. Despite heightened fears on the part of the white population, however, they did not engage in the sort of massive uprising that occurred in Saint Domingue during the French Revolution.[55]

It was more rational for Southern slaves to look to the Union army, with its new black contingents, to lead the assault on the slave order.

The emancipation policy certainly helped in Europe, rendering public opinion in Britain and France more hostile to recognizing the rebels. The fledgling labor and socialist movements were not completely united, but the most dynamic and representative currents now rallied against the Confederacy. Marx and Engels based their efforts to develop the International Workers Association on this trend. Marx believed that the willingness of Manchester workers to rally in support of the North, even though the "cotton famine" menaced their own livelihood, showed the moral superiority of a rising class.

Lincoln was dismayed when General Meade failed to aggressively follow up his victory over the rebels at Gettysburg. Instead, Meade issued a proclamation saying that the country "looks to the army for greater efforts to drive from our soil every vestige of the presence of the invader." Lincoln was dismayed to find that he had yet another general who entirely failed to grasp the simple idea that

---

55   Peter Kolchin, "Slavery and Freedom in the Civil War South," in James McPherson and William Cooper, eds. *Writing the Civil War*, Charleston 1998, pp. 241–60.

"the whole country is our soil."[56] But above and beyond the importance of defending the whole territory of the former Union was the claim that the North was defending a new Union that would correspond more closely to the democratic nation state cherished by so many nineteenth-century nationalists.[57] In his famous address at Gettysburg Lincoln underlined the "new birth of freedom" that must inform and infuse the military struggle. He used the word *nation*, with its warm resonance, five times, in preference to the flatter term *union*. Was this rebirth defined by slave emancipation or was it simply a vindication of American "principles of self-government"? Both interpretations were available. The rebirth of the national spirit was something that many immigrants as well as natives would be able to understand, because they came from lands like Germany and Ireland where the national revolution was as yet unconsummated. (The Irish Fenians strongly supported the North, helping to organize a number of units). And as revolutionary and democratic nationalists, they were less inclined to be fixated by given political forms, such as the US Constitution.

European nationalisms, with their dominant ethnicities and religions, had their own problems with reconciling rival concepts and recognizing minorities. The Republicans had shied away from crude nativism, but without embracing the radical abolitionist call for equality. The formulas expressed by Lincoln at Gettysburg did not offer citizenship to the freedmen (nor to American Indians), though Northern European Protestant immigrants somehow fit in. Dorothy Ross urged that Gettysburg marks a step back from the universalism of the Declaration of Independence:

> Lincoln transforms a truth open to each man as man into something he shares by virtue of his partnership in the nation…Lincoln solved the moral conflict he faced between principles and national survival by linking human rights to national allegiance, but human rights became the subordinate partner.[58]

---

56 James McPherson, "A. Lincoln, Commander in Chief," in *Our Lincoln*, Eric Foner, ed., New York 2009, p. 33.
57 For the evolution of Unionist nationalism, see Bensel, *Yankee Leviathan*, pp. 18–47.
58 Dorothy Ross, "Lincoln and the Ethics of Emancipation: Universalism,

However, one could say that lofty statements of rights desperately need to be brought down to earth and that at least Lincoln was pushing in that direction (Marx inclined to this conclusion). But at the time of Gettysburg, slavery was not yet finished, and what remained of it might still be given a new lease of life in the event of the Northern peace party gaining the upper hand. The Radical concern to get some sweeping and thorough antislavery measure agreed upon—perhaps a Thirteenth Amendment—stemmed from this fear.

The leaders of the North faced more dissidence than did those of the South. The war's heavy toll on life and the North's failure to inflict decisive defeats on the Confederate forces led "copperhead" Democrats to hanker for peace talks. Conscription led to violent draft riots in 1863 in New York and other urban centers, with the rioters attacking blacks as the supposed cause of the conflict. But even New England abolitionists with impeccable patriot credentials could doubt whether war was the right way to impose their section's superior civilization. The avowed abolitionist (and future chief justice) Oliver Wendell Holmes Jr., as a young officer who had just experienced several terrible, bloody engagements, wrote to his orthodox Republican father:

> If it is true that we represent civilization wh. is in its nature, as well as slavery, diffuse & aggressive, and if civn and progress are better things why they will conquer in the long run, we may be sure, and will stand a better chance in their proper province—peace—than in war, the brother of slavery—it is slavery's parent, child and sustainer all at once.[59]

What Holmes here refers to as civilization and progress are forces that Marx would have seen as capitalism or the advance of bourgeois social relations. The sentiments expressed point to pacifism rather than anti-imperialism. The idea is that one way or another the North is going to prevail, so why not do so in a kinder, gentler way? The North's ownership of the future is set down to the

Nationalism and Exceptionalism," *Journal of American History*, 96: 2, September 2009, p. 346.
59   Louis Menand, *The Metaphysical Club: A Story of Ideas in America*, New York 2001, p. 45.

extraordinary locomotive of its capitalist economy. Marx himself probably would have agreed that the North would prevail in any case, but would have added that 300,000 slaveholders were not going to give up their human property without a continuing fight.

Holmes's letter was written in December 1862, at a time when the consequences and character of the emancipation policy were not yet clear. Without abandoning all his misgivings, Holmes became more committed to the war over the next year or two. His enthusiasm for the Union cause was boosted by the bravery of the black soldiers in the assault of Fort Wagner, by revulsion at the racial attacks in New York, and, finally, by the growing effectiveness of the Northern war machine, which at last made all the bloodshed seem to be to some purpose after all.[60] The fluctuations of Northern morale illustrated the old saw that nothing succeeds like success.

The gradual improvement in the Union's military position, especially the taking of Vicksburg in July 1863, allowed for a greater application of the emancipation policy, as Union forces broke through into territories where there were large numbers of slaves. A static war, and one focused on set-piece engagements, meant that the slaves in the Confederate rear areas had little chance of playing any role. The majority of African Americans who enrolled, including slaves, came from areas already controlled by the Union. Indeed, many tens of thousands of them came from Kentucky, since, as the loyal slaveholders had warned, Union commanders had no way of knowing whether a black recruit was someone's property or, if he was, what the home state or political stance of that property owner might be. Heavy troop losses—and black losses were very heavy—meant that commanders were disinclined to ask awkward questions. For their part, the new recruits saw enlistment as a good way to escape bondage, even if it was also an illegal one. (Legal slavery actually outlasted the Confederacy and was only formally ended towards the close of 1865, when the Thirteenth Amendment, introduced by the Congressional Radicals, was finally endorsed by the requisite qualified majority of states.)

The advantages of an "aggressive" emancipation policy—one that aimed to penetrate Confederate lines—were logistical, as well

---

60 Menand, *The Metaphysical Club*, pp. 52–3.

as military in the narrow sense, as may be inferred from Grant's account of the advantages of a war of movement in North Carolina. It would, Grant wrote, "give us possession of many Negroes who are indirectly aiding the rebellion."[61] In practice, of course, the appearance of Union columns led the slaves to act no longer as mere "possessions," but as Union scouts, auxiliaries, and recruits eager to see the Confederacy defeated. The Emancipation policy was always premised on the view that slaves would respond to it. So long as slaves were still unarmed in the face of mounted patrols and blood-hounds, there was little they could do, but once Union troops thrust into Confederate territory the black population became an invaluable ally, helping the Union at last to crush the stubborn rebellion. There had been intimations of this in 1862 and 1863 but, partly because of excessive caution, the emancipation policy was not pursued with sufficient vigor until the last six months of the war. [62]

From time to time Lincoln hankered for an aggressive military policy linked to emancipationism. As early as March 1863 he wrote to Governor Andrew Johnson of Tennessee warmly endorsing the idea of Johnson taking command of a "negro military force" since "[t]he colored population is the great *available*, yet *unavailed of*, force for the restoration of the union." He was especially supportive of this since Johnson was the governor of a slave state, and "[himself] a slaveholder." Lincoln was convinced that "[t]he bare sight of fifty thousand armed and drilled black soldiers on the banks of the Mississippi would end the rebellion at once."[63] Wendell Phillips had pointed out in an influential lecture that Toussaint Louverture had raised precisely such a drilled black force in Saint Domingue in the 1790s and trounced the Spanish and British.[64] But, unlike Andrew Johnson, Toussaint was black and a former slave.

---

61   Quoted Archer Jones, "Jomini and the Strategy of the American Civil War: a Reinterpretation," *Military Affairs*, December 1970, pp. 127–31, p. 130.
62   See Steven Hahn, "Did We Miss the Greatest Rebellion in Modern History," *The Political Worlds of Slavery and Freedom*, Cambridge, MA, 2009, pp. 55–114. See also James Oakes, *Slavery and Freedom: an Interpretation of the Old South*, New York 1990, pp. 185–92.
63   Letter to Gov. Johnson 26 March 1863, Abraham Lincoln, *Speeches and Writings*, pp. 694–5.
64   Mathew Clavin, *Toussaint Louverture and the American Civil War: the Promise and the Peril of a Second Haitian Revolution*, New York 2010, pp. 6–7.

Frederick Douglass, 1852

Lincoln later returned to the idea of an unorthodox force that might get behind enemy lines. In August 1864, he invited Frederick Douglass, the black abolitionist, to visit him to discuss whether there might be some way of bringing the emancipation message to the mass of still enslaved blacks and of encouraging them to desert the plantations. He explained, "The slaves are not coming as rapidly and numerously to us as we had hoped."[65] Lincoln seems to have envisioned a small, highly mobile force, but it is not clear whether he intended that the commander be black, nor what rules of engagement the unit might have. The president was keen to avoid any hint or imputation of race war (the Proclamation's injunction against violence toward slaveholders was prompted by this concern). The encounter with Douglass did not come to anything. Douglass thought a propagandist column would soon be overwhelmed. The

---

65   Frederick Douglass, *Life and Times of Frederick Douglas*, quoted by James Oakes in *The Radical and the Republican*, New York 2007, p. 231.

two men did not meet again for several months during which General Sherman's capture of Atlanta and march to the sea at last brought the possibility of escape to masses of slaves on his route. Union successes also ensured Lincoln's victory in the election of 1864, something that had seemed—to Lincoln as well as his critics and opponents—very much in doubt in the summer of that year.

THE ADDRESS OF THE INTERNATIONAL TO PRESIDENT LINCOLN

It is at this point that we should consider the brief and mediated exchange between Marx and the US president. The two men were both averse to wordy rhetoric and conventional pieties, and yet both discovered an emancipatory potential in a bloody and often sordid Civil War. Lincoln did not indulge in flowery language. When it came to justifying slave emancipation, Lincoln was bound by political and constitutional considerations, the need to retain the loyalty of the border states, and the legal obligation to take only such actions as conformed to his war powers as president. So neither the Emancipation Proclamation nor the Gettysburg address avow an abolitionist objective, even if both had an implicit antislavery message for those willing to hear it.

The Radical Republicans liked the Emancipation Proclamation but saw it as incomplete. It left in bondage some 800,000 slaves owned by loyal masters—and, of course, those in rebel territory— so the final fate of slavery still remained to be decided. Radical Republicans debated different options, and in January 1864 they introduced a Thirteenth Amendment that, if approved by the necessary majorities, would end slavery and override any peace negotiations or Supreme Court rulings that might salvage slavery's considerable remnants.[66]

Lincoln was aware that the Proclamation might be vulnerable, and this awareness may explain why he invited the artist Francis Carpenter to stay a few months at the White House and paint a

66 Michael Vorenberg, *Final Freedom: The Civil War, the Abolition of Slavery, and the Thirteenth Amendment,* Cambridge 2001, 197–210.

picture of the first reading of the Proclamation to Lincoln's cabinet. The painting makes it clear that the measure was backed by the cabinet's weightiest members, with Seward prominently depicted addressing his colleagues. Lincoln was obviously proud of the Proclamation—he described it as "the central event of my administration and the great event of the nineteenth century"—but he also wanted to display the backing it enjoyed from all his distinguished colleagues. Seward himself saw matters differently, explaining to the painter that the Emancipation Proclamation was "merely incidental" and that the most important cabinet meeting was the one that followed the firing on Fort Sumter. However, the painting, usually in a lithograph version, was to be widely adopted, becoming one of the most widely diffused of national images in subsequent decades.[67]

Lincoln's course following the Emancipation Proclamation aimed not just to maintain and invigorate the Unionist coalition but also to appeal to public opinion in the wider Atlantic world and to head off the inclination of the governments in Paris and London to recognize the Confederacy or, later, to offer mediation. Lincoln's carefully constructed appeals to abolitionism were a vital part of this. Since the International Workingmen's Association (IWA) embraced several British and French trade unions, it was evidently worthy of some diplomatic acknowledgment. The General Council of the IWA asked Karl Marx to draft a message of congratulation to Lincoln on the occasion of his reelection. The Republican watchword "Free Labor, Free Soil, Free Men" was designed to indict the "Slave Power" and, however vaguely, to offer rights, land, and recognition to the laborer. This was not anticapitalism, but it was, in Marx's terms, a step in the right direction.

Marx found drafting the International's Address to Lincoln more difficult than he had anticipated. He complained to Engels that such a text was "much harder [to draft] than a substantial work," since he was anxious that "the phraseology to which this sort of scribbling is restricted should at least be distinguished from the

---

67 Harold Holzer, "Picturing Freedom," in *The Emancipation Proclamation*, Harold Holzer, E. G. Medford and Frank Williams, eds., Baton Rouge 2006, pp. 83–136.

democratic, vulgar phraseology ..."[68] Nevertheless he allowed himself the following resonant, if complex, paragraph:

> When an oligarchy of 300,000 slaveholders dared to inscribe, for the first time in the annals of the world, "slavery" on the banner of armed revolt; when on the very spots where hardly a century ago the idea of one great democratic republic had first sprung up, whence the first Declaration of the Rights of Man was issued, and the first impulse given to the European revolution of the eighteenth century ... then the working classes of Europe understood at once, even before the fanatic partisanship of the upper classes for the Confederate gentry had given warning, that the slaveholders' rebellion was to sound the tocsin for a general holy crusade of property against labor ...

The address also warned that so long as the republic was "defiled by slavery," so long as the Negro was "mastered and sold without his concurrence," and so long as it was "the highest prerogative of the white-skinned laborer to sell himself and choose his own master," they would be "unable to attain the true freedom of labor." [69]

The repeated invocation of the cause of labor in the address thus gave its own more radical twist to the "free labor" argument characteristic of Lincoln and other Republicans. In the address, Marx observed:

> The workingmen of Europe feel sure that as the American War of Independence initiated a new era of ascendancy for the middle class, so the American antislavery war will do for the working classes. They consider it an earnest of the epoch to come, that it fell to the lot of Abraham Lincoln, the single-minded son of the working class, to lead his country through matchless struggle for the rescue of an enchained race and the reconstruction of the social world.[70]

---

68 Marx and Engels, *The Civil War in the United States*, p. 273.
69 "The Address," Marx and Engels, *The Civil War in the United States*, pp. 260–1.
70 Ibid, p. 281. The meanings of the address are rarely addressed, so it is all the more regrettable to find it interpreted in a tendentious way, as it is in Timothy Messer-Kruse's book *The Yankee International, 1846–1876: Marxism and the American Reform Tradition*, Chapel Hill 1998, pp. 54–6. This author

The US ambassador to Britain, Charles Francis Adams, replied to the address, on behalf of the president, a month later, writing, "I am directed to inform you that the address of the Central Council of your Association, which was duly transmitted through this legation to the President of the United States, has been received by him. So far as the sentiments expressed by it are personal, they are accepted by him with a sincere and anxious desire that he may be able to prove himself not unworthy of the confidence which has recently been extended to him by his fellow citizens." Adams went on to declare that "the United States regard their cause in the present conflict with slavery-maintaining insurgents as the cause of human nature and…they derive new encouragement to persevere from the testimony of the workingmen of Europe."[71] Thus both the address and the reply refer to labor with the greatest respect and both assert the rights of labor, embedding them in, respectively, the "rights of man" and "the cause of human nature."

THE STATUS OF THE FREEDMEN AND WOMEN

As emancipation advanced on the military and legislative fronts, the question was raised were the freedmen and women US citizens and did they have the vote? In the months before he unveiled his emancipation policy, Lincoln had gone out of his way to reiterate his support for colonization of those freed from slavery. He had invited black leaders to the White House to lecture them on the wisdom of leaving a land where they would never be accepted as real equals. This was the summer of 1862 and may charitably be interpreted as an attempt to placate Northern racism. But in 1864–5, as the emancipation policy led to large-scale escapes and as

notes Marx complaining at the "bother" of having to write something of such little importance as this address and claims that he only consented to do so because "[in] Marx's view, slavery had to be destroyed in order to allow for the historical development of the white working class" (p. 54). This illogically insinuates that Marx was privileging the white workers by insisting that the more oppressed blacks should be freed first. In reality, Marx was rejecting the idea of a preordained sequence.
71   "The American Ambassador's Reply," in *The Civil War in the United States*, Marx and Engels, pp. 262–3.

the Thirteenth Amendment gathered support, a new abolitionist and antiracist agenda emerged concerning the civic status of those who were to be freed from slavery. Lincoln had repeatedly declared that slaves were part of humankind and that it was blasphemy to belittle or deny this, as he thought Stephen Douglas and other Democratic leaders did. But Lincoln's vehemence on the equal humanity of the former slaves did not mean that they were all simply Americans who were entitled, once released from slavery, to equal citizenship. As we have seen, he long believed that they would remain a sort of alien or stranger and should be invited to leave North America and found a land of their own in Africa or the Caribbean.[72]

In a speech at Charleston on September 18, 1858—part of his famous debating duel with Stephen Douglas—Lincoln had insisted, "I am not, nor have I ever been, in favor of making voters or jurors of negroes, nor of qualifying them to hold office, nor to intermarry with white people."[73] This view of the Negro and his rights was not lightly held, but it did change in the course of the conflict.

In the last year of the war Lincoln gave up his long-held attachment to the policy of encouraging freed people to leave the United States and find a new life in Africa. He found that colonization was rejected not only by black abolitionists and church leaders but also by the "contrabands" who had fled the Confederacy. Elizabeth Keckley, seamstress and confidante to the president's wife, Mary Todd Lincoln, and herself a former slave, headed the Contraband Relief Association in Washington, D.C.[74] The president was

---

72   Lincoln's long attachment to the colonization idea is documented by Eric Foner in "Lincoln and Colonization," in *Our Lincoln: New Perspectives on Lincoln and His World*, Eric Foner, ed., New York 2008, pp. 135–66.

73   Speech of September 18, 1858, taken from Harold Holzer's *The Lincoln-Douglas Debates*, New York 1993, p. 189. This was not an offhand remark, but rather forms part of a careful introduction to his speech. However, on one point it jars with the positive terms he used more than a year before to refer to the enfranchisement of some blacks in the early United States. In a speech on June 26, 1857, on the Dred Scott ruling he cites the dissenting opinion by Judge Curtis, which had shown that some free blacks in five states in the 1780s did exercise the vote. While not advocating giving the vote to free blacks Lincoln seemed keen to stress that, contra Chief Justice Taney, some free blacks did have (voting) rights in the early republic.

74   Foner, *Fiery Trial*, p. 257.

curious about the outlook of the contrabands and Keckley arranged for a few to visit the White House. As we have noted, the "contrabands" had pressured the Union authorities to take a stand on slavery. Now they helped to persuade Lincoln to give up the idea of colonization, which African Americans had many reasons to reject. A point they sometimes made that may have had a special appeal to Lincoln was the argument of "unrequited labor." After all, the slaves' toil had built the seat of government in Washington, D.C., and many fortunes in both South and North.[75] There was also the emphatic rejection voiced by the black leader Edward Thomas: "Are you an American? Are you a Patriot? So are we. Would you spurn all absurd, meddlesome, impudent propositions for your colonization in a foreign country? So do we."[76]

By the time of the Lincoln's second inauguration, in March 1865, the president was less constrained than on earlier occasions and placed slavery as central to the conflict in a way that he had previously avoided. He gave vent to his sense of the heavy wrong that his nation had committed by permitting an extremity of human bondage. He declared that each side in the still unfinished conflict had looked for "an easier triumph" but had not been able to contrive "a result less fundamental and astounding." He saw the carnage of the war as perhaps God's punishment for the nation's "offences" and concluded that he could only hope and pray that "this mighty scourge of war" would come to a speedy end. He added: "Yet if God wills that it continue, until all the wealth piled up by the bondman's two hundred and fifty years of unrequited toil shall be sunk, and until every drop of blood drawn with the lash shall be paid by another drawn with the sword, as was said three thousand years ago, so still it must be said, 'the judgments of the Lord are true and righteous altogether.'"

75　See Foner's essay in *Our Lincoln,* Eric Foner, ed., pp. 135–66. Manisha Sinha's contribution to this volume also cites the African Americans' influence in changing his mind on the question. See her "Allies for Emancipation: Lincoln and Black Abolitionists," pp. 167–98. In this same volume James Oakes argues that the "unrequited labor" strand in Lincoln's rejection of slavery became more marked in the late 1850s and the war years, in his essay "Natural Rights, Citizenship Rights, States' Rights, and Black Rights: Another Look at Lincoln and Race," pp. 109–34.

76　Allen Guelzo, *Lincoln's Emancipation Proclamation: the End of Slavery in America,* New York 2004, p. 19.

This passage certainly put "American slavery" at the center, and strikingly memorialized its enormity as a system for the exploitation of labor. But the Second Inaugural Address did not mention the black soldiers or outline any ideas as to the future fate of the emancipated slave. In the preceding months Radical members of Congress had urged that the freedmen should be given the vote as part of the reconstruction of the rebel states. Lincoln had been noncommittal to begin with, but as he explained himself, he became more positive. Writing to the governor of Louisiana at a time when that state was establishing franchise qualifications, he gently observed, "I barely suggest for your private consideration whether some of the colored people may not be let in—as for instance the very intelligent, and especially those who have fought gallantly in our ranks."[77] In this attempt to cajole the Louisiana governor, using a moderate tone was no doubt advisable, and the enfranchisement of black soldiers would already establish a considerable bloc of black voters. If Lincoln had lived, it seems quite possible that as the situation evolved, so would his views on this matter. James Oakes has noted that Lincoln, in the last year of his life, went out of his way to seek out Frederick Douglass, the outstanding black abolitionist, as on the occasion noted already. Given the racism that permeated the North as much as the South, Lincoln's willingness to solicit the views of the veteran abolitionist and treat him as an equal was a significant development. When Douglass was stopped at the door of the reception held following Lincoln's second inaugural, the president went over publicly to greet him and make clear to all how welcome this black leader was in the White House.[78]

Douglass himself later wrote, "Viewed from genuine abolition ground, Mr. Lincoln seemed tardy, cold, dull, and indifferent, but measuring him by the sentiment of his country, a sentiment he

---

77 Charles Vincent, *Black Legislators in Louisiana During Reconstruction*, Baton Rouge 1976, p. 22.
78 Oakes, *The Radical and the Republican*, pp. 238–43. Oakes explains that Douglass had declined an invitation from the president about a week after his meeting at the Oval Office in August 1864 on the grounds of a prior speaking engagement. Their third (very friendly) encounter was not until six months later. While both men were very busy the apparent lack of follow-through to the second meeting remains puzzling.

was bound as a statesman to consult, he was swift, zealous, radical, and determined." This verdict doesn't directly refer to race, but we may assume that racial feeling is also covered by the term *sentiment*. Lincoln's attempts to reach out to Douglass in the last year of his life seem to signal the stirring of an awareness of the need for African American agency if freedom were really to be won.

By the time of the Second Inaugural the Confederacy was collapsing. The North's belated victory reflected growing success in mobilizing its potential resources—and the Confederacy's increasing failure to do so. The emancipation policy, black enlistment and Union strikes deep inside rebel territory allowed black courage and toil to favor and fortify the Union. So long as it could maintain 400,000 men in the field—as it did until the last months of 1864—the Confederacy still had a hope of exploiting one of the waves of Northern defeatism that periodically swept the North and bringing it to terms. But while the North was at last bringing its resources to bear the Confederacy was dragged down by problems that stemmed directly from the slave regime. Confederate nationalism and the battlefield effectiveness of the rebel forces were sapped by severe shortages, hyperinflation and market collapse. The Southern armies possessed the war materiel they needed to maintain the fight. Indeed, if he had known about it, Marx could have been impressed by the success of the state-directed Southern war industries. But the class-egoism of the planters—their tax allergy and their obsession with growing cotton—led to financial chaos and agricultural dearth. The planter-dominated government resorted to printing bank notes and haphazard requisitions. The resulting hyperinflation disorganized production and exchange. The planters stockpiled some 7 million bales of the commodity in the hope of selling at a good price once the war had ended. The depreciating currency robbed producers of any incentive to grow food for sale, leading to desperate food shortages—in an agricultural state. The Southern desertion rate overtook that of the North. Eventually the Southern military decided to negotiate surrender rather than to pursue a guerrilla struggle that might once again have put wind in the sails of a Northern peace movement. Educated Americans knew about the major role played by "guerrilla" struggle in the Spanish resistance to Napoleon. They also knew about Toussaint Louverture's victory over the British and the defeat of the French by the Haitian republic. But the Southern elite had no stomach for such a fight since it would have imperilled the entire social order of the South. By surrendering when they did the Southern officers were able to retain their side-arms, their horses and some hope of keeping their land and, as we have seen, of rebuilding their local leadership and cross-sectional alliances. [79]

The assassination of Lincoln prompted the International to send another "Address," this time to Andrew Johnson, the new American president.[80] This address closed with the observation that the way was now open to a "new era of the emancipation of labor." But Marx and Engels were soon alarmed by the actions of Lincoln's successor. On July 15, 1865, Engels writes to his friend attacking Johnson: "His hatred of Negroes comes out more and more violently...If things go on like this, in six months all the old villains of secession will be sitting in Congress at Washington. Without colored suffrage, nothing whatever can be done there."[81] The IWA General Council sent a protest to President Johnson in September 1865 and urged that the freedmen should not be denied the vote. In April 1866 Marx writes to Engels, "After the Civil War the United States are only now really entering the revolutionary phase."[82] A clash between president and Congress drove the Republicans to

79 For social conditions in the Confederacy and of the reasons for its defeat, see James Roark, "Behind the Lines: Confederate Society and Economy," in *Writing the Civil War: the Quest to Understand*, James McPherson and William Cooper, eds., Charleston 1998, pp. 201–27. Famine led to bread riots and contributed to the collapse in morale. See Paul Escott, *After Secession: Jefferson Davis and the Failure of Confederate Nationalism*, Baton Rouge 1978, pp. 137–8. See also Mary DeCredico, "The Confederate Home Front," in Ford, *A Companion to the Civil War and Reconstruction*, pp. 258–76 and David Williams, *Rich Man's War*, Athens GA 1998, pp. 98–103.

80 This address, like the first written by Marx, heaps praise on Lincoln as "a man neither to be browbeaten by adversity nor intoxicated by success; inflexibly pressing on to his great goal, never compromising it by blind haste; slowly maturing his steps, never retracing them; carried away by no surge of popular favor, disheartened by no slackening of the popular pulse" and so forth. "Address of the International Workingmen's Association to President Johnson," *The Civil War in the United States*, Marx and Engels, p. 358.

81 Marx and Engels, *The Civil War in the United States*, pp. 276–7.

82 Marx and Engels, *The Civil War in the United States*, p. 277.

more radical measures just as the ending of the war was marked by a multiplication of movements and demands.

CONSEQUENCES OF VICTORY

Marx and Engels expected more from the victory of the Union than an end to slavery, momentous as that was. They also expected the producers to assert new political and social rights. If the freedmen moved simply from chattel slavery to wage slavery, if they were denied the right to vote, or to organize, or to receive an education, then the term *emancipation* would be a mockery. Some Union commanders were already settling freedmen on public or confiscated land. The decision to set up a Bureau of Refugees, Freedmen, and Abandoned Lands in March 1865 seemed to mark a recognition that the occupying power was to take responsibility for an extraordinary situation.

As it turned out, the era of Reconstruction did indeed bring a radical surge in both South and North, with the Republican party seeking to keep abreast of events by adopting the ideas of radical abolitionists, black as well as white, and with pressure being exerted by a shifting coalition of labor unions, social reformers, African American conventions, feminists, and last but not least, the multiplying American sections of the IWA. The martyred president's acknowledgment of its earlier address, and the warm, not to say fulsome, nature of Marx's tribute to the "son of the working class" helped to make the International a quite respectable and visible body. The post–Civil War radicalization in North America in some ways may be compared with the British experience of slave emancipation and home political reform in the 1830s.[83] In both countries, abolitionism and the "free labor" doctrine seemed at a certain juncture to consecrate wage labor and its central role in the capitalist order, only to give rise to popular movements—Chartism in Britain,

---

83 I sketch British slave emancipation in *The Overthrow of Colonial Slavery*, London 1988, pp. 294–330. For a brilliant reading of the social meanings of British abolitionism, see David Brion Davis's *The Problem of Slavery in the Age of Revolution*, New York 1975, and *Slavery and Human Progress*, New York 1984.

a wave of class struggles and popular radicalism in the US—that challenged the given form of the bourgeois order. Although the banner of free labor expressed bourgeois hegemony at one moment, it furnished a means of mobilizing against it at another. In one register, the ideal of free labor encouraged the aspiration of workers to become independent small producers, with their own workshops and farms. Hence the Republican slogan "Free soil, free labor, free men" and its embodiment in the Homestead Act of 1862.[84] But in the United States of the 1860s and 1870s, as in the Britain of the 1840s, there were increasing numbers of wageworkers who did not want to become farmers and who looked to a collective improvement in the rights of working people. David Montgomery, taking a sample of over seventy labor organizers of the later 1860s about whom information is available, found that most of them were second-generation wageworkers, about half of them British immigrants. Their efforts focused not on acquiring land but on regulating the conditions of labor and securing political and industrial representation of the workingman.[85] Of course some workers did take up the offer of land, but many realized that this could prove a trap. Already by the middle and late 1860s the farmers' Grange movement was complaining about exorbitant railroad freight rates and cutthroat competition from large producers.

David Fernbach points out that the "Address to President Lincoln" was one of the first public acts of the International.[86] Lincoln's reply was a publicity coup. Moreover, the campaign to radicalize the resistance to Southern secession—to turn the Civil War into a social revolution—seems to have had a major impact on Marx's thinking and vocabulary. The addresses written by Marx for the International, including the association's own inaugural address, make repeated use of the term "emancipation," a word that

---

84 The classic study of the free labor doctrine is Eric Foner's *Free Soil, Free Labor, Free Men: The Ideology of the Republican Party Before the Civil War*, New York 1970.
85 David Montgomery, *Beyond Equality: Labor and the Radical Republicans, 1862–1872*, New York 1967.
86 Karl Marx, "Introduction," *The First International and After*, Political Writings Vol. 3, edited and introduced by David Fernbach, London 1974, p. 14.

Marx used in his early writings but which did not figure in the *Communist Manifesto* or in his writings in the 1850s. Marx's return to the concept also involved a modification of the way it was used by abolitionists. For most abolitionists the word *emancipation* conjured up the idea of an Emancipator, an external agent carrying out the process of liberation. Marx believed that the new working class would be the agent of its own liberation. He did sometimes take note of slave resistance and slave revolt, but he did not study the Haitian example and tended to believe that slaves needed external deliverance. Given that people of color were a minority—albeit a large one—in the Southern US, this was very likely to be the case in North America. But the notion of emancipation also contains within it the idea that the person or social group to be emancipated is self-standing, capable of exercising freedom, and has no need of an exploiter. Marx had always seen the modern industrial working class as the first exploited class that—because of the social and political rights it had, or would, conquer, and because it was schooled and organized by capitalism itself—could take its destiny into its own hands. The agent here was the "collective worker," all those who contributed to social labor. Marx argues in the IWA's inaugural address that "the emancipation of the working class will be the task of the working class itself." In a word, it will be self-emancipation. Marx saw the fostering of working-class organization as the International's most crucial task, and he believed that class struggle would set up a learning process that would lead them sooner or later to see the need for working-class political power.[87] Even this modification of the emancipation concept may have contained some small, unconscious echo of Lincoln at Gettysburg, as when Marx commends the Paris Commune for embodying "the people acting for itself, by itself."[88]

Raya Dunayevskaya argues in *Marxism and Freedom* that the US agitation for an eight-hour day during and immediately after the Civil War prompted Marx to deepen and elaborate his analysis of

---

87   As Carol Johnson points out, this leaves little room for long-term reformism. See Carol Johnson, "Commodity Fetishism and Working Class Politics," *New Left Review*, 1:119 (1980).
88   Hal Draper, *Karl Marx's Theory of Revolution*, Vol. III, *The Dictatorship of the Proletariat*, New York 1986, p. 273.

the length of the working day in *Das Kapital,* published in 1867.[89] The early US labor movement, like Britain's, sought, and sometimes won, laws limiting the length of the working day. In the years 1864–8 this campaign achieved a new scale and intensity in the United States. Some employers argued that this would be ruinous, since they made all their profits in the last two hours of the day—an argument Marx refuted. He showed that the more efficient employers would be able to thrive under such regulation. As we will see below, struggles over this issue were to play a major role in US labor organizing in the postbellum world. The eight-hour day movement was important to Marx because it expanded the free time available to the laborer.

Marx was well aware that the forced labor of the slave meant very long hours for all, whether old or young, male or female. And in the scarce hours left to them the slaves were as far as possible denied uses of their time that would pose any risk to the system. Thus rigorous laws sought to prevent slaves from learning to read or write, or to venture outside the plantation without a pass. The wageworker, even though intensely exploited, had greater opportunities for education and communication. When Joseph Wedemeyer organized the *Arbeitsbund* that organization sought to develop the workers' access to culture, to press for universal public education, and to oppose "all laws that violate anyone's natural rights, like temperance, Sabbath, or other prohibitionist laws." [90]

The discretion available to the wageworker in the sphere of consumption, culture, and reproduction was registered as a vital point in Marx's work for *Das Kapital.* Slaves were superexploited because they did not receive any monetary reward for toil that yielded a huge flow of premium commodities. With little or no cash, they had no claim on social wealth. Although the wageworkers received much less than the value of their work, they were able to shape their own "extended reproduction," that is, not only to reproduce themselves and their families in ways of their own choosing but also to achieve a level of social communication beyond that—for example, by buying newspapers and even helping to produce them. [91] Plantation

---

89   Raya Dunayevskaya, *Marxism and Freedom*, London 1971, pp. 81–91.
90   Levine, *The Spirit of 1848*, p. 145.
91   See, for example, Karl Marx, "Results of the Immediate Process of

slaves were, by contrast, permitted only "simple reproduction" within a narrow locality—a subsistence defined by allowances from the planter and by what they could themselves produce in garden plots. Marx and the abolitionists sometimes went too far in attributing an abject state to the slaves. They were not sufficiently aware of the reality of a slave community that produced its own culture of survival and resistance. But they were nevertheless quite right to indict the tight invigilation of the slaves, the narrow space allowed them, the daily violence of the slave system, and the constant disruption of the slave community as the plantation economy advanced. The controversies over North American slavery brought home to Marx the relatively broader possibilities of class struggle open to the wageworker even in normal times.

The political antecedents and consequences of slavery and emancipation in the US republic also had a deep impact on Marx and other nineteenth-century socialists. Marx was far from admiring the US political system, which he regarded as continuing to exhibit extreme degrees of corruption, demagoguery, and humbug. But he was impressed by the vast scale and almost elemental character of the social struggles that had been unleashed there. Curiously, Marx and Engels devoted little attention to the aspects of the Constitution and its functioning that rendered it so vulnerable to abuses. For example, they did not note the vagaries of the electoral college or the indirect election of senators. Nevertheless Lincoln's conduct during the Civil War crisis illustrated important points, in Marx's view. The challenge of a "slaveholders' revolt" justified resort to military means. Karl Kautsky and other Marxists were later to argue that any workers' government elected within a bourgeois democratic regime should expect there to be the capitalist equivalent of a "slaveholders' revolt" and should prepare to suppress it by any means necessary. Lincoln's preparedness to suspend habeas corpus and to impose presidential Reconstruction showed that democracy might need to be defended by emergency measures. The example of the Paris Commune reminded Marx of the term "dictatorship of the proletariat," a term that he had not used between 1852 and

---

Production," published as an appendix to Karl Marx, *Capital*, Vol. 1, [Penguin Marx Library], London 1976, p. 1033.

1871. Like the Romans, Marx saw dictatorship as different from tyranny in that the dictator wielded extraconstitutional powers for a brief emergency period. Lincoln's actions were justified by socialists using such arguments as Hal Draper points out in his discussion of the evolution of Marx's ideas.[92]

At the close of the Civil War, Engels wrote to Wedemeyer with the following prophecy:

> Once slavery, the greatest shackle on the political and social development of the United States, has been broken, the country is bound to receive an impetus from which it will acquire quite a different position in world history within the shortest possible time, and a use will then soon be found for the army and navy with which the war is providing it.[93]

Northern capitalism did indeed receive great impetus from the war, after which it embarked on headlong continental expansion. For three decades this proved to be such an absorbing task that little was done to project US power outside the country's own borders. William Seward wanted Caribbean acquisitions, but the Radical Republicans were not interested.[94] Troops were sent to repress the resistance of the Sioux, Cheyenne, and Apache, and steps were taken to modernize the navy, but the terrible losses of the Civil War bequeathed a great distrust of military adventures that lasted for a generation.

Instead, the main focus was on three intimately interlinked processes that were of supreme interest to Marx and Engels: the advance of capitalism in North America, the unfolding of an epic class struggle, and the progress made toward building a genuine workers' party. The outcome of this mighty contest was to determine the possibility, timing and character of any US bid for empire.

---

92   Hal Draper, *The Dictatorship of the Proletariat*, New York 1987, p. 15.
93   Engels to Joseph Wedemeyer, November 24, 1864, Marx and Engels, *The Civil War in the United States*.
94   Walter LaFeber, *The New Empire: an Interpretation of American Expansion*, Ithaca 1963, pp. 24–32.

RECONSTRUCTION AND LABOR FERMENT

In the post–Civil War era, the recently reunited United States was the most dynamic and soon the largest capitalist state in the world. No country illustrated Marx's ideas with greater precision and purity. Great railroads spanned the continent, and vast factories sprouted up, producing steel, agricultural machinery, sewing machines. The emancipation of four million slaves, the demobilization of three million soldiers, and the arrival of a stream of new immigrants swelled the size of the most diverse laboring class in the world. Marx predicted that capitalist conditions would generate class conflict as workers were brought into contact with one another and discovered their common condition. Though they might at first follow their employers, their attempts to acquire security and improved pay or conditions would repeatedly bring them into conflict with them. This would teach the workers the need to organize and seek political representation. And since capitalism would create wealth at one pole and misery at another, and since it would be gripped by recurrent crises, the workers would be drawn to support increasingly radical measures. The Gilded Age served as a laboratory test of such ideas, and with its robber-baron capitalists and titanic labor conflicts, it vindicated many of them.[95] But despite several attempts, no broad-based working-class party emerged in the United States, and the country proved a laggard in developing a welfare state. In these respects much greater progress was made in Europe, especially in Marx's native Germany, where the rise of a Social Democratic Party inspired by Marx's ideas persuaded Chancellor Otto von Bismarck to begin construction of a social security system.

Marx had observed that labor in the white skin would not be truly free so long as labor in the black skin was in chains. This should be understood as a complex sociological proposition as much as a simple moral statement. In 1865, the Thirteenth Amendment, which abolished slavery in the United States, ended a formal legal status that was already crumbling because of massive slave desertions, the Emancipation Proclamation, and deep, disruptive inroads by the Union armies. The greater part of the Confederate forces had

---

95 Matthew Josephson, *The Robber Barons*, New York 1934.

melted away and the planter class was reeling from its spectacular defeat. But, paradoxically, local white power emerged in some ways stronger than before. Alarmed at the sight of free black people, former Confederate officers and men formed militia and patrols designed to defend white families from luridly imagined threats and to deny land and hunting rights to the freemen, to ensure that they were still available for work. Union officers enforced a ban on the whip, but they could not be everywhere. Moreover, the coercion applied to the freed people was increasingly economic rather than physical. Many were obliged to enter very lopsided contracts, with minimal pay until the crop had been sold and with wages paid in "checks" that could only be redeemed at the local store.

The new president in Washington condoned and shared the Southern whites' reaction to black freedom. Johnson urged white-only Southern assemblies to endorse the Thirteenth Amendment, saying that if they did their states could then reenter the Union. He was angered by the continuing demands of the Radical Republicans and the actions of some Union officers who had taken over properties abandoned by Confederate officials and begun distributing land to the freedmen. Johnson believed that the freedmen now needed to be taught their place. He sympathized with the actions of all-white assemblies who enacted strict new labor codes, obliging the freedmen to accept work where it was offered and penalizing "vagrants." Leading Southern gentlemen and ladies paid court to Johnson in the White House, hailing him as the harbinger of reconciliation and the savior of his country. So although Johnson did press Southerners to accept the Thirteenth Amendment, he did so while assuring them that their acceptance would smooth their state's path to rapid reentry into the Union. The idea that the original secessions had been illegal, null, and void potentially opened the way to arguing that the seceders could now simply return. The Republicans insisted that it should fall to Congress to set out the terms of "Reconstruction." They passed resolutions stripping former Confederate officials and officers of their political rights and laying down procedures for fines and confiscations. But the president found ways to frustrate them.

Using his presidential power, Johnson issued thousands of pardons to Confederate military and civilian officials. He also issued a decree halting the distribution of land to the freedmen (of course the estates of whites who had been pardoned could not be seized anyway). The Republican Radicals were able to pass a series of Reconstruction Acts by margins large enough to make the measures immune to presidential veto. In 1866 the Republicans had shied away from giving the freedmen the vote, but the conflict with Johnson and their own plans for Reconstruction persuaded them that only extending the franchise could bring about the election of genuinely loyal assemblies in the Southern states. The presence of an occupying Union Army certainly helped, but the Republicans also needed to mobilize as much political support as possible in the states undergoing Reconstruction.

The Republicans failed (by a narrow margin) to impeach Johnson for treason, but nevertheless were able to impose much of their own vision of Reconstruction on the former slave states, thanks to the presence of Union troops and to the emergence of Union Leagues drawing support from the freedmen and from Southern whites who resented the power of the planters. But the Republican leaders set too much store by the ballot, underestimating the need for measures to tackle the severe economic problems of the South. So long as Union troops were on hand, the freedmen braved intimidation and went out to vote, but occupation was not a long-term solution. Returning Confederate soldiery lurked in the shadows and bided their time.[96]

As the Northern public became aware of the new President's gross indulgence of traitors and of the planters' resort to violence in their attempt to rebuild a coercive labor regime, support for the Radicals grew. Northern outrage at the presidential pardons and at the vicious racial revanchism of the Ku Klux Klan and kindred groups led the Congressional Republican majority to support more radical measures and to propose extending the vote to the freedmen of the South. The Fourteenth Amendment of 1868 promoted the enfranchisement of black males. In 1866–8 the Radical Republicans had the wind in their sails and managed to overrule the president on key issues. But the momentum of the Radicals was

96 Foner, *Reconstruction*, pp. 228–81, and William McKee Evans, *Open Wound: the Long View of Race in America*, Urbana 2009, pp. 147–74. See also David Roediger, *How Race Survived US History*, New York 2009.

checked by the defeat of their attempt to impeach Johnson, with the appearance of moderates who refused to back the measure. The Republican Party recovered in 1868 by endorsing General Ulysses S. Grant, the hugely popular Union commander, as its candidate in the presidential election. Though this ensured a Republican victory, it gave the White House to a man who lacked political experience and judgment, surrounded himself with mediocrities, and failed to include a single Southern Republican in his cabinet. However, as a military commander Grant had at least learned how fickle, short-sighted, and cowardly was the "public opinion" manufactured by the newspapers.

President Grant lent his backing to a Republican strategy of restoring some of the sanctions on former Confederate officials and obliging the reconstructed states to give freedmen the vote as the price of reentry into the Union. For a while the Radical Republicans could still influence Grant, but they failed to register that the revolution in the South was generating its own counterrevolution and could only be sustained by strong and constant support from Washington, and by a far-reaching mobilization of those who supported the new order in the South.

Reconstruction set out to make freedom and equality more tangible, and for a while it succeeded in curbing white terror and promoting black representation and equality. Congressional Reconstruction had given the vote to the freedmen, and the result was to be Republican majorities in the occupied states and the election of some 600 black legislators and officials throughout the occupied South. By itself this was an extraordinary development. African Americans now sat in the Senate and House of Representatives in Washington as well as in the state assemblies.[97]

In Louisiana attempts had been made to segregate public space and means of transport. The state's 1868 Constitutional Convention asserted the novel concept of "public rights," which would give equal access to public space. The Constitution's Bill of Rights declared that all citizens of the state should enjoy "the same civil, political, and public rights and privileges, and be subject to the same pains and penalties." The concept of public rights was clarified by a pro-

---

97   Foner, *Reconstruction*, pp. 351–63.

hibition of racial discrimination on public transport and in places of public resort or accommodation. Rebecca Scott, quoting the document, contrasts this clear requirement with the "oblique language" of the Fourteenth Amendment.[98]

Many abolitionists and Radical Republicans believed that the suppression of slavery was not enough and that the freedmen deserved at least free education, and preferably land and the vote as well. In this situation it was important that some Union Leagues were responsive to abolitionist appeals and that a convention of 150 colored men from 17 states met in Syracuse, New York, in October 1864. The Syracuse convention and subsequent gatherings in Charleston and New Orleans framed a broad program for equal civic and political rights. Many of the participants in these events were already free before the war. They articulated the aspirations of colored communities in Louisiana, South Carolina, and Tennessee—areas occupied by Unionist forces long before the final collapse. Their leaders argued that black soldiers had earned citizenship by helping to save the Union. They also paid their taxes, and therefore deserved representation. At Syracuse, Charleston, and elsewhere the call was not simply for rights in the abstract but for tangible expressions of a new status—the right to vote and serve on juries—and a Homestead Act for the South that would give land to the freedmen. A "Declaration of Rights and Wrongs," adopted at both Syracuse and Charleston, warned that passing measures favorable to the freedmen would be a hollow mockery if planters were still free to intimidate and dragoon them.[99]

The Reconstruction administrations were elected by precarious majorities, achieved by the votes of black men, and also by reaching out to whites who had never owned slaves or supported the Secession, or who had found the Confederacy a nightmare. The Freedmen's Bureau, established in 1865, was wound up in 1870. Radical Republicans and abolitionists were too inclined to believe that once slavery had been struck down a new regime of wages

---

98   Rebecca Scott, *Degrees of Freedom: Louisiana and Cuba after Slavery*, Cambridge, MA, 2005, pp. 43–5.
99   Steven Hahn, *A Nation Under Our Feet: Black Political Struggles in the Rural South from Slavery to the Great Migration*, Cambridge, MA, 2003, pp. 103–5.

and "free labor" would automatically follow. Many freedmen and women devoted more time to cultivating tiny plots that they rented or claimed as squatters. Though some entered into agreements with the planters, who still owned the best land, their new employers complained that the freed people thought that they could withdraw their labor whenever convenient or demand higher pay just when the harvest had to be brought in. An early recovery of the Southern economy was not sustained because of a credit famine. Merchants were only willing to advance credit for staple production, leading to shortfalls in the production of subsistence crops. The plantation economy went into decline, with many landowners in the cotton belt offering sharecropping arrangements to the freedmen. In some cases the sharecropper would be the tenant of a piece of land, some of which could be used for subsistence production. But to begin with it was more common for the sharecropper to work on a planter's land for a modest wage and the promise of further pay once the crop was sold. Thus the sharecropper bore the risk of a poor market on his own shoulders, and this was not the end of his problems. Tenants and sharecroppers often needed to borrow money, and they became indebted to store owners, who would charge them high rates of interest on loans as well as high prices for merchandise. These arrangements narrowed the scope of the Southern market, fostered stagnation and decline, and caused economic pain to white farmers as well as black laborers and tenants.[100]

With Union soldiers on call, the freedmen voted in new officials and sent black representatives and senators to Washington. The Reconstruction administrations also fostered a variety of social programs. These regimes, lasting from four to ten years, were innovative. As Eric Foner explains, they sought to introduce social institutions that the old slave-state authorities had neglected: "Public schools, hospitals, penitentiaries, and asylums for orphans and the insane were established for the first time or received increased funding. South Carolina funded medical care for poor citizens, and Alabama

---

100 The postbellum miseries of the freed people are trenchantly explored by Roger Ransom and Richard Sutch in *One Kind of Freedom: the Economic Consequences of Emancipation*, second ed., Cambridge 2001, especially pp. 244–53.

funded free legal counsel for indigent defendants."[101] With some charitable assistance, the Reconstruction administrations laid the basis for an educational system that was to comprise university colleges as well as high schools, open to the freed people and their descendants. The social programs of Reconstruction demanded resources that were in chronically short supply. Raising taxes alienated potential supporters. The South experienced a credit famine, as banks and storekeepers would advance supplies only for cotton cultivation and did so in far more modest installments than they had before the war, when slave property could be offered as collateral.

The empowerment of the freedmen was carried through in the teeth of continuing resistance from white "rifle clubs," the Ku Klux Klan, and kindred organizations. The Reconstruction administrations fared best—at least for a while—in states where there was either a large black population (South Carolina and Louisiana) or a solid phalanx of white Republicans (Texas and Arkansas).[102] Much depended on the quality and energy of local political leadership. What was needed was an alternative to Federal troops as guarantors of the new order.

In the few areas where there were not only Union soldiers but also black elected officials and police, there were instances of freedmen's labor associations successfully taking over and running the plantations. This occurred on several of the rice plantations along the rivers of coastal South Carolina. The planters' practice of paying wages in "checks" at high-priced stores that they controlled had bred hostility to the wage system: "In Colleton County, by the early 1870s, several large plantations were operating under what a newspaper called "a sort of 'communism,'" with black laborers forming societies, electing officers, and purchasing estates collectively.[103] But such enclaves of labor power were precarious, and in the later 1870s black organization and ownership was to be targeted in South Carolina as it was elsewhere.

The Northern public had been disturbed by white terrorism and so-called "race riots" (really ethnic cleansing), but it had little

101   Foner, *Reconstruction*, p. 364.
102   Eric Foner, *Reconstruction*, pp. 439–40.
103   Eric Foner, *Nothing But Freedom: Emancipation and its Legacy*, Baton Rouge 1983, p. 85.

patience for the heavy costs of an extended occupation of the South and was demoralized by reports of carpetbagger corruption. Prior to the 1872 election, a group of "reform" or Liberal Republicans, led by Horace Greeley, mustered a challenge to Grant, but they argued for less rather than more engagement in the South. Grant's reelection gave a little extra time, but neither the president nor the Republicans gave decisive support to the Reconstruction administrations. To do so would have been expensive and contrary to the growing view that the time had come for a reconciliation with Southern elites. The size of Union forces in the South was continually being whittled down, and white vigilantism was emboldened. Some attempts were made in South Carolina to defend Reconstruction by relying on a local mixed militia, but eventually in the key states the Republican governors had to rely on Federal troops.[104]

THE RESTORED UNION AND A
THWARTED REVOLUTION

The Civil War had landed Washington with a debt of $2.8 billion, and the bankers had extracted exceedingly favorable terms.[105] Schuyler Colfax, from Indiana, proposed that the huge war effort required new taxes—a progressive income tax and a levy on the shareholders of the banks and the new corporations. Colfax pointed out that the farmer had to pay a tax on his property, so justice demanded that there should be a tax on capital—especially that of shareholders—as well as on employees and cultivators.[106] The income tax was agreed upon but the plan for a tax on capital was vetoed by Wall Street

---

104 Steven Hahn, *A Nation Under Our Feet*, pp. 302–13.

105 The total cost of the war has been estimated at $6.5 billion by Claudia Goldin and Frank Lewis, prompting Phillip Paludan's comment, "That amount would have allowed the government to purchase and free all the 4,000,000 slaves (at 1860 prices) give each family 40 acres and a mule and still have provided $3.5 billion as reparations to former slaves for a century of lost wages." Paludan, "What Did the Winners Win?" in *Writing the Civil War*, McPherson and Cooper, p. 181.

106 W. Elliot Brownlow, *Federal Taxation in America*, Cambridge 1996, p. 26. Colfax was at this time in the Radical camp. Also see Vorenberg, *Final Freedom*, pp. 206–7.

and the treasury secretary. The income tax was set at 3 percent and much war expenditure was paid for either by issuing war bonds or by printing greenbacks. Some urged that the public debt be paid off in the same way, although the value of the paper currency had fallen by about a third. The Republicans, having contracted the debt, argued that paying it off with devalued paper would be a sorry reward for the patriotism of those who had subscribed, whether bankers or ordinary citizens. Their decision to pay off that debt in gold left the Treasury bare, unable to pay for Reconstruction in the South or ensure steady growth in the North. Neither the Lincoln administration nor its Republican successors seized the opportunity to introduce a central bank or effectively to regulate the thousands of private banks. This was to be a source of future financial instability and meant that farmers and small or medium businesses did not have access to reliable and reasonably-priced credit. In a book of letters addressed to Colfax in 1865, Henry Carey, the noted critic of free-trade economics, warned that a credit famine would ruin all hopes for successful Reconstruction.[107] Yet nothing was done to meet this problem, Southern producers were starved of credit and by 1880 per capita income in the US South was only 50 percent of the national average, and it would remain so for many decades after. The weakness of the Southern economy was a drag on national performance, but the national economy also suffered because of the primitive banking regime. One rather understated criticism of the postbellum US financial system concludes: "The main costs to the US economy of not having a central bank were a less efficient payments system and a greater potential for instability."[108] The North's master financier, Jay Cooke, who had marketed the Union's war bonds, was himself to be bankrupted by the crisis of 1873.

As it happened, by 1869 Schuyler Colfax was vice president and, one might have hoped, ready to devise a way of taxing the new breed of robber barons. Unfortunately, it was soon discovered that he was implicated in the Credit Mobilier scandal. The Credit Mobilier had issued shares to large numbers of legislators,

---

107   Henry Carey, *Letters to the Honorable Schuyler Colfax*, Philadelphia 1865.
108   Richard Sylla, "Reversing Financial Reversals," in *Government and the American Economy*, Price Fishback et al., Chicago 2007, pp. 115–47, p. 133.

backing return for their backing on its railroad projects. (From the days of John Law onward, there has always been a connection between financial innovation and swindling.)

During the heyday of Radical Reconstruction Northern white workingmen made some gains of their own. The freed people were in a struggle for the control of *space*, both public and private; the Northern workers sought to control *time*. In this industrializing era the average working day lasted more than eleven hours. In 1868 Congress was persuaded to establish an eight-hour legal working day for Federal employees. Eight states had similar laws, though implementation was weak. Radical Reconstruction also favored the first attempts to regulate the railroads. The stirrings of a new social utopianism and a very practical trade union movement were encouraged by the polarizations around Radical Republicanism. Wendell Phillips led prominent abolitionists and Radicals in supporting Eight Hour Leagues. In demanding the eight-hour day the "labor reformers" were accepting "clock time" and a degree of labor discipline as part of a wider scheme of improvement. Starting from free labor principles, Ira Steward argued that shorter hours meant higher pay and that higher pay would combat unemployment and the erosion of wages by inflation. As he bluntly put it, "new employments depend upon a more expensive style of living."[109]

In 1867 a National Labor Union was formed to spread the eight-hour day demand. At its first national meeting the NLU declared: "The National Labor Union knows no north, no south, no east, no west, neither color nor sex, on the question of the rights of labor."[110] The London headquarters of the International sent a warning in May 1869 attacking both ill-founded rumors of war (between Britain and the US) and the all-too-real domestic threat to living standards:

> The palpable effect of the Civil War was, of course, to deteriorate the position of the American workman. In the United States, as in Europe, the monster incubus of a national debt was shifted

109   Quoted in David Roediger and Philip Foner's *Our Own Time: A History of American Labor and the Working Day*, London 1989, p. 85.
110   Quoted in Messer-Kruse's *Yankee International*, p. 191.

from hand to hand, to settle down on the shoulders of the working class.[111]

However, it ventured to anticipate that there would be resistance, and resistance that would have been enhanced by what had already been achieved: "For all this, the Civil War did compensate by freeing the slave and [by] the consequent moral impetus this gave to your own class movement."[112]

Phillip Paludan urges that the war's deleterious impact on labor, and labor's reaction, have not received sufficient attention. The immiseration of Northern workers as a consequence of the great inflation of the 1860s prompted hundreds of strikes and the emergence of many new workers' organizations. Indeed for a while there was a sharp discrepancy between the squeezing of these workers and the improvements accruing to both farmers and former slaves. The Homestead program allowed farmers' sons to acquire land cheaply. Farmers could pay off debts with depreciated currency, and the building of new railroads soon gave them easier access to markets. As for the former slaves, the disintegration of a formidable apparatus of labor coercion had immediate benefits, as families reunited and some withdrew from the labor force while others received at least modest payment.[113] But in both cases these improvements were precarious, as Northern and Northwestern railroads raised freight rates, Southern landowners drove a harder bargain, and white vigilantes sought to intimidate the freedmen.

Some Southern black workers sought to join the eight hours movement. The New Orleans *Tribune*, published by black journalists, supported the campaign, and a State Labor Convention in South Carolina called for a nine-hour day. But true wage labor was of limited significance in the South, so the impact of these moves was small. A Colored Workers Convention in New York in 1869 sought to build a bridge between organized labor and the freedmen. The "Declaration of Rights and Wrongs" framed by African

111 "Address to the National Labour Union of the United States," in *Karl Marx on America and the Civil War*, Saul K. Padover, ed., p. 144.
112 Ibid.
113 Paludan, What Did the Winners Win?" in *Writing the Civil War*, pp. 178, 183, 187.

American conventions at Syracuse and Charleston denounced seg-
regation in public places and warned that measures favorable to
the freedmen would be a hollow mockery if planters were still free
to intimidate and dragoon them.[114] But the differing problems of
workers in the South and North made it more difficult to promote
an alliance between them.

THE POSTWAR RADICALIZATION

Marx's addresses had increased awareness of the International
Workingmen's Association in the United States. The IWA attracted
a diverse range of supporters there, and even as senior a figure as
Senator Charles Sumner was occasionally prepared to support
events staged by the International. By the early 1870s the IWA had
fifty sections in a dozen urban areas, ranging from Boston and New
York in the East, to such crucial hubs as St. Louis and Chicago in
the Midwest, to San Francisco on the West Coast. In New York
there were militia companies led by supporters of the International,
and an African American militia was also said to have become
affiliated. But there is no mention of sections in the South, even
in those areas like South Carolina where there was labor militancy.
The reason for this was very likely the threatening security situation, which obliged all supporters of Reconstruction to cleave to
the Republican Party and its militia. (During the early 1870s the
young Albert Parsons—subsequently a strong supporter of the
International, advocate of independent working-class politics, and
Haymarket martyr—was a colonel in the Texas National Guard,
which was in effect a Republican militia).

Some leading female abolitionists declined to support the
Fourteenth Amendment on the ground that while promoting the
enfranchisement of black men it left women without the vote.[115]
This was an argument about priorities, since nearly all abolitionists supported women's suffrage. The great majority of abolitionists
believed that any chance of achieving black male enfranchisement
should be supported. The 1868 elections, allowing voters their first

114   Hahn, *A Nation Under Our Feet*, pp. 103–5.
115   See Angela Davis, *Women, Race and Class*, New York 1983, pp. 30–86.

opportunity to respond to Johnson's conduct and to news of white brutality in the South, was a good year for Republicans in most parts of the North and West, and confirmed the Republican Congress's desire for black suffrage in the South. Where the Republican leadership had the courage to fight for black male suffrage in the North and West, then they had a good prospect of winning it at home as well as for the South. The fact that so many African Americans had risked their lives for the Union carried great weight with Northern voters. In Iowa, a proposal to give black men the vote passed in a referendum in 1868 though a similar proposal had failed there in 1857. However, the skill and conviction with which the Iowa Republicans seized the "egalitarian moment" was not seen everywhere.[116]

The vulnerability of the black communities in the South also furnished an added argument for black male enfranchisement. The women of the North and West had certainly rallied to support the war effort and were shortly to gain the right for themselves to vote for school boards in Kansas and elsewhere. But whereas the racial order was—at least momentarily—disputed, gender divisions had not been challenged by the war. (Though, as we will see below, this began to change with the advent of peace.) The dispute over this issue soon subsided, as most socialists and abolitionists did support votes for women. This cleared the way for new attempts in the 1870s to explore the makings of a progressive coalition.[117]

The appearance of the labor movements encouraged the view that a fresh start could be made in the 1870s, with the emergence of new

---

116   Robert Dykstra shows that military service was a trump card in the debate over enfranchising black men in Iowa. See Robert Dykstra, *Bright Radical Star: Black Freedom and White Supremacy on the Hawkeye Frontier*, Cambridge, MA, 1993.

117   Women had been lauded for their contributions to the war as nurses and homemakers, but the passage from this to enfranchisement proved more difficult. See also Elizabeth Cady Stanton and Susan B. Anthony, *Correspondence, Writings, Speeches*, Ellen Dubois, ed., New York 1981, pp. 92–112; 166–9. Dubois, in her editorial presentation, argues that Anthony and Cady Stanton were, in different ways, both trying to adapt the women's movement to the need for wider alliances. While Anthony drew on "free labor" ideology to criticize women's dependence, Stanton sketched the programmatic basis for an alliance between the women's and labor movements.

issues and voices. Racism, sexism, and conscious or unconscious bourgeois ideology continued to hold much of the population in thrall and to weaken progressive movements. But much more remarkable than this predictable state of affairs was the emergence of challenges to it: to racism, including institutional racism; to male privilege in the home and workplace as well as at the ballot box; and to the divine right of employers to dictate to their employees and to accumulate vast personal fortunes.

For a brief span—about half a dozen years—the US sections of the IWA became the sounding board and banner for a diverse series of radical initiatives. The IWA and the National Labor Union were seen as sister organizations. The German American Marxists wielded what was then a very novel doctrine—the idea that if labor were only sufficiently well organized it would became a mighty lever for social advances, opening the way to all sections of the oppressed. The privileges of white and male workers were not addressed: all attention was focused on the great concentration of privilege represented by capital. In theory, female and black workers were welcome to join the workers' organizations and would enjoy equal rights within them, though the practice often lagged some way behind. Some of the IWA's US sections developed a primitive and sectarian Marxism that contrasts with the program and practice of the German Social Democratic Party. Marx and Engels were often uneasy at the narrow-mindedness of their American followers, but they were themselves partly responsible for this, since they had not yet developed a conception of the different character and goals of trade unions on the one hand and political parties on the other. The fact that the International embraced, or mixed, both types of organization was no bad thing, but because there had been no theorization of their distinct and different purposes the result was often confusion and tension. There was also the dilemma posed by the scope for social alliances. The workers needed to organize themselves as a distinct body, yet they also needed to reach out to potential allies—farmers, farm laborers, progressive members of the middle class, home workers—on a range of issues. The implicit labor metaphysic of some of the German American Marxists failed to tackle these issues. Nevertheless, in the short run the International actually thrived by avoiding a clear stance on such questions and simply allowing each section to organize in its own way and according to its own priorities.

The German American Marxists might have been narrow-minded, but still they were committed to the principles of racial and gender equality, though they soft-pedaled these issues when seeking to recruit *bona fide* wageworkers such as the Irish of Pennsylvania, New York, and elsewhere who did not share these principled commitments, arguing that it would be easier to educate them once they had joined the IWA. Marx and Engels, familiar with anti-Irish discrimination in England, readily agreed that special efforts should be made to win over the Irish workers. They may not fully have realized that in the US the Irish workers—especially the Pennsylvania miners—had been stigmatized as "copperheads" and traitors because they were believed to have lacked enthusiasm for the Northern cause. The International's strong Unionist credentials and welcoming attitude toward the Irish proved a good combination.

The IWA became a rallying point for many of the disparate forces of emancipation seeking to take part in the reconstruction of the social order. It attracted the attention of Victoria Woodhull—in some ways the Arianna Huffington of the 1870s—who edited the widely selling and much discussed *Woodhull & Claflin's Weekly* and used it to publicize the initiatives of the IWA. Tennie Claflin, Victoria's sister, was elected colonel of a militia after urging that the workers would need a force to defend them in the struggles to come. In 1870 and 1871 the *Weekly* published several articles summarizing the *Communist Manifesto* or explaining the documents of the IWA. It exposed the schemes of the railway promoters and argued that the greed of the owners of the Staten Island ferry led them to skimp on safety, and their negligence eventually caused a disaster in which a hundred passengers perished. An editorial evoked the new spirit:

> This is the age of rights, when, for the first time in human history, the rights of all living things are, in some way, recognized as existing. We are far enough yet from according to all their rights, but we talk about them, we see them, and thought is busy to determine how best they should be secured.[118]

---

118   "The Rights of Children," *Woodhull & Claflin's Weekly*, December 6, 1870.

A series of articles entitled "Man's Rights, or How Would you Like It?" explored the idea of women taking leading positions in economic affairs while it became the turn of men to be "housekeepers and kitchen girls."[119] Other articles sought to reconcile a needed collectivism with the rights of the individual. The banks and the corporations should be taken into truly public ownership, and democratic institutions should ensure "the personal participation of each in the preparation, administration, and execution of the laws by which all are governed." But the state should not seek to prescribe how people lived: "Social freedom means the absolute immunity from impertinent intrusion in all affairs of exclusively personal concernment, such as scientific or religious belief, the sexual relationship, habits of dress, diet or the like."[120]

With her sister, Woodhull was the founder of Wall Street's first female brokerage, and used her rewards from this to finance the *Weekly*, "the lady broker's paper." Eclectic and radical, the *Weekly* showed a lively interest in socialism and new forms of collective self-government and published a special edition of Marx's "Address on the Civil War in France." Marx wrote a friendly note to Woodhull and suggested that his daughter Jenny could supply an article on her experiences in France following the suppression of the Paris Commune.[121]

After the European panic occasioned by the Commune uprising, Marx and his followers had moved the IWA's headquarters to New York. This is often seen as a ploy by Marx and his followers to prevent the IWA failing into the hands of the anarchists. No doubt there is truth in this. Yet there was indeed, as Marx claimed, a promising opening in the United States in which the International could begin to sink real roots in North America.

---

119 "Man's Rights, or How Would You Like It?" ibid., September 8, 1870.
120 "The International: Appeal of Section No. 12," ibid., September 23, 1871.
121 Unfortunately this cordial tone was not maintained. Primed by the doctrinaire Internationalists, in a later letter Marx casually refers to Woodhull as "a banker's woman, free lover and general humbug"; so far as sexual matters were concerned, Marx, the likely father of Frederick Demuth, was more deserving of the term "humbug" than Woodhull.

In Europe, respectable opinion was outraged by the supposed excesses of the Communards in 1871. But in the United States it was the bloody suppression of the Commune that provoked outrage, and sympathy for the victims. Marx's *Civil War in France* was widely read by reformers and radicals. The IWA mustered a demonstration of 70,000 or more in New York in December 1871 to pay tribute to the Commune's tens of thousands of martyrs. The parade brought together the Skidmore Guards (a black militia), the female leadership of Section 12 (Woodhull and Claflin), an Irish band, a range of trade unions, supporters of Cuba's fight for independence marching under the Cuban flag, and a broad spectrum of socialist, feminist, Radical, and Reform politics. In its aftermath, Section 12 and its supporters in the Equal Rights Association, a new reform body, proposed running a ticket in the forthcoming presidential election, with Victoria Woodhull and Frederick Douglass as the candidates. For a brief moment an attempt was made to present a progressive alternative in the 1872 elections, but it passed.[122]

Many of Marx's US followers distrusted Woodhull. She was president of the American Society of Spiritualists, and her Wall Street brokerage had the support of Cornelius Vanderbilt, the richest man in America. The IWA Council declared that wage earners should comprise at least 60 percent of the membership in all sections. Section 12 was suspended for failing to reach this figure. The failure to distinguish between trade union and party was part of the problem here. So, too, was the conception that workers' interests were somehow natural and sociologically given without benefit of ideology or politics. The sectarian exclusion of Section 12 weakened the International, though in the short run the dissension it aroused was eclipsed when Woodhull and her *Weekly* became embroiled in an unrelated obscenity suit. Incensed by hypocritical attacks on her philosophy of "free love," she ran a story in the *Weekly* exposing the extramarital affair of New York's most prominent preacher. The scandal briefly led to Woodhull's imprisonment and prevented her from developing her political profile. Feminist and

---

122 The classic study is Montgomery's *Beyond Equality*; the IWA is discussed on pp. 414–21. But see also Herbert Gutman, *Work, Culture and Society in Industrializing America*, Oxford 1976, pp. 293–343, and Samuel Bernstein, *The First International in America*, New York 1962.

spiritualist leaders followed the socialists in keeping their distance from her.[123]

There was to be a legacy of distrust and factional strife between those of Marx's German American followers who believed that party building was the priority, and others who saw the trade unions as the priority. Both "Yankee" and German Internationalists deplored racial violence and supported female enfranchisement, but the trade unionists gave low priority to such issues, and many Socialists despised the narrowness and caution of the trade union leaders. On the other hand the rumblings of class conflict split the radical Republicans, as some sided with the employers, others with the workers, some supporting the eight-hour demand, and others hostile to it. Then the postwar boom was brought to a shuddering halt by the crash of 1873. The wages of workers had been eroded by the depreciating purchasing power of greenbacks. With their own living standards falling by as much as a third in a few years, the workers of the North and West were first and foremost concerned about bread-and-butter issues. The Republicans lost ground, as they seemed incapable of defending either the wages of Northern workers or the political gains of Southern freedmen. Ultimately the Republicans had deferred to the large property holders in both sections.

AN EXPLOSION OF CLASS STRUGGLE: 1877 AND AFTER

The presidential election of 1876 was deadlocked in the electoral college. The Republicans had failed to find anyone with even remotely Grant's appeal and received many fewer votes, but there was an even tie in the college. This eventually led to a deal—the Wormley House pact of 1877—whereby the Republican went to the White House but the Federal Army was withdrawn from the South. The last Reconstruction governments there collapsed, to be replaced by white "Redeemers," but the spirit of radicalism unleashed by the Civil War and its outcome had not yet been laid to rest.

---

123 For a rounded assessment see Amanda Frisken, *Victoria Woodhull's Sexual Revolution*, Philadelphia 2004.

The deal hatched by the Republicans and Democrats was not a pretty one. It sent the less popular candidate to the White House and allowed him to find jobs in Washington for a horde of displaced Southern Republicans. The press was full of reports of payoffs involving the award of railroad franchises. The new administration soon catered to bankers and bondholders by resuming specie payments. These developments confirmed the scathing assessments of the most dogmatic Marxists of the Socialist Party. The bosses were using the two main parties as blatant spoils machines, and in most areas they were oblivious to the plight of the growing working class. To the socialists, the need for a quite new party—a farmer-labor party—could not have been clearer. The Internationalists moved to form a Workers Party. Robin Archer has recently shed new light on why this possibility was nipped in the bud. He sees it as happening because of a combination of ferocious repression, Socialist sectarianism, and the reluctance of workers' organizations to address political questions, since to do so would risk antagonizing the large number of religious workers with their ties to the existing party system.[124]

The existing party system was difficult to beat because it adjusted to the threat of third parties either by stealing their slogans or by ganging up against them—as the Republicans and Democrats did with their joint slate in Illinois in the 1880s. Successful labor leaders were wooed as candidates by the two established parties. But both parties took handouts from the robber barons, with state assemblies becoming the pawns of railway promoters awarding them large tracts of public land in return for kickbacks. The state authorities also frequently allowed the state militia to be used as strike breakers. Although striking workers sometimes enjoyed public support, the newspapers and middle class opinion easily turned against them.

However, it was an employers' offensive and an across-the-board 10 percent cut in rail workers' pay that detonated the Great Rail Strike of 1877. Many of the rail workers were Union Army

---

124   Robin Archer, *Why Is There No Labor Party in the United States?*, Oxford 2008. This carefully researched and argued study is the most provocative work on its theme since Mike Davis's *Prisoners of the American Dream* (London 1985) and extends the latter's comparison of the US and Australia.

veterans, and the rail companies sought to encourage their loyalty by issuing them uniforms and placing well-known generals on the board. But with this further pay cut such petty palliatives could no longer hold them in check. The Great Strike of 1877 has been described as "one of the bitterest explosions of class warfare in American history."[125] It reached inland to the great rail hubs and soon gripped the greater part of the North and West. Though it erupted three months after the ending of Reconstruction, the Great Strike did not come out of a blue sky. The employers had acted in a concerted fashion and counted on support from Washington, now that the political crisis had been resolved and the troops withdrawn from the South. The rail workers had much public sympathy, and their action encouraged others to down tools and take to the streets in urban areas.[126] Workers in mines and steel plants joined in. The strike gathered momentum because some militia units were loath to threaten lives. One commander explained, "Meeting an enemy in the field of battle, you go there to kill ... But here you have men with fathers and brothers and relatives mingled in the crowd of rioters. The sympathy of the people, of the troops, my own sympathy, was with the strikers proper. We all felt that these men were not receiving enough wages."[127]

In St. Louis, the strike, orchestrated by the Workingmen's Party, an offshoot of the International, had control of the city for several days. Burbank reports:

> The British Consul in St. Louis noted an example of how society was being turned upside down: on a railroad in Ohio, the strikers "had taken the road into their own hands, running the trains and collecting the fares" and felt that they deserved praise because they turned over the proceeds to company officials. The consul commented stiffly that "it is ... to be deplored that a large part of

---

125   Eric Foner, *Reconstruction*, p. 383. For this momentous event see also Robert Bruce, *1877: Year of Violence*, New York 1959, and Philip Foner, *The Great Labor Uprising of 1877*, New York 1977.
126   David Stowell, *The Great Strike of 1877*, Urbana, IL., 2006.
127   Quoted in John P. Lloyd's "The Strike Wave of 1877," in *The Encyclopedia of Strikes in American History*, Aaron Brenner, Benjamin Day and Immanuel Ness, eds., Armonk, NY, 2009, p. 183.

the public appear to regard such conduct as a legitimate mode of warfare."[128]

The strikers produced their own newspaper, the St. Louis *Times*, which attacked the voice of the city's leaders:

> The St. Louis *Times* jeered at *The Republican*'s solemn warnings, quoting the phrase about the railroad men striking "at the very vitals of society": on the contrary, said the *Times*, it was "the very vitals of society' which were on strike, 'and hungry vitals they are too!'"[129]

African Americans played a prominent role in the St. Louis action, a fact harped on by municipal authorities and the local press in their attacks on the strike. A report of the general meeting convoked by the strike leadership noted: "The chairman introduced the Negro speaker, whose remarks were frequently applauded."[130] The strike leadership required the authorities to enact a series of radical measures, including restoration of wage cuts and the generalization of the eight-hour day, but were thwarted when a Committee of Public Safety set up by the leading men of the city raised a militia and sent it to crush the rebellion and end the strike. However, the black population of St. Louis remained a force to be reckoned with—in 1879 blacks fleeing Southern repression, the "Exodusters," were able to shelter in St. Louis prior to leaving for Kansas.[131]

Just as the withdrawal of Federal troops abandoned the field to semiprivate white militia in the South, so the employers in the North were able to pay for thousands, sometimes tens of thousands, of National Guards, specially recruited "deputy marshals," and Pinkerton men to break the strike, which had spread until it had national scope.[132] One hundred strikers lost their lives in the course of the 1877 strike. The employers were also able to bring in

---

128   David Burbank, *Reign of the Rabble: the St. Louis General Strike of 1877*, New York 1966, p. 64.
129   Ibid., p. 25.
130   Ibid., p. 33.
131   For the role of African Americans in the strike and later see Bryan Jack, *The St. Louis African American Community and the Exodusters*, Columbia, MO, 2007, especially pp. 142–50.
132   Samuel Yellin, *American Labor Struggles*, 1877–1934, New York 1937.

black workers to take the place of strikers. The more far-seeing and enlightened labor organizers had urged that blacks be welcomed and organized, too, but it took time for formal recognition to be translated into practical action.[133]

The new president, Rutherford B. Hayes, noted in his diary that the 1877 strike had been suppressed "by *force*." Grant, the man he replaced, was vacationing in Europe—he found these proceedings "a little queer." During his own administration, Grant noted, the entire Democratic Party and "the morbidly honest and 'reforma- tory' portion of the Republicans had thought it 'horrible' to employ Federal troops 'to protect the lives of negroes.' Now, however, there is no hesitation about exhausting the whole power of the govern- ment to suppress a strike on the slightest intimation that danger threatened."[134]

By the 1880s there were 30,000 Pinkerton men, making them a larger force than the Army of the Republic. The latter's strength had dropped to less than 27,000, with those soldiers not in the West reduced to strikebreaking roles. By 1877 the Democrats were calling for Army strength to be further reduced to no more than 20,000. The robber barons of the North and West and the planters of the South had found brutally effective ways to cow the direct producers. Both distrusted the Army and both hated the Federal taxing power. The steep reductions in the Federal military establish- ment reflected both an economy drive and the conviction of some that an Army that stemmed from the Civil War and Reconstruction was not well adapted to enforcing labor discipline.

An unsavory alliance of politicos and robber barons had beaten the rail workers into submission, but this was just the start of two decades of large-scale clashes. From actions by the Illinois and Pennsylvania dockers, lumbermen, miners, and steelworkers of the 1880s to the Pullman and Homestead strikes of the 1890s, the United States was shaken by epic and desperate industrial strug- gles. These battles involved tens, sometimes hundreds, of thousands of workers and had no equal in Europe. In the great battles of the 1880s and 1890s, hundreds of strikers were killed, thousands

---

133 Gutman, *Work, Culture and Society*, pp. 131–208.
134 Quoted in Foner's *Reconstruction*, p. 586.

imprisoned, and tens of thousands blacklisted. These grueling labor battles sometimes seemed like a civilian echo of the Civil War, with the strikers cast as copperheads, or even rebels, and the army, police, and deputy marshals as the loyalists. The Republicans, encouraged by Unionist veterans organizations like the GAR, sought to retain the support of their followers by voting pensions for veterans. Black veterans also qualified. Thanks to this, by 1914 the US provision for public pensions was larger than Germany's, but it was destined steadily to diminish as the old soldiers died. This was a sectional welfare state; the Southern authorities did not have the resources to match it on behalf of Confederate veterans.[135]

Stephen Skowronek describes the closing decades of the nineteenth century as the epoch of the "patchwork state" and emphasizes the role of labor struggles in shaping its peculiar formation.[136] The antebellum regime had defended plantations without regulating them; the postbellum regime did similar service for the new corporations. It is sometimes believed that the Civil War, whatever else it did—or did not do—at least modernized and strengthened the US Federal state. But the authority of the state remained very uneven, the civilian administration was in hock to party placemen, and the legislatures were in league with the money power. These features had survived the war and been intensified by Reconstruction and its overturning. The frustration of "bourgeois" revolution brought no gain to Northern workers or Southern freedmen.

DEFEAT AND TRIUMPH FOR AMERICAN WORKERS

The double defeat of Reconstruction had suppressed black rights in the South and curtailed labor rights in the North. Jim Crow in the South and the widespread use of Pinkerton's men and other goons in the North were both victories for privatized violence and a minimal view of the state. They were a defeat for the republican

135   Theda Skocpol, *Protecting Soldiers and Mothers: the Political Origins of Social Security*, Cambridge, MA, 1992.
136   Stephen Skowronek, *Building a New American State: the Expansion of National Administrative Capacities*, Cambridge 1982, pp. 38–84.

ideal of a unified and responsible federal authority. It was most particularly a defeat for Lincoln's idea that the rule of law should be the "political religion" of all Americans.

There was orchestrated violence in the North, but it was put into the shade by Jim Crow. During the years 1884–1899, between 107 and 241 African Americans were murdered each year by lynch mobs, with total victims numbering more than 3,000. Lynchings were concentrated in the South and a great majority of the victims were black, but they were not unknown elsewhere and they sometimes targeted white labor organizers, Chinese, and Mexicans. Along the Mexican border dozens of Hispanics were lynched during these years. And there were also lynchings of whites in other parts of the Union, especially the "wild" West.[137] The intensification of Jim Crow in the South was accompanied by the spread of onerous, if less extreme, practices of racial exclusion in other sections, affecting residence, employment, and education.[138]

The freed people of the South and the labor organizers of the North not only faced physical threats but also found their attempts to organize and negotiate assaulted in the name of the same conservative strain in free labor ideology—that which construed any regulation or combination as a violation of "freedom of contract." The Republicans and Democrats deferred to this doctrine and the Supreme Court codified it. These rulings pulverized the workers and sharecroppers, leaving them to negotiate only as individuals.

Without a political order capable of regulating the employers, the case for a social democratic party was more difficult to make, and to some a syndicalist perspective seemed more realistic. Another obstacle to proposals for a labor party was the fact that the federal state was fiscally hamstrung, rendering impractical projects for a welfare state. The Union's vast Civil War outlays had been met in part, as

---

137 Joel Williamson, *The Crucible of Race: Black-White Relations in the American South Since Emancipation*, Oxford 1984, pp. 117–8, 185–9; Ida B. Wells-Barnet, *On Lynchings*, with an introduction by Patricia Hill Collins, New York 2002 (first ed. 1892), pp. 201–2.
138 Desmond King and Stephen Tuck, "De-Centering the South: America's Nationwide White Supremacist Order After Reconstruction," *Past and Present*, February 2007, pp. 213–53.

noted above, by the progressive income tax.[139] However, in the early 1870s the income tax was dropped—and then declared unconstitutional by the Supreme Court. The Fourteenth Amendment had promised "all persons" the equal protection of the laws. Though this proved a dead letter so far as the freedmen were concerned, the corporations—who enjoyed the legal status of persons—successfully invoked it against measures for corporate taxation and regulation.

These and other reactionary developments might themselves have increased the willingness of the trade unions to back a labor party. Indeed, those trying to organize general or industrial unions aimed at the mass of workers realized that they needed the support of government. But Archer argues that many key craft leaders—especially Samuel Gompers—had greater industrial bargaining power and feared that their organizations might be put at risk if they teamed up with political adventurers.

Several key trade unions had been inspired by the agitation surrounding the IWA and Marx's writings on the importance of self-organization by the workers. Several US unions were to describe themselves as International organizations—the International Longshoremen or International Garment Workers Union and so forth—an echo of the IWA. Sometimes the "International" was justified by its reference to organizing in Canada, but it had a resonance beyond this. If Marx's followers—many of them German Americans—can take a share of the credit for the impetus given to trade union organization, they must also accept some of the blame for the failure of the US workers' movement to develop a labor party and for the related tardy development and weakness of the US welfare state. Indeed, some blame the influence of Karl Marx for these failures.[140]

Yet Marx favored both trade unions and social democratic or socialist parties in the 1870s, as may readily be seen in the case of Germany. The German SPD was clearly linked to and supportive of organized labor, but its Erfurt program committed it to

---

139   W. Elliot Brownlee, *Federal Taxation in America*, Cambridge 1996, p. 26.
140   Messer-Kruse in *Yankee International* and Archer in *Why Is There No Labor Party in the United States?* come close to this but ultimately concede that on such questions there was a large gap between Marx and those in the US who regarded themselves as his followers. (These included Samuel Gompers.)

revolutionary and democratic objectives and to immediate reforms. It campaigned for votes for women and the defense of the German forests. It supported rights for homosexuals and an end to Germany's imperial exploits in Africa, and it debated the "agrarian question."[141] The breadth of the SPD's program did not, of course, wholly stem from Karl Marx but came also from several other currents, including the Lassalleans. Though Marx had tenaciously fought against what he saw as Lassalle's misguided belief in the progressive character of the German state, he nevertheless went out of his way to cultivate Lassalle's acquaintance, gently to warn him of his mistakes, and above all to remain in touch with the tens of thousands of German socialists who were influenced by him. Marx stressed the great potential and attractive power of the working class, but in his "Critique of the Gotha Programme" he combated the idea that labor was the only source of value, insisting that land (by which he meant nature) was a vital source of use values.[142]

The programmatic scope of the SPD is not the only evidence of the approach favored by Marx and Engels. The program of the French workers party was directly inspired by a conversation with Marx. Its very first clause declared, "the emancipation of the class of producers involves all mankind, without distinction of sex or race."[143] Its immediate program committed it to universal suffrage and equal pay for equal work. No doubt that economism still lurks in it, but in 1879 a platform like this was not such a bad starting point. The idea that trade unions and political organization are mutually exclusive put supposedly Marxian US Socialists and trade unionists at odds with their mentor.

The paternalist ethos of the early socialist movement rendered its commitment to equal rights for women ethereal and abstract.

---

141   I have a very brief discussion of the programmatic ideas of the SPD in "Fin de Siècle: Socialism After the Crash," *New Left Review*, 1:185, January/February 1991. For the evolution of the party's positions on sexuality in the late nineteenth and early twentieth century, see David Fernbach, "Biology and Gay Identity," *New Left Review*, 1:228, 1998.
142   Marx and Engels, "Critique of the Gotha Programme," in Marx, *The First International and After*, pp. 339–59.
143   "Introduction to the Program of the French Workers Party," *The First International and After*, p. 376.

But as women were drawn into the labor movement in the 1880s, female activists challenged the idea that a woman's place was in the home. While male labor organizers were prone to support the notion that the male worker should earn a "family wage," the socialist organizations, especially those influenced by the German SPD, took a different stance: they urged that women would not be truly emancipated until they entered the world of paid labor on equal terms with men. August Bebel, one of the historic leaders of the SPD, wrote a book on the topic, *Woman Under Socialism* (1879), which was widely read in both German and English. Bebel urged that domestic labor should be lightened, and women's employment promoted, by the provision of free communal child-care facilities and restaurants. Though they did not anticipate twentieth-century feminism and often romanticized patriarchal features of the family, the socialists of this era did pay some attention to the issue of gender equality.[144] Female members of the Socialist Labor Party were able to offer a feminist interpretation of Bebel's ideas and to use them to argue for the importance of organizing women workers. Given the employment of large numbers of women in new branches of the economy, socialist women became a significant force.

In 1887 Engels paid tribute to the giant strides being made by the American workers movement, embracing momentous class battles in Illinois and Pennsylvania, the spread of the Eight Hour Leagues, the growth of the Knights of Labor, the sacrifices that had established May 1 as International Labor Day, and the electoral achievements of the first state-level labor parties.[145] But appreciative as he was, he insisted that the whole movement would lose its way unless it could develop a transformative program: "A new party must have a distinct platform," one adapted to American conditions. Without this, any "new party would have but a rudimentary existence." However, beyond saying that the kernel of this program would have to be public ownership of "land, railways, mines, machinery, etc." he did not speculate as to what problems that program should address. Engels rebuked the doctrinaires of the heavily German American Socialist Labor Party for their hostility to unions and their failure

144   Mari Jo Buhle, *Women and American Socialism*, Urbana 1981, pp. 1–48.
145   See Frederick Engels, "Preface to the American Edition," *The Condition of the Working Class in England*, New York 1887, reprinted in this volume.

to grapple with American reality. He urged them to "doff every remnant of their foreign garb," "go to the Americans who are the vast majority" and "on all accounts learn English."[146]

The advice Engels offered, though entirely justified, was also elementary and even simplistic. Programmatic thinking was not entirely lacking in the United States, but it was throttled by the given forms of the labor movement. In many trade unions there was a formal ban on any political discussion, on the grounds that it would prove divisive. The largest working-class organization, the Noble Order of the Knights of Labor, had a similar ban. The Knights of Labor only emerged from clandestinity in 1881 and never entirely shook off its roots as a secret society. Security threats distracted them from public debate of their objectives. Terence Powderley, the Knights' leader, was intensely hostile to foreign-born doctrinaires and strove to exclude or neutralize them. The unions and the Knights made efforts to organize African American and female workers but had no discussion of how to campaign for respect for their rights.[147]

Engels's text was most likely to be read by the members of the Socialist Labor Party, but he did not go far enough in pressing them to become relevant to US conditions. His insistence that the US labor party would have to commit itself to public ownership of the railways and steel was timely—and if it had been heeded by some progressive coalition it might have averted the disaster awaiting these industries in the mid to late twentieth century. His brief list should have included the banks, since they were critical to industry and agriculture. His call for the nationalization of land short-circuited the tangled problems of the county's three million farmers and four million tenants and laborers. By the time of the 1870 census there were 4.9 million wage earners, some of them white-collar, but the agricultural sector was still hugely important. The spread of the Farmers' Alliance in the 1880s and 1890s showed the huge scope there was for mobilizing indebted farmers and rack-rented tenants or sharecroppers, both black and white. Engels endorsed the idea that a US labor party should aim to win a majority in Congress and elect its candidate to the White House, but without

---

146   Ibid., p. 14.
147   Davis, *Prisoners of the American Dream*, pp. 30–1.

an appeal to farmers, tenants, and rural laborers—and many others besides—this was a pipe dream. While Marx and Engels were quite right to shun many of the "Sentimental reformers" with their patented cure-alls, some of these individuals focused on critical issues of taxation and banking, or security and democracy. The milieu of labor reformers had identified and skillfully exploited the issue of the eight-hour day, a programmatic demand that had a mobilizing and universalist impulse (though enforcement was often difficult under US conditions).

The London International had cordial relations with Richard Hinton, a labor reformer and organizer of the Washington, D.C., Section. When the German Marxist leader Sorge sought to bring this section under his control, the General Council in London declared that this was going too far and that the Washington Section should run its own affairs. This section refused to back Sorge's expulsion of Section 12. The British-born Hinton was a former companion of John Brown's and officer of the First Kansas Colored Regiment, and he was fascinated by Edward Kellogg's plan for a network of public banks and Osborn Ward's proposals for cooperative agriculture and industry. In late-nineteenth-century conditions the smallholder was on a hiding to nothing—cooperatives with some public support could have made a lot of sense. Hinton's section included many civil servants, who would actually have to implement any massive program of nationalization. They were probably aware that the country only had 60,000 civil servants and any socialist plan must stimulate local publicly or socially owned enterprises and bottom-up initiatives.[148] Hinton was later to be associated with Eugene Debs's Socialist Party, as editor of its magazine.

In his survey Engels developed a very polite critique of the ideas of Henry George, even conceding that the land tax might have some role. Another radical taxation proposal that merited examination was Schuyler Colfax's idea (mentioned above) of a levy on all shareholding capital.[149] Finally, there was the issue of Lincoln's very unfinished revolution in the American South. Prior to the triumph

---

148   Montgomery, *Beyond Equality*, pp. 387–477.
149   Brownlee, *Federal Taxation*, p. 26.

of the ultraracists in 1900 there were several movements which showed that white and black farmers and laborers could support the same goals; these included the Readjusters movement, which gained power in Virginia in the late 1870s, the Farmers' Alliance, the "fusion" movement in North Carolina, and many branches of Populism. It is striking that these moments of interracial cooperation were targeted at the banks, the railroad corporations, and (in the case of Virginia) the large bondholders.[150] The coal mines of Tennessee also witnessed trade union battles that brought together black and white workers opposed to their employers' leasing of convict labor.[151]

The years 1886–96 witnessed the rise and fall of the People's Party, mounting the most serious third party challenge to the post–Civil War US political regime. The Populist movement was born out of bitterness at the depressed condition of farming and at the venality of Wormley House politics. Farmers in all parts of the Union, but most particularly in the Midwest and South, called on the Federal and state authorities to come to the aid of farmers devastated by low prices, high freight rates and expensive credit. Among the demands launched by the movement were nationalization of the railroads, the coining of silver and the setting up of "sub-treasuries" at state and federal level which would serve as marketing boards for the main cash crops. The farmers' produce would be held in public warehouses in each county; against this collateral they would be able to take out publicly-guaranteed, low interest loans. The People's Party proved attractive enough to elect some Senators and Governors, and scores of state level legislators. It did particularly well in the South, especially where it reached tacit agreements with the Republican party to combine forces against the dominant Democrats. The party's standard bearers were white but it received significant black support, partly thanks to tactical deals with the Republicans. The Democratic party responded with alarm and ferocity to Populist success, on the one hand adopting some of its more eye-catching proposals (e.g. monetizing silver in order to avoid "crucifying mankind on a cross of gold") and on the other

---

150   Evans, *Open Wound*, pp. 175–87.
151   Karen Shapiro, *A New South Rebellion, 1871–1896*, Chapel Hill 1998.

unleashing a campaign of physical intimidation against Southern Populists (in the Georgia campaign in 1892 fifteen men were killed because of their politics). Carl Degler suggests that the Democrat leaders saw the Populist challenge as a "second Reconstruction" and were determined to stamp it out.[152] The defeat of the Southern Populists was accompanied by a further tightening of racial oppression and the consolidation of the Democrats as the unquestioned ruling party of the South. The Populists did try to reach out to the urban workers. They supported two policies cherished by organized labor—the eight hour agitation and opposition to the leasing of convicts to private employers. A group of Populists wanted Eugene Debs, the labor organizer, to become the party's presidential candidate in the 1896 election but he declined. The Populists did not challenge the racial order and were easily deterred from coming to the defense of blacks. Their leaders sometimes couched their appeals in a stridently Protestant idiom that did not appeal to Catholics. The party's most radical proposal was for the "sub-treasury" scheme but key leaders kept their distance from this. The rise and fall of the Populists showed that the idea of a Farmer-Labor party was not just an ideological figment but it also demonstrated the resilience of the reigning political regime.[153]

In private correspondence Engels had a poor view of the theoretical grasp of the American Marxists and socialists. However, Engels was hugely impressed by the anthropological studies of Lewis Henry Morgan and Marx took seriously Henry Carey's economic writings. Within a little more or less than a decade of Engels's death, three outstanding works appeared that would very likely have improved his view of critical thought in the United States: Louis Boudin, *The Theoretical System of Karl Marx* (1907); Thorsten Veblen, *The Theory of Business Enterprise* (1904); and W.E.B. Du Bois, *The Souls of Black Folk* (1903).

The eruption of titanic class struggles also had an impact on

---

152 Carl Degler, *The Other South: Southern Dissenters in the Nineteenth Century*, Boston 1982, pp. 316–70.
153 See Lawrence Goodwyn, *Democratic Promise: The Populist Movement in America*, New York 1976; Michael Kazin, *The Populist Persuasion*, Ithaca 1998; Ernesto Laclau, *On Populist Reason*, London 2005, pp. 200–08; Robert McMath, *American Populism: a Social History, 1877–98*, London 1990.

currents in US intellectual life far removed from Marxism. Eugene
Debs's American Railway Union (ARU) broke with the caution of
craft unionism and tried to organize the entire railroad industry. In
1892 the ARU forced major concessions from the Northern Union
railroad, and its membership grew to 150,000. However, when the
ARU showed that it could paralyze one half of the entire rail network, the administration of Grover Cleveland stepped in to break
the strike through injunctions and imprisonments. A conversation
with an ARU picket had an electrifying impact on the philosopher
John Dewey: "My nerves were more thrilled than they had been for
years; I felt as if I had better resign my job teaching and follow him
round till I got into life. One lost all sense of the right and wrong
of things in admiration of his absolute, almost fanatic, sincerity
and earnestness, and in admiration of the magnificent combination
that was going on. Simply as an aesthetic matter, I don't believe the
world has been but few times such a spectacle of magnificent union
of men about a common interest, as this strike evinces...The govt
is evidently going to take a hand in and the men will be beaten
almost to a certainty—but it's a great thing and the beginning of
greater."[154]

Eugene Debs was arrested for defying the government injunction,
and read Marx's work in jail. Marx's ideas were themselves beginning to influence the culture of US radicalism, just as they were also,
in their turn, shaped by the American experience of robber baron
capitalism and desperate class struggle. Marx's dark vision clearly
supplies the central themes of Jack London's extraordinarily powerful novel *The Iron Heel*, a book read by millions in a large number
of languages—and which many claimed had changed their lives.
The history of the United States in the Gilded Age had resonated
with such epic class struggles that they fleshed out the social imaginary of socialists and other radicals, not just in North America but
also in Europe and far beyond—Latin America, Asia, and Africa.
The New World had always tapped into European utopian longings, sometimes accompanied by dystopian fears. The United States
of the great capitalist trusts and their Congressional marionettes

154   Menand, *The Metaphysical Club*, p. 295; see also Archer, *Why Is There No
Labor Party in the United States?*, pp. 112–42.

offered an awesome spectacle—but so did the resistance of US workers and farmers. The international day of the working class, May 1, after all, memorializes US workers—the Haymarket martyrs of May 1886. So just as the US capitalist, with his top hat and cigar, typified the boss class, so the US workingman, with his shirt and jeans or overalls, became the image of the proletarian (and Lucy Parsons, Mother Jones, and "Rosie the Riveter" supplied his female counterpart). The set-piece battles in industrial America between the two sides were typically on a larger scale than European industrial disputes. There is, of course, irony in the fact that the iconic US worker was ultimately defeated or contained, while organized labor in Europe and the antipodes secured representation and even some social gains.

Albert Parsons, the Haymarket martyr, and his wife, Lucy Parsons, who did so much to defend the memory of her husband and his colleagues, had both participated in the Internationalist movement of the 1870s. They first met in Texas. Albert had volunteered for the Confederate army at the age of 13, but later came to apologize for this. Because of his military experience, he was made colonel of a militia regiment formed to defend Reconstruction. Lucy Parsons was a woman of mixed race (with indigenous, African and European forbears), who may have been born a slave. They moved to Chicago in the mid-1870s, where they were at first active as socialist agitators in the International Working People's Association (IWPA), which saw itself first as a branch of the International and later were self-described anarchists. They were strongly committed to the idea that the workers needed to emancipate themselves. They were subsequently associated with a double attempt to radicalize the program and method of the trade unions. They insisted that the eight-hour day should mean "eight for ten," that is, ten hours' pay for eight hours' work, or an eight-hour day with no loss of pay. This way of shaping the demand had not always been so sharply pursued before. They also propagated the idea that workers should support one another's struggles with boycotts and sympathy strikes.

Albert Parsons was a gifted orator and journalist, but he also assisted in the formation of a workers' militia that would protect political meetings and demonstrations. The Chicago businessmen had already formed their own militia, equipped with carbines and a Gatling gun. However, the famous Haymarket massacre involved neither of these formations. The workers' rally was unarmed and unprotected. An individual, perhaps a provocateur, threw a bomb, and four policemen were killed in the resulting melee. Albert and Lucy, who were unarmed, had taken their children to the rally. The Chicago police responded to the bomb throwing by indiscriminate shooting, killing perhaps a dozen and may have caused some of their own casualties. The anarchist and socialist movement had rhetorically posed the question of revolutionary violence without clearly deciding and explaining the circumstances that might require and justify it.

The eight-hour movement in Chicago had huge support in May 1886, but that support was disoriented by the carefully orchestrated media hysteria claiming an anarchist terror plot. The subsequent trial of the supposed ringleaders of an armed uprising was a judicial lynching rather than a legal process—as the pardons later issued to those who had been imprisoned (rather than hanged) acknowledged and documented. The issuing of this pardon just eight years after the trial illustrates an interesting aspect of the Chicago anarchists: namely, that they did not abstain from electoral politics. Mayor Harrison testified in favor of Albert Parsons, and Parsons urged his followers to vote for Harrison—who lost in 1886 but was reelected in 1893. When Peter Altgelt, the Governor of Illinois, issued pardons to the surviving Haymarket leaders in 1892, he did not suffer electorally.[155] Though generally scornful of politicians, Lucy Parsons expressed her high regard for Altgelt's courage.

Lucy Parsons was a dedicated and accomplished orator, agitator, and organizer, roles that she sustained for half a century after her husband was hanged. She had a special gift for encapsulating the syndicalist worldview. From today's perspective, her identity as a woman and a person of mixed ancestry—Mexican, white and black—makes her a symbol of multiculturalism. However, her own self-conception stressed her identity as a neo-abolitionist exposing "wage slavery." In the 1890s she launched a journal called *The Liberator*, a deliberate echo of William Lloyd Garrison's famous

---

155   James Green, *Death in the Haymarket: A Story of Chicago, the First Labor Movement and the Bombing that Divided America*, New York 2006.

abolitionist magazine. She expressed her horror at Southern lynchings and other attacks on African Americans. But she believed that it was class, not color, that defined the exploited and the oppressed. She urged the Southern blacks to organize and resist without fully registering that white violence was designed to make this impossible. Her anarchist or syndicalist beliefs led her to warn Southern blacks that neither preachers nor politicians would help them. She became a member of Industrial Workers of the World, the syndicalist organization, at its founding conference in Chicago in 1905. For her, the redemptive power of "One Big Union" was needed to crush and scatter the bosses, whether the latter owned factories, railroads, or plantations.[156]

Another product of Reconstruction and the International milieu was Timothy Thomas Fortune, a New York journalist who had been born a slave in Florida and freed by the Emancipation Proclamation and who later served as an aide to his father, a Radical Republican. Fortune's writings, especially *White and Black: Land, Labor and Politics in the South* (1884), analyzed the racial formation of class in the postbellum South. Fortune saw racial and class privilege as mutually supportive. His focus on the historic confrontation between "labor and capital" betrayed some Marxist influence, but he was also founder of the Afro-American League, one of the successors to the Black Convention Movement of 1830–70 and a precursor of the NAACP.[157] In the 1890s he worked for Booker T. Washington and advocated measures favorable to black business and a black middle class.

Both color-blindness and conscious racism prevented US labor from taking up the cause of the victims of white oppression in the South. Employers were often able to exploit and foster racial antagonism. Booker T. Washington sometimes urged employers to take on black employees with the argument that they would be good workers who would spurn the troublemakers. Blinkered as they were, the more ideological wing of German American socialism never recanted their commitment to human unity. Even a writer as

---

156 Lucy Parsons, *Freedom Equality and Solidarity: Writings, and Speeches, 1878–1937*, edited and introduced by Gale Ahrens, Chicago 2004.
157 T. Thomas Fortune, "Labor and Capital," in *Let Nobody Turn Us Around*, Manning Marable and Leith Mullings, eds., pp. 143–6.

critical of the German American Marxists as Messer-Kruse concedes that they "never renounced their devotion to the principle of racial equality,"[158] something which cannot be said of several traditions of Anglo-American socialism.[159]

If the nonappearance of a US labor party marked a critical defeat for Karl Marx, the failure of the Republican Party to emerge from Reconstruction and its sequel as a party of bourgeois rectitude and reform registered a spectacular defeat for Lincoln's hopes for his party and country. After dominating Washington for half a century the Republicans were the party of cartels and corruption. The Democrats were also no slouches when it came to ingratiating themselves with Big Money or persecuting social reformers. Both parties failed US capitalism by offering neither honest stewardship nor the regulatory institutions that might have checked abuse and underpinned progressive development. Instead, as Matthew Josephson showed so vividly, venal "politicos" became the handmaidens of the new corporations and the enemies of social improvement.[160] Moreover, no event so well exhibited the vices of the US political class as the Wormley House deal that ended Reconstruction in 1877. The violence of Southern whites was rewarded, the freedmen and women were abandoned, the wishes of the voters were flouted, and railroad contracts were forwarded or thwarted. The participants in these proceedings sought to camouflage their sordid character by claiming that "reform" would be promoted, but this had become a code word for spending cuts, not integrity and authority in Federal

---

158 Messer-Kruse, *Yankee International*, p. 188.
159 Whatever their other failings, twentieth-century American Marxists, white as well as black, were to make an outstanding contribution to the battle against white racism and for civil rights. No other political current has such an honorable and courageous record. It is to this tradition and a Marxist US New Left that we owe the term *political correctness*. Despite occasional excesses, PC has nevertheless proved to be a hugely progressive force, establishing a basic etiquette of respect and collaboration. Mocked though it sometimes is, its achievement is a noble one. This having been said, Marx—at least in his private correspondence—furnishes a field day for PC critics, though they should notice that his negative characterizations are bestowed impartially on Germans and French, Yankees and South Americans, blacks and Jews. Cherishing universalism, he is excessively hostile to any type of partiality.
160 Matthew Josephson, *The Politicos*, New York 1963.

administration. The freed people were left on their own, while Republican placemen forced to flee the South were found jobs in the Treasury Department in Washington.[161]

But the real problem was that in each recession many banks failed and even in good times the service offered to farmers was miserably inadequate. The modest resources available to the Federal government were also a significant factor in the failure of Reconstruction, as we have seen. Abraham Lincoln gave considerable latitude to his treasury secretaries, but by inclination he favored private sector solutions and was wary of giving too much scope to publicly controlled entities. If the US postbellum record was much weaker than it should have been, the decisions taken—and not taken—by his administration help to explain this. However, it was the retreat from Reconstruction, the granting of virtual autonomy to Southern Dixiecrats, and the blunting of Federal powers by the Supreme Court that gave free rein to robber baron capitalism.

Marx and Engels themselves were often scornful of Republican leaders, including Lincoln, and generally distrusted the machinations of large states. But, with occasional misgivings, they had placed a wager that the Civil War would lead to slave emancipation, and that emancipation would in its turn pose the issue of votes for the freedmen. They further predicted more and larger labor struggles. Their predictions were borne out, although the new unions were eventually contained or defeated. The American Federation of Labor was founded, but it turned its back on the formation of a labor party. The example and watchwords of the Internationalists and of the Haymarket martyrs helped to encourage worker resistance in Shanghai, Petrograd, Calcutta, Havana, Turin, Barcelona, Berlin, Vienna, and Glasgow. In the years before the outbreak of the great slaughter in 1914, socialists, anarchists, and syndicalists worked to oppose imperial war, and to foster internationalism and class solidarity. And though they underestimated the power of nationalism and militarism, they were right about imperialism.

---

161   Foner, *Reconstruction*, pp. 580–1; Josephson, *Politicos*, pp. 234–6.

New York City IWA parade to commemorate martyrs of the Paris Commune, December 17, 1871 (original woodcut from Frank Leslie's Illustrated Newspaper, *New York 1872).*

MARX IN THE US?

It remains only to address a final problem. Karl Marx's conception of history bequeathed a theoretical puzzle to later historical materialists, namely, what is the role of the individual in history? Such powerful writers and thinkers as Georgi Plekhanov, Isaac Deutscher, Jean-Paul Sartre, and Ernest Mandel debated the topic, often drawing attention to the fact that even deep-laid historical processes often depend on highly personal capacities and decisions. Considering the remarkable sequence of events I have surveyed here, it is clear that some individuals are so placed that they can influence the course of history. Lincoln did so with the Emancipation Proclamation. He thereby started a revolution, but he did not live to finish it. The freed people, the former abolitionists of whatever race, sex, or class had to contend with the consequences—angry white men in the South and greedy businessmen in the North. Through

the IWA, Karl Marx had an impact on a generation of American workers and radicals, but despite heroic battles to do so, the IWA proved unable to build a political workers' movement to compare with those in Europe and the antipodes.

This leads me to a final thought. What would have happened if Marx or Engels had themselves sailed from England to make their home in New York or Chicago? It would have provoked a sensation. Marx would have earned good fees as a lecturer, and his family, including his daughters and sons-in-law, would very likely have flourished. Engels was hugely invigorated by the trip he did make to New York and Boston in 1887, but he declined to give public lectures there, and he did not return.[162]

But the truly tantalizing issue is whether they would have been able to find a more promising path for the American left. Obviously, there is no real way of knowing. But if their conduct in Germany in 1848–9, or in the 1860s, is any guide, Marx and Engels would have

---

162   Eleanor Marx and Edward Aveling also visited the US in 1887, and their combined lecture tour was very well received by the public. However, the visit was to be marred by controversies over the expenses claimed by Aveling. See Yvonne Kapp, *Eleanor Marx*, volume 2, London 1976, pp. 141–91.

strongly opposed any policy of subordinating the real movement to some socialist shibboleth. They might well have helped to consolidate the International's achievements. They would very likely have favored opening the unions to the generality of workers and they would surely have given exceptional importance to curbing the freelance violence of the Southern "rifle clubs" and Northern company goons. Marx would have urged workers to develop their own organizations. But, just as he saw the importance of the slavery issue at the start of the Civil War, so he would surely have focused on "winning the battle of democracy," securing the basic rights of the producers—including the freedmen—in all sections as preparation for an ensuing social revolution. Eschewing reactionary socialism or the counterfeit anti-imperialism of some Southern slaveholders, Marx and Engels would have insisted that only the socialization of the great cartels and financial groups could enable the producers and their social allies to confront the challenges of modern society and to aspire to a society in which the free development of each is the precondition for the free development of all.

Abraham Lincoln

First Inaugural Address

Fellow Citizens of the United States:

In compliance with a custom as old as the Government itself, I appear before you to address you briefly and to take in your presence the oath prescribed by the Constitution of the United States to be taken by the President before he enters on the execution of this office.

I do not consider it necessary at present for me to discuss those matters of administration about which there is no special anxiety or excitement.

Apprehension seems to exist among the people of the Southern States that by the accession of a Republican Administration their property and their peace and personal security are to be endangered. There has never been any reasonable cause for such apprehension. Indeed, the most ample evidence to the contrary has all the while existed and been open to their inspection. It is found in nearly all the published speeches of him who now addresses you. I do but quote from one of those speeches when I declare that I have no purpose directly or indirectly to interfere with the institution of slavery in the States where it exists. I believe I have no lawful right to do so, and I have no inclination to do so.

Those who nominated and elected me did so with full knowledge that I had made this and many similar declarations and had never recanted them; and more than this, they placed in the platform for my acceptance, and as a law to themselves and to me, the clear and emphatic resolution which I now read:

> Resolved, that the maintenance inviolate of the rights of the States, and especially the right of each State to order and control its own domestic institutions according to its own judgment exclusively, is essential to that balance of power on which the perfection and endurance of our political fabric depend, and we denounce the lawless invasion by armed force of the soil of any State or Territory, no matter what pretext, as among the gravest of crimes.

I now reiterate these sentiments, and in doing so I only press upon the public attention the most conclusive evidence of which the case is susceptible that the property, peace, and security of no section are to be in any wise endangered by the now incoming Administration. I add, too, that all the protection which, consistently with the Constitution and the laws, can be given will be cheerfully given to all the States when lawfully demanded, for whatever cause—as cheerfully to one section as to another.

There is much controversy about the delivering up of fugitives from service or labor. The clause I now read is as plainly written in the Constitution as any other of its provisions:

No person held to service or labor in one State, under the laws thereof, escaping into another, shall in consequence of any law or regulation therein be discharged from such service or labor, but shall be delivered up on claim of the party to whom such service or labor may be due.

It is scarcely questioned that this provision was intended by those who made it for the reclaiming of what we call fugitive slaves, and the intention of the lawgiver is the law. All members of Congress swear their support to the whole Constitution—to this provision as much as to any other. To the proposition, then, that slaves whose cases come within the terms of this clause "shall be delivered up" their oaths are unanimous. Now, if they would make the effort in good temper, could they not with nearly equal unanimity frame and pass a law by means of which to keep good that unanimous oath?

There is some difference of opinion whether this clause should be enforced by national or by State authority, but surely that difference is not a very material one. If the slave is to be surrendered, it can be of but little consequence to him or to others by which authority it is done. And should anyone in any case be content that his oath

Abraham Lincoln, 1860

shall go unkept on a merely unsubstantial controversy as to how it shall be kept?

Again: In any law upon this subject ought not all the safeguards of liberty known in civilized and humane jurisprudence to be introduced, so that a free man be not in any case surrendered as a slave? And might it not be well at the same time to provide by law for the enforcement of that clause in the Constitution which guarantees that "the citizens of each State shall be entitled to all privileges and immunities of citizens in the several States"?

I take the official oath today with no mental reservations and with no purpose to construe the Constitution or laws by any hypercritical rules; and while I do not choose now to specify particular acts of Congress as proper to be enforced, I do suggest that it will be much safer for all, both in official and private stations, to conform to and abide by all those acts which stand unrepealed than to violate any of them trusting to find impunity in having them held to be unconstitutional.

It is seventy-two years since the first inauguration of a President under our National Constitution. During that period fifteen different and greatly distinguished citizens have in succession administered the executive branch of the Government. They have conducted it through many perils, and generally with great success. Yet, with all this scope of precedent, I now enter upon the same task for the brief constitutional term of four years under great and peculiar difficulty. A disruption of the Federal Union, heretofore only menaced, is now formidably attempted.

I hold that in contemplation of universal law and of the Constitution the Union of these States is perpetual. Perpetuity is implied, if not expressed, in the fundamental law of all national governments. It is safe to assert that no government proper ever had a provision in its organic law for its own termination. Continue to execute all the express provisions of our National Constitution, and the Union will endure forever, it being impossible to destroy it except by some action not provided for in the instrument itself.

Again: If the United States be not a government proper, but an association of States in the nature of contract merely, can it, as a contract, be peaceably unmade by less than all the parties who made it? One party to a contract may violate it—break it, so to speak—but does it not require all to lawfully rescind it?

Descending from these general principles, we find the proposition that in legal contemplation the Union is perpetual confirmed by the history of the Union itself. The Union is much older than the Constitution. It was formed, in fact, by the Articles of Association in 1774. It was matured and continued by the Declaration of Independence in 1776. It was further matured, and the faith of all the then thirteen States expressly plighted and engaged that it should be perpetual, by the Articles of Confederation in 1778. And finally, in 1787, one of the declared objects for ordaining and establishing the Constitution was "to form a more perfect Union."

But if destruction of the Union by one or by a part only of the States be lawfully possible, the Union is less perfect than before the Constitution, having lost the vital element of perpetuity.

It follows from these views that no State upon its own mere motion can lawfully get out of the Union; that resolves and ordinances to that effect are legally void; and that acts of violence within any State or States against the authority of the United States are insurrectionary or revolutionary, according to circumstances.

I therefore consider that in view of the Constitution and the laws the Union is unbroken, and to the extent of my ability I shall take care, as the Constitution itself expressly enjoins upon me, that the laws of the Union be faithfully executed in all the States. Doing this I deem to be only a simple duty on my part, and I shall perform it so far as practicable unless my rightful masters, the American people, shall withhold the requisite means or in some authoritative manner direct the contrary. I trust this will not be regarded as a menace, but only as the declared purpose of the Union that it will constitutionally defend and maintain itself.

In doing this there needs to be no bloodshed or violence, and there shall be none unless it be forced upon the national authority. The power confided to me will be used to hold, occupy, and possess the property and places belonging to the Government and to collect the duties and imposts; but beyond what may be necessary for these objects, there will be no invasion, no using of force against or among the people anywhere. Where hostility to the United States in any interior locality shall be so great and universal as to prevent competent resident citizens from holding the Federal offices, there will be no attempt to force obnoxious strangers among the people for that object. While the strict legal right may exist in the Government to enforce the exercise of these offices, the attempt to do so would be so irritating and so nearly impracticable withal that I deem it better to forego for the time the uses of such offices.

The mails, unless repelled, will continue to be furnished in all parts of the Union. So far as possible the people everywhere shall have that sense of perfect security which is most favorable to calm thought and reflection. The course here indicated will be followed unless current events and experience shall show a modification or change to be proper, and in every case and exigency my best discretion will be exercised, according to circumstances actually existing and with a view and a hope of a peaceful solution of the national troubles and the restoration of fraternal sympathies and affections.

That there are persons in one section or another who seek to destroy the Union at all events and are glad of any pretext to do it I will neither affirm nor deny, but if there be such, I need address no word to them. To those, however, who really love the Union may I not speak?

Before entering upon so grave a matter as the destruction of our national fabric, with all its benefits, its memories, and its hopes, would it not be wise to ascertain precisely why we do it? Will you hazard so desperate a step while there is any possibility that any portion of the ills you fly from have no real existence? Will you, while the certain ills you fly to are greater than all the real ones you fly from, will you risk the commission of so fearful a mistake?

All profess to be content in the Union if all constitutional rights can be maintained. Is it true, then, that any right plainly written in the Constitution has been denied? I think not. Happily, the human mind is so constituted that no party can reach to the audacity of doing this. Think, if you can, of a single instance in which a plainly written provision of the Constitution has ever been denied. If by the mere force of numbers a majority should deprive a minority of any clearly written constitutional right, it might in a moral point of view justify revolution—certainly would if such right were a vital one. But such is not our case. All the vital rights of minorities and of individuals are so plainly assured to them by affirmations and negations, guarantees and prohibitions in the Constitution that controversies never arise concerning them. But no organic law can ever be framed with a provision specifically applicable to every question which may occur in practical administration. No foresight can anticipate nor any document of reasonable length contain express provisions for all possible questions. Shall fugitives from labor be surrendered by national or by State authority? The Constitution does not expressly say. May Congress prohibit slavery in the Territories? The Constitution does not expressly say. Must Congress protect slavery in the Territories? The Constitution does not expressly say.

From questions of this class spring all our constitutional controversies, and we divide upon them into majorities and minorities. If the minority will not acquiesce, the majority must, or the Government must cease. There is no other alternative, for continuing the Government is acquiescence on one side or the other. If a minority in such case will secede rather than acquiesce, they make a precedent which in turn will divide and ruin them, for a minority of their own will secede from them whenever a majority refuses to be controlled by such minority. For instance, why may not any portion of a new confederacy a year or two hence arbitrarily secede again, precisely as portions of the present Union now claim to secede from it? All who cherish disunion sentiments are now being educated to the exact temper of doing this.

Is there such perfect identity of interests among the States to compose a new union as to produce harmony only and prevent renewed secession?

Plainly the central idea of secession is the essence of anarchy. A majority held in restraint by constitutional checks and limitations and always changing easily with deliberate changes of popular opinions and sentiments is the only true sovereign of a free people. Whoever rejects it does of necessity fly to anarchy or to despotism. Unanimity is impossible. The rule of a minority, as a permanent arrangement, is wholly inadmissible; so that, rejecting the majority principle, anarchy or despotism in some form is all that is left.

I do not forget the position assumed by some that constitutional questions are to be decided by the Supreme Court, nor do I deny that such decisions must be binding in any case upon the parties to a suit as to the object of that suit, while they are also entitled to very high respect and consideration in all parallel cases by all other departments of the Government. And while it is obviously possible that such decision may be erroneous in any given case, still the evil effect following it, being limited to that particular case, with the chance that it may be overruled and never become a precedent for other cases, can better be borne than could the evils of a different practice. At the same time, the candid citizen must confess that if the policy of the Government upon vital questions affecting the whole people is to be irrevocably fixed by decisions of the Supreme Court, the instant they are made in ordinary litigation between parties in personal actions, the people will have ceased to be their own rulers, having to that extent practically resigned their Government into the hands of that eminent tribunal. Nor is there in this view any assault upon the court or the judges. It is a duty from which they may not shrink to decide cases properly brought before them, and it is no fault of theirs if others seek to turn their decisions to political purposes.

One section of our country believes slavery is right and ought to be extended, while the other believes it is wrong and ought not to be extended. This is the only substantial dispute. The fugitive-slave clause of the Constitution and the law for the suppression of the foreign slave trade are each as well enforced, perhaps, as any law can ever be in a community where the moral sense of the people imperfectly supports the law itself. The great body of the people abide by the dry legal obligation in both cases, and a few break over in each. This, I think, cannot be perfectly cured, and it would be worse in both cases after the separation of the sections than before. The foreign slave trade, now imperfectly suppressed, would be ultimately revived without restriction in one section, while fugitive slaves, now only partially surrendered, would not be surrendered at all by the other.

Physically speaking, we cannot separate. We cannot remove our respective sections from each other nor build an impassable wall between them. A husband and wife may be divorced and go out of the presence and beyond the reach of each other, but the different parts of our country cannot do this. They cannot but remain face to face, and intercourse, either amicable or hostile, must continue between them. Is it possible, then, to make that intercourse more advantageous or more satisfactory after separation than before? Can aliens make treaties easier than friends can make laws? Can treaties be more faithfully enforced between aliens than laws can among friends? Suppose you go to war: you cannot fight always, and when, after much loss on both sides and no gain on either, you cease fighting, the identical old questions, as to terms of intercourse, are again upon you.

This country, with its institutions, belongs to the people who inhabit it. Whenever they shall grow weary of the existing Government, they can exercise their constitutional right of amending it or their revolutionary right to dismember or overthrow it. I cannot be ignorant of the fact that many worthy and patriotic citizens are desirous of having the National Constitution amended. While I make no recommendation of amendments, I fully recognize the rightful authority of the people over the whole subject, to be exercised in either of the modes prescribed in the instrument itself, and I should, under existing circumstances, favor rather than oppose a fair opportunity being afforded the people to act upon it. I will venture to add that to me the convention mode seems preferable, in that it allows amendments to originate with the people themselves, instead of only permitting them to take or reject propositions originated by others, not especially chosen for the purpose, and which might not be precisely such as they would wish to either accept or refuse. I understand a proposed amendment to the Constitution—which amendment, however, I have not seen—has passed Congress, to the effect that the Federal Government shall never interfere with the domestic institutions of the States, including that of persons held to service. To avoid misconstruction of what I have said, I depart from my purpose not to speak of particular amendments so far as to say that, holding such a provision to now be implied constitutional law, I have no objection to its being made express and irrevocable.

The Chief Magistrate derives all his authority from the people, and they have referred none upon him to fix terms for the separation of the States. The people themselves can do this if also they choose, but the Executive as such has nothing to do with it. His duty is to administer the present Government as it came to his hands and to transmit it unimpaired by him to his successor.

Why should there not be a patient confidence in the ultimate justice of the people? Is there any better or equal hope in the world? In our present differences, is either party without faith of being in the right? If the Almighty Ruler of Nations, with His eternal truth and justice, be on your side of the North, or on yours of the South, that truth and that justice will surely prevail by the judgment of this great tribunal of the American people.

By the frame of the Government under which we live this same people have wisely given their public servants but little power for mischief, and have with equal wisdom provided for the return of that little to their own hands at very short intervals. While the people retain their virtue and vigilance no Administration by any extreme of wickedness or folly can very seriously injure the Government in the short space of four years.

My countrymen, one and all, think calmly and well upon this whole subject. Nothing valuable can be lost by taking time. If there be an object to hurry any of you in hot haste to a step which you would never take deliberately, that object will be frustrated by taking time, but no good object can be frustrated by it. Such of you as are now dissatisfied still have the old Constitution unimpaired, and, on the sensitive point, the laws of your own framing under it, while the new Administration will have no immediate power, if it would, to change either. If it were admitted that you who are dissatisfied hold the right side in the dispute, there still is no single good reason for precipitate action. Intelligence, patriotism, Christianity, and a firm reliance on Him who has never yet forsaken this favored land are still competent to adjust in the best way all our present difficulty.

In your hands, my dissatisfied fellow countrymen, and not in mine, is the momentous issue of civil war. The Government will not assail you. You can have no conflict without being yourselves the aggressors. You have no oath registered in heaven to destroy the Government, while I shall have the most solemn one to "preserve, protect, and defend it."

I am loath to close. We are not enemies, but friends. We must not be enemies. Though passion may have strained it must not break our bonds of affection. The mystic chords of memory, stretching from every battlefield and patriot grave to every living heart and hearthstone all over this broad land, will yet swell the chorus of the Union, when again touched, as surely they will be, by the better angels of our nature.

March 4, 1861

Emancipation Proclamation

Whereas, on the twenty-second day of September, in the year of our Lord one thousand eight hundred and sixty-two, a proclamation was issued by the President of the United States, containing, among other things, the following, to wit:

> That on the first day of January, in the year of our Lord one thousand eight hundred and sixty-three, all persons held as slaves within any State or designated part of a State, the people whereof shall then be in rebellion against the United States, shall be then, thenceforward, and forever free; and the Executive Government of the United States, including the military and naval authority thereof, will recognize and maintain the freedom of such persons, and will do no act or acts to repress such persons, or any of them, in any efforts they may make for their actual freedom.
>
> That the Executive will, on the first day of January aforesaid, by proclamation designate the States and parts of States, if any, in which the people thereof, respectively, shall then be in rebellion against the United States; and the fact that any State, or the people thereof, shall on that day be, in good faith, represented in the Congress of the United States by members chosen thereto at elections wherein a majority of the qualified voters of such State shall have participated, shall, in the absence of strong countervailing testimony, be deemed conclusive evidence that such State, and the people thereof, are not then in rebellion against the United States.

Now, therefore, I, Abraham Lincoln, President of the United States, by virtue of the power in me vested as Commander in Chief of the

Army and Navy of the United States in time of actual armed rebellion against the authority and government of the United States, and as a fit and necessary war measure for suppressing said rebellion, do on this first day of January in the year of our Lord one thousand eight hundred and sixty-three, and in accordance with my purpose so to do publicly proclaimed for the full period of one hundred days from the day first above mentioned, order and designate as the States and parts of States wherein the people thereof respectively are this day in rebellion against the United States, the following, to wit:

> Arkansas, Texas, Louisiana (except the Parishes of St. Bernard, Plaquemines, Jefferson, St. John, St. Charles, St. James Ascension, Assumption, Terrebonne, Lafourche, St. Mary, St. Martin, and Orleans, including the City of New Orleans), Mississippi, Alabama, Florida, Georgia, South Carolina, North Carolina, and Virginia (except the forty-eight counties designated as West Virginia, and also the counties of Berkley, Accomac, Northampton, Elizabeth City, York, Princess Ann, and Norfolk, including the cities of Norfolk and Portsmouth, and which excepted parts, are for the present, left precisely as if this proclamation were not issued).

And by virtue of the power and for the purpose aforesaid, I do order and declare that all persons held as slaves within said designated States, and parts of States, are, and henceforward shall be free; and that the Executive government of the United States, including the military and naval authorities thereof, will recognize and maintain the freedom of said persons.

And I hereby enjoin upon the people so declared to be free to abstain from all violence, unless in necessary self-defense; and I recommend to them that in all cases when allowed, they labor faithfully for reasonable wages.

And I further declare and make known, that such persons of suitable condition will be received into the armed service of the United States to garrison forts, positions, stations, and other places, and to man vessels of all sorts in said service.

And upon this act, sincerely believed to be an act of justice, warranted by the Constitution, upon military necessity, I invoke the considerate judgment of mankind, and the gracious favor of Almighty God.

In witness whereof I have hereunto set my hand and caused the seal of the United States to be affixed.

Done at the City of Washington, this first day of January in the year of our Lord one thousand eight hundred and sixty three, and of the Independence of the United States of America the eighty-seventh. By the President: ABRAHAM LINCOLN WILLIAM H. SEWARD, Secretary of State.

January 1, 1863

Gettysburg Address

Fourscore and seven years ago, our fathers brought forth on this continent a new nation, conceived in liberty and dedicated to the proposition that all men are created equal. Now we are engaged in a great civil war, testing whether that nation or any nation so conceived and so dedicated can long endure. We are met on a great battlefield of that war. We have come to dedicate a portion of that field as a final resting place for those who here gave their lives that that nation might live. It is altogether fitting and proper that we should do this. But in a larger sense, we cannot dedicate, we cannot consecrate, we cannot hallow this ground. The brave men, living and dead, who struggled here have consecrated it far above our poor power to add or detract. The world will little note nor long remember what we say here, but it can never forget what they did here. It is for us the living, rather, to be dedicated here to the unfinished work which they who fought here have thus far so nobly advanced. It is rather for us to be here dedicated to the great task remaining before us: that from these honored dead we take increased devotion to that cause for which they gave the last full measure of devotion; that we here highly resolve that these dead shall not have died in vain, that this nation under God shall have a new birth of freedom, and that government of the people, by the people, for the people shall not perish from the earth.

November 19, 1863

Second Inaugural Address

Fellow Countrymen:

At this second appearing to take the oath of the Presidential office there is less occasion for an extended address than there was at the first. Then a statement somewhat in detail of a course to be pursued seemed fitting and proper. Now, at the expiration of four years during which public declarations have been constantly called forth on every point and phase of the great contest which still absorbs the attention and engrosses the energies of the nation, little that is new could be presented. The progress of our arms, upon which all else chiefly depends, is as well known to the public as to myself, and it is, I trust, reasonably satisfactory and encouraging to all. With high hope for the future, no prediction in regard to it is ventured.

On the occasion corresponding to this four years ago, all thoughts were anxiously directed to an impending civil war. All dreaded it; all sought to avert it. While the inaugural address was being delivered from this place, devoted altogether to saving the Union without war, insurgent agents were in the city seeking to destroy it without war—seeking to dissolve the Union and divide effects by negotiation. Both parties deprecated war, but one of them would make war rather than let the nation survive, and the other would accept war rather than let it perish, and the war came.

One eighth of the whole population were colored slaves, not distributed generally over the Union but localized in the southern part of it. These slaves constituted a peculiar and powerful interest. All knew that this interest was somehow the cause of the war. To strengthen, perpetuate, and extend this interest was the object for which the insurgents would rend the Union even by war, while the Government claimed no right to do more than to restrict the territorial enlargement of it. Neither party expected for the war the magnitude or the duration which it has already attained. Neither anticipated that the cause of the conflict might cease with, or even before, the conflict itself should cease. Each looked for an easier triumph and a result less fundamental and astounding. Both read the same Bible and pray to the same God, and each invokes His aid against the other. It may seem strange that any men should dare to ask a just God's assistance in wringing their bread from the sweat of other men's faces, but let us judge not, that we be not judged. The prayers of both could not be answered. That of neither has been answered fully. The Almighty has His own purposes. "Woe unto the world because of offenses; for it must needs be that offenses come, but woe to that man by whom the offense cometh." If we shall suppose that American slavery is one of those offenses which, in the providence of God, must needs come, but which, having continued through His appointed time, He now wills to remove, and that He gives to both North and South this terrible war as the woe due to those by whom the offense came, shall we discern therein any departure from those divine attributes which the believers in a living God always ascribe to Him? Fondly do we hope, fervently do we pray, that this mighty scourge of war may speedily pass away. Yet if God wills that it continue until all the wealth piled by the bondsman's two hundred and fifty years of unrequited toil shall be sunk, and until every drop of blood drawn with the lash shall be paid by another drawn with the sword, as was said three thousand years ago, so still it must be said "the judgments of the Lord are true and righteous altogether."

With malice toward none, with charity for all, with firmness in the right as God gives us to see the right, let us strive on to finish the work we are in, to bind up the nation's wounds, to care for him who shall have borne the battle and for his widow and his orphan, to do all which may achieve and cherish a just and lasting peace among ourselves and with all nations.

March 4, 1865

Karl Marx

The North American Civil War

London, October 20, 1861

For months now, the leading London papers, both weekly and daily, have been repeating the same litany on the American Civil War. While they insult the free states of the North, they anxiously defend themselves against the suspicion of sympathizing with the slave states of the South. In fact, they continually write two articles: one in which they attack the North, another in which they excuse their attacks on the North. *Qui s'excuse, s'accuse.*

Their extenuating arguments are basically as follow. The war between North and South is a tariff war. Furthermore, the war is not being fought over any issue of principle; it is not concerned with the question of slavery but in fact centers on the North's lust for sovereignty. In the final analysis, even if justice is on the side of the North, does it not remain a futile endeavor to subjugate eight million Anglo-Saxons by force! Would not a separation from the South release the North from all connection with Negro slavery and assure to it, with its 20 million inhabitants and its vast territory, a higher level of development up to now scarcely dreamed of? Should the North not then welcome secession as a happy event, instead of wanting to crush it by means of a bloody and futile civil war?

Let us examine point by point the case made out by the English press.

The war between North and South—so runs the first excuse—is merely a tariff war, a war between a protectionist system and a free-trade system, and England, of course, is on the side of free trade. Is the slave owner to enjoy the fruits of slave labor to the full, or is he to be cheated of part of these fruits by the Northern protectionists? This is the question at issue in the war. It was reserved for the *Times* to make this brilliant discovery; the *Economist, Examiner, Saturday Review* and the like have elaborated on the same theme. It is characteristic that this discovery was made not in Charleston, but in London. In America everyone knew, of course, that between 1846 and 1861 a system of free trade prevailed and that Representative Morrill only carried his protectionist tariff through Congress after the rebellion had already broken out. Secession did not take place, therefore, because Congress had passed the Morrill tariff; at most, the Morrill tariff was passed by Congress because secession had taken place. To be sure, when South Carolina had its first attack of secessionism, in 1832, the protectionist tariff of 1828 served as a pretext; but that a pretext is all it was is shown by a statement made by General Jackson. This time, however, the old pretext has in fact not been repeated. In the secession Congress at Montgomery,[1] every mention of the tariff question was avoided, because in Louisiana, one of the most influential Southern states, the cultivation of sugar is based entirely on protection.

But, the London press pleads further, the war in the United States is nothing but a war aimed at preserving the Union by force. The Yankees cannot make up their minds to strike off fifteen stars from their banner.[2] They want to cut a colossal figure on the world stage. Indeed, it would be quite a different matter if the war were being fought in order to abolish slavery. But the slavery question, as the *Saturday Review*, among others, categorically declares, has absolutely nothing to do with this war.

It must be remembered above all that the war was started not by the North but by the South. The North is on the defensive. For months it had quietly stood by and watched while the secessionists took possession of forts, arsenals, shipyards, customs houses, pay offices, ships, and stores of arms belonging to the Union, insulted

---

1 On February 4, 1861, the Congress of Montgomery founded the Confederate States of America, with eleven member states under the presidency of Jefferson Davis.

2 This total includes the contested border states that the South also claimed.

Karl Marx, 1849

its flag, and took Northern troops prisoner. The secessionists finally decided to force the Union government out of its passive stance by means of a blatant act of war; *for no other reason than this* they proceeded to bombard Fort Sumter near Charleston. On April 11 [1861] their General Beauregard had learned in a meeting with Major Anderson, the commander of Fort Sumter, that the fort only had rations for three more days and that it would therefore have to be surrendered peacefully after this period. In order to forestall this peaceful surrender the secessionists opened the bombardment early the next morning (April 12), bringing about the fall of the place after a few hours. Hardly had this news been telegraphed to Montgomery, the seat of the secession Congress, when War Minister Walker declared publicly, in the name of the new Confederacy, "No man can say where *the war opened today* will end." At the same time he prophesied that before the first of May the flag of the Southern Confederacy would wave from the dome of the old Capitol in Washington and within a short time perhaps also from the Faneuil

Hall in Boston. Only then did Lincoln issue the proclamation summoning 75,000 men to protect the Union. The bombardment of Fort Sumter cut off the only possible constitutional way out: the summoning of a general convention of the American people, as Lincoln had proposed in his inaugural address. As it was, Lincoln was left with the choice of fleeing from Washington, evacuating Maryland and Delaware, surrendering Kentucky, Missouri, and Virginia, or of answering war with war.

The question as to the principle underlying the American Civil War is answered by the battle slogan with which the South broke the peace. [Alexander H.] Stephens, the Vice President of the Southern Confederacy, declared in the secession Congress that what fundamentally distinguished the constitution recently hatched in Montgomery from that of Washington and Jefferson was that slavery was now recognized for the first time as an institution good in itself and as the foundation of the whole political edifice, whereas the revolutionary fathers, men encumbered by the prejudices of the eighteenth century, had treated slavery as an evil imported from England and to be eradicated in the course of time. Another Southern matador, Mr. Spratt, declared, "For us it is a question of the foundation of a great slave republic." Thus if the North drew its sword only in defense of the Union, had not the South already declared that the continuance of slavery was no longer compatible with the continuance of the Union?

Just as the bombardment of Fort Sumter gave the signal for the opening of the war, the electoral victory of the Northern Republican party, Lincoln's election to the presidency, had given the signal for secession. Lincoln was elected on November 6, 1860. On November 8 the message was telegraphed from South Carolina, "Secession is regarded here as an accomplished fact"; on November 10, the Georgia legislature occupied itself with plans for secession, and on November 13 a special sitting of the Mississippi legislature was called to consider secession. But Lincoln's election was itself only the result of a split in the Democratic camp. During the election campaign the Northern Democrats concentrated their votes on Douglas, the Southern Democrats on [John C.] Breckinridge; the Republican party owed its victory to this split in the Democratic vote. How, on the one hand, did the Republican party achieve this dominant position in the North; how, on the other hand, did this division arise *within* the Democratic party, whose members, North and South, had operated in conjunction for more than half a century?

Buchanan's presidency[3] saw the control which the South had gradually usurped over the Union, as a result of its alliance with the Northern Democrats, reach its peak. The last Continental Congress of 1787 and the first constitutional Congress of 1789–90 had legally excluded slavery from all territories of the republic northwest of Ohio. (Territories are the colonies lying within the United States which have not yet achieved the population level laid down in the Constitution for the formation of autonomous states.) The so-called Missouri Compromise (1820), as a result of which Missouri entered the ranks of the United States as a slave-owning state, excluded slavery from all other territories north of 36° 30′ latitude and west of the Missouri [River]. As a result of this compromise the area of slavery was extended by several degrees of longitude while, on the other hand, quite definite geographical limits seemed to be placed on its future propagation. This geographical barrier was in turn torn down by the so-called Kansas-Nebraska Bill, whose author, Stephen A. Douglas, was at the time leader of the Northern Democrats. This bill, which passed both Houses of Congress, repealed the Missouri Compromise, placed slavery and freedom on an equal footing, enjoined the Union government to treat both with indifference, and left it to the sovereign people to decide whether slavery was to be introduced in a territory or not. Thus, for the first time in the history of the United States, every geographical and legal barrier in the way of an extension of slavery in the territories was removed. Under this new legislation the hitherto free territory of New Mexico, an area five times greater than New York State, was transformed into a slave territory, and the area of slavery was extended from the Mexican republic to latitude 38° north. In 1859 New Mexico was given a legal slave code which vies in barbarity with the statute books of Texas and Alabama. However, as the 1860 census shows, New Mexico does not yet have fifty slaves in a population of about 100,000. The South therefore only had to send over the border a few adventurers with some slaves and, with

---

3 James Buchanan was US president from 1857 to 1861.

the help of the central government in Washington, get its officials and contractors to drum up a sham representative body in New Mexico, in order to impose slavery and the rule of the slaveholders on the territory.

However, this convenient method proved inapplicable in the other territories. The South, therefore, went one step further and appealed from Congress to the Supreme Court of the United States. This Supreme Court, which numbers nine judges, five of whom are Southerners, had long been the most amenable instrument of the slaveholders. In 1857, in the notorious Dred Scott case, it decided that every American citizen had the right to take with him into any territory any property recognized by the Constitution. The Constitution recognizes slaves as property and commits the Union government to the protection of this property. Consequently, on the basis of the Constitution, slaves could be forced by their owners to work in the territories, and thus every individual slaveholder was entitled to introduce slavery into territories hitherto free against the will of the majority of the settlers. The territorial legislatures were denied the right to exclude slavery, and Congress and the Union government were charged with the duty of protecting the pioneers of the slave system.

While the Missouri Compromise of 1820 had extended the geographical boundaries of slavery in the territories, and while the Kansas-Nebraska Bill of 1854 had eliminated all geographical boundaries and replaced them by a political barrier, the will of the majority of the settlers, the Supreme Court's decision of 1857 tore down even this political barrier and transformed all territories of the republic, present and future, from nurseries of free states into nurseries of slavery.

At the same time, under Buchanan's administration, the more severe law of 1850 on the extradition of fugitive slaves was ruthlessly carried out in the Northern states. It seemed to be the constitutional calling of the North to play slave-catcher for the Southern slaveholders. On the other hand, in order to hinder as far as possible the colonization of the territories by free settlers, the slaveholders' party frustrated all so-called free-soil measures, that is, measures intended to guarantee the settlers a fixed amount of uncultivated public land free of charge.

As in domestic policy, so also in the foreign policy of the United States the interests of the slaveholders served as the guiding star. Buchanan had in fact purchased the presidential office by issuing the Ostend Manifesto,[4] in which the acquisition of Cuba, whether by payment or by force of arms, is proclaimed as the great political task of the nation. Under his administration northern Mexico had already been divided up among American land speculators, who were impatiently awaiting the signal to fall upon Chihuahua, Coahuila, and Sonora. The incessant piratical filibusters against the Central American states were no less carried out under the direction of the White House in Washington.[5] Closely connected with this foreign policy, which was manifestly aimed at conquering new territory for the expansion of slavery and the rule of the slaveholders, was the *resumption of the slave trade*, secretly supported by the Union government. Stephen A. Douglas himself declared in the American Senate on August 20, 1859, that during the previous year more Negroes had been requisitioned from Africa than ever before in any single year, even at the time when the slave trade was still legal. The number of slaves imported in the last year amounted to 15,000.

Armed propaganda abroad on behalf of slavery was the avowed aim of national policy; the Union had in fact become the slave of the 300,000 slaveholders who rule the South. This state of affairs had been brought about by a series of compromises which the South owed to its alliance with the Northern Democrats. All the periodic attempts made since 1817 to resist the ever increasing encroachments of the slaveholders had come to grief against this alliance. Finally, there came a turning point.

Hardly had the Kansas-Nebraska Bill been passed, erasing the geographical boundary of slavery and making its introduction into new territories subject to the will of the majority of the settlers, when armed emissaries of the slaveholders, border rabble from Missouri and Arkansas, fell upon Kansas, a bowie-knife in one hand and a revolver in the other, and with the most atrocious barbarity

---

4   The Ostend Manifesto was issued in 1854 by the United States ambassadors to Spain, France, and England (the latter being Buchanan); it contained an offer to purchase Cuba from Spain and threatened to seize it by force if Spain refused.
5   Nicaragua was the particular object of these expeditions.

tried to drive out its settlers from the territory which they had colonized. As these raids were supported by the central government in Washington, a tremendous reaction ensued. In the whole of the North, but particularly in the Northwest, a relief organization was formed to provide support for Kansas in the shape of men, weapons, and money. Out of this relief organization grew the Republican party, which thus has its origins in the struggle for Kansas. After the failure of the attempts to transform Kansas into a slave territory by force of arms, the South tried to achieve the same result by way of political intrigue. Buchanan's administration, in particular, did its utmost to maneuver Kansas into the ranks of the United States as a slave state by the imposition of a slave constitution. Hence a new struggle took place, this time conducted for the most part in the Washington Congress. Even Stephen A. Douglas, leader of the Northern Democrats, now (1857–8) entered the lists, against the administration and against his Southern allies, because the imposition of a slave constitution would contradict the principle of settlers' sovereignty passed in the Nebraska Bill of 1854. Douglas, senator for Illinois, a northwestern state, would naturally have forfeited all his influence if he had wanted to concede to the South the right to steal by force of arms or acts of Congress the territories colonized by the North. Thus while the struggle for Kansas gave birth to the Republican party, it simultaneously gave rise to the first split within the Democratic party itself.

The Republican party issued its first program for the presidential election of 1856. Although its candidate, John Frémont, did not win, the huge number of votes cast for him demonstrated the rapid growth of the party, particularly in the Northwest. In their second national convention for the presidential election (May 17, 1860), the Republicans repeated their program of 1856, enriched by only a few additional points. Its main contents were that not a foot of new territory would be conceded to slavery, and that the filibustering[6] policy abroad must cease; the resumption of the slave trade was condemned, and lastly, free-soil laws would be enacted in order to further free colonization.

---

6 The term "filibuster" here denotes American insurrectionist activities carried out in a foreign country.

The point of decisive importance in this program was that slavery was not to be conceded another foot of new ground; rather, it was to remain confined once and for all within the limits of the states where it already legally existed. Slavery was thus to be interned for good. However, permanent territorial expansion and the continual extension of slavery beyond its old borders is a law of existence for the slave states of the Union.

The cultivation of the Southern export crops, i.e., cotton, tobacco, sugar, etc., by slaves is only profitable so long as it is conducted on a mass scale by large gangs of slaves and in wide areas of naturally fertile soil requiring only simple labor. Intensive cultivation, which depends less on the fertility of the soil and more on capital investment and on intelligent and energetic labor, runs contrary to the nature of slavery. Hence the rapid transformation of states such as Maryland and Virginia, which in earlier times employed slavery in the production of export commodities, into states which raise slaves in order to export them to states lying further south. Even in South Carolina, where slaves form four-sevenths of the population, the cultivation of cotton has remained almost stationary for years, due to the exhaustion of the soil. Indeed, South Carolina has become partly transformed into a slave-raising state by pressure of circumstances insofar as it already sells slaves to the states of the deep South and Southwest to a value of four million dollars annually. As soon as this point is reached, the acquisition of new territory becomes necessary, so that one section of the slaveholders can introduce slave labor into new fertile estates and thus create a new market for slave raising and the sale of slaves by the section it has left behind. There is not the least doubt, for example, that without the acquisition of Louisiana, Missouri, and Arkansas by the United States, slavery would long ago have disappeared in Virginia and Maryland. In the secession Congress at Montgomery, one of the Southern spokesmen, Senator Toombs, strikingly formulated the economic law that necessitates the constant expansion of the slave territory. "In fifteen years more," he said, "without a great increase in slave territory, either the slaves must be permitted to flee from the whites, or the whites must flee from the slaves."

As is well known, individual states are represented in the Congressional House of Representatives according to the size of their respective populations. Since the population of the free states is growing incomparably more quickly than that of the slave states, the number of Northern representatives has inevitably overtaken the number of Southerners. The actual seat of Southern political power, therefore, is being transferred more and more to the American Senate, where every state, whether its population is great or small, is represented by two senators. In order to assert its influence in the Senate and, through the Senate, its hegemony over the United States, the South thus needed a continual formation of new slave states. But this could only be brought about by conquering foreign countries, as in the case of Texas, or by transforming the United States territories first into slave territories, later into slave states, as in the case of Missouri, Arkansas, etc. John Calhoun, whom the slaveholders admire as their statesman *par excellence*, declared in the Senate as early as February 19, 1847 that only the Senate offered the South the means of restoring a balance of power between South and North, that the extension of the slave territory was necessary to restore this balance, and that therefore the attempts of the South to create new slave states by force were justified.

When it comes down to it, the number of actual slaveholders in the South of the Union is not more than 300,000, an exclusive oligarchy confronted by the many million so-called poor whites, whose number has constantly grown as a result of the concentration of landed property, and whose situation can only be compared with that of the Roman plebeians in the direst period of Rome's decline. Only with the acquisition of new territories, the prospect of such acquisition, and filibustering expeditions is it possible to harmonize the interests of these "poor whites" successfully with those of the slaveholders, to channel their restless thirst for action in a harmless direction, and to tempt them with the prospect of becoming slave-holders themselves one day.

As a result of economic laws, then, to confine slavery to the limits of its old terrain would inevitably have led to its gradual extinction; politically it would have destroyed the hegemony exercised by the slave states by way of the Senate; and finally it would have exposed the slaveholding oligarchy to ominous dangers within their own states from the "poor whites." With the principle that every further extension of slave territories was to be prohibited by law, the Republicans therefore mounted a radical attack on the rule of the slaveholders. Consequently, the Republican election victory could not help but lead to open struggle between North and South. However, as has already been mentioned, this election victory was itself conditioned by the split in the Democratic camp.

The Kansas struggle had already provoked a split between the slave party and its Democratic allies in the North. The same quarrel now broke out again in a more general form with the presidential election of 1860. The Northern Democrats, with Douglas as their candidate, made the introduction of slavery into the territories dependent upon the will of the majority of settlers. The slaveholders' party, with Breckinridge as its candidate, asserted that the Constitution of the United States, as the Supreme Court had also declared, made legal provision for slavery; slavery was in actual fact already legal in all territories and did not require special naturalization. Thus, while the Republicans prohibited any growth of slave territories, the Southern party laid claim to all territories as legally warranted domains. What they had tried, for instance, with Kansas—imposing slavery on a territory against the will of the settlers themselves, by way of the central government—they now held up as a law for all Union territories. Such a concession lay beyond the power of the Democratic leaders and would only have caused their army to desert to the Republican camp. On the other hand, Douglas's "settlers' sovereignty" could not satisfy the slaveholders' party. What the slaveholders wanted to achieve had to be brought about in the next four years under the new President; it could only be brought about by means of the central government and could not be delayed any longer. It did not escape the slaveholders' notice that a new power had arisen, the Northwest, whose population, which had almost doubled between 1850 and 1860, was already more or less equal to the white population of the slave states—a power which neither by tradition, temperament, nor way of life was inclined to let itself be dragged from compromise to compromise in the fashion of the old Northern states. The Union was only of value for the South insofar as it let it use federal power as a means of implementing its slave policy. If it did not, it was better to break now than to watch the development of the Republican party and the rapid growth of the Northwest for another four years, and to begin the struggle under less favorable conditions. The slaveholders' party, therefore, now staked its all! When the Northern Democrats refused to play the role of the Southern "poor whites" any longer, the South brought about Lincoln's victory by splitting the votes and used this victory as an excuse for drawing the sword.

As is clear, the whole movement was and is based on the *slave question*. Not in the sense of whether the slaves within the existing slave states should be directly emancipated or not, but whether the twenty million free Americans of the North should subordinate themselves any longer to an oligarchy of 300,000 slaveholders; whether the vast territories of the Republic should become the nurseries of free states or of slavery; finally, whether the foreign policy of the Union should take the armed propaganda of slavery as its device throughout Mexico and Central and South America.

In a foreign article we shall examine the assertion of the London press that the North should sanction secession as the most favorable and only possible solution of the conflict.[7]

Die Presse, October 25, 1861

---

7   See the following chapter, "The American Question in England."

The American Question in England

London, September 18, 1861

Mrs. Beecher Stowe's letter to Lord Shaftesbury, whatever its intrinsic merit may be, has done a great deal of good, by forcing the anti-Northern organs of the London press to speak out and lay before the general public the ostensible reasons for their hostile tone against the North and their ill-concealed sympathies with the South, which looks rather strange on the part of people affecting an utter horror of slavery. Their first and main grievance is that the present American war is "not one for the abolition of slavery," and that therefore the high-minded Britisher, used to undertaking wars of his own, and interesting himself in other people's wars only on the basis of "broad humanitarian principles," cannot be expected to feel any sympathy with his Northern cousins. "In the first place," says the *Economist*, "the assumption that the quarrel between the North and South is a quarrel between Negro freedom on the one side, and Negro slavery on the other, is as impudent as it is untrue." "The North," says the *Saturday Review*, "does not proclaim abolition, and never pretended to fight for antislavery. The North has not hoisted for its oriflamme the sacred symbol of justice to the Negro; its *cri de guerre*[1] is not unconditional abolition." "If," says the *Examiner*, "we have been deceived about the real significance of the sublime movement, who but the Federalists themselves have to answer for the deception?"

Now, in the first instance, the premise must be conceded. The war has not been undertaken with a view to putting down slavery,

---

1 War cry.

and the United States authorities themselves have taken the greatest pains to protest against any such idea. But then, it ought to be remembered that it was not the North but the South which undertook this war, the former acting only on the defense. If it be true that the North, after long hesitation and an exhibition of forbearance unknown in the annals of European history, drew at last the sword not for crushing slavery, but for saving the Union, the South, on its part, inaugurated the war by loudly proclaiming "the peculiar institution" as the only and main end of the rebellion. It confessed to fighting for the liberty of enslaving other people, a liberty which, despite the Northern protests, it asserted to be put in danger by the victory of the Republican Party and the election of Mr. Lincoln to the Presidential chair. The Confederate Congress boasted that its newfangled Constitution, as distinguished from the Constitution of the Washingtons, Jeffersons, and Adamses, had recognized for the first time slavery as a thing good in itself, a bulwark of civilization, and a divine institution. If the North professed to fight but for the Union, the South gloried in rebellion for the supremacy of slavery. If antislavery and idealistic England felt not attracted by the profession of the North, how came it to pass that it was not violently repulsed by the cynical confessions of the South?

The *Saturday Review* helps itself out of this ugly dilemma by disbelieving the declarations of the seceders themselves. It sees deeper than this, and discovers "*that slavery had very little to do with secession,*" the declarations of Jeff [erson] Davis and company to the contrary being mere "conventionalisms" with "about as much meaning as the conventionalisms about violated altars and desecrated hearths, which always occur in such proclamations."

The staple of argument on the part of the anti-Northern papers is very scanty, and throughout all of them we find almost the same sentences recurring, like the formulas of a mathematical series, at certain intervals, with very little art of variation or combination. "Why," exclaims the *Economist*, "it is only yesterday, when the Secession movement first gained serious head, on the first announcement of Mr. Lincoln's election, that the Northerners offered to the South, if they would remain in the Union, every conceivable security for the performance and inviolability of the obnoxious institution— that they disavowed in the most solemn manner all intention of interfering with it—that their leaders proposed compromise after compromise in Congress, all based upon the concession that slavery should not be meddled with." "How happens it," says the *Examiner*, "that the North was ready to compromise matters by the largest concessions to the South as to slavery? How was it that a certain geographical line was proposed in Congress within which slavery was to be recognized as an essential institution? The Southern states were not content with this."

What the *Economist* and the *Examiner* had to ask was not only why the Crittenden and other compromise measures were *proposed* in Congress, but why they were not *passed*? They affect to consider those compromise proposals as accepted by the North and rejected by the South, while in point of fact they were baffled by the Northern party that had carried the Lincoln election. Proposals never matured into resolutions, but always remaining in the embryo state of *pia desideria*,[2] the South had of course never any occasion either of rejecting or acquiescing. We come nearer to the pith of the question by the following remark of the *Examiner*:

> Mrs. Stowe says: "The slave party, finding they could no longer use the Union for their purposes, resolved to destroy it." There is here an admission that up to that time the slave party had used the Union for their purposes, and it would have been well if Mrs. Stowe could have distinctly shown where it was that the North began to make its stand against slavery.

One might suppose that The *Examiner* and the other oracles of public opinion in England had made themselves sufficiently familiar with the contemporaneous history to not need Mrs. Stowe's information on such all-important points. The progressive abuse of the Union by the slave power, working through its alliance with the Northern Democratic Party, is, so to say, the general formula of United States history since the beginning of this century. The successive compromise measures mark the successive degrees of the encroachment by which the Union became more and more transformed into the slave of the slave owner. Each of these compromises denotes a new encroachment of the South, a new concession of the

2 Pious wishes.

North. At the same time none of the successive victories of the South was carried but after a hot contest with an antagonistic force in the North, appearing under different party names with different watchwords and under different colors. If the positive and final result of each single contest told in favor of the South, the attentive observer of history could not but see that every new advance of the slave power was a step forward to its ultimate defeat. Even at the time of the Missouri Compromise, the contending forces were so evenly balanced that Jefferson, as we see from his memoirs, apprehended the Union to be in danger of splitting on that deadly antagonism. The encroachments of the slaveholding power reached their maximum point, when by the Kansas-Nebraska bill, for the first time in the history of the United States—as Mr. Douglas himself confessed—every legal barrier to the diffusion of slavery within the United States territories was broken down; when afterward a Northern candidate bought his presidential nomination by pledging the Union to conquer or purchase in Cuba a new field of dominion for the slaveholder; when later on by the Dred Scott decision diffusion of slavery by the Federal power was proclaimed as the law of the American Constitution; and lastly, when the African slave trade was de facto reopened on a larger scale than during the times of its legal existence. But concurrently with this climax of southern encroachments, carried by the connivance of the Northern Democratic Party, there were unmistakable signs of Northern antagonistic agencies having gathered such strength as must soon turn the balance of power. The Kansas war, the formation of the Republican party, and the large vote cast for Mr. Frémont during the Presidential election of 1856 were so many palpable proofs that the North had accumulated sufficient energies to rectify the aberrations which United States history, under the slave owners' pressure, had undergone for half a century, and to make it return to the true principles of its development. Apart from those political phenomena, there was one broad statistical and economical fact indicating that the abuse of the Federal Union by the slave interest had approached the point from which it would have to recede forcibly or *de bonne grace*.[3] That fact was the growth of the Northwest,

---

3   With good grace.

the immense strides its population had made from 1850 to 1860, and the new and reinvigorating influence it could not but bear on the destinies of the United States.

Now, was all this a secret chapter of history? Was "the admission" Mrs. Beecher Stowe wanted to reveal to the *Examiner* and the other political illuminati of the London press the carefully hidden truth that "up to that time the slave party had used the Union for their purposes?" Is it the fault of the American North that the English pressmen were taken quite unawares by the violent clash of the antagonistic forces, the friction of which was the moving power of its history for half a century? Is it the fault of the Americans that the English press mistake for the fanciful crotchet hatched in a single day what was in reality the matured result of long years of struggle? The very fact that the formation and progress of the Republican Party in America have hardly been noticed by the London press speaks volumes as to the hollowness of its antislavery tirades. Take, for instance, the two antipodes of the London press, the London *Times* and *Reynolds's Weekly Newspaper*, the one the great organ of the respectable classes and the other the only remaining organ of the working class. The former, not long before Mr. Buchanan's career drew to an end, published an elaborate apology for his Administration and a defamatory libel against the Republican movement. Reynolds, on his part, was during Mr. Buchanan's stay at London one of his minions, and since that time never missed an occasion to write him up and to write his adversaries down. How did it come to pass that the Republican Party, whose platform was drawn up on the avowed antagonism to the encroachments of the slaveocracy and the abuse of the Union by the slave interest, carried the day in the North? How, in the second instance, did it come to pass that the great bulk of the Northern Democratic party, flinging aside its old connections with the leaders of slaveocracy, setting at naught its traditions of half a century, sacrificing great commercial interests and greater political prejudices, rushed to the support of the present Republican Administration and offered it men and money with an unsparing hand? Instead of answering these questions, the *Economist* exclaims:

Can we forget that Abolitionists have habitually been as ferociously persecuted and maltreated in the North and West as in the South? Can it be denied that the testiness and halfheartedness, not to say insincerity, of the Government at Washington have for years supplied the chief impediment which has thwarted our efforts for the effectual suppression of the slave trade on the coast of Africa, while a vast proportion of the clippers actually engaged in that trade have been built with Northern capital, owned by Northern merchants, and manned by Northern seamen?

This is, in fact, a masterly piece of logic. Antislavery England cannot sympathize with the North breaking down the withering influence of slaveocracy because she cannot forget that the North, while bound by that influence, supported the slave trade, mobbed the Abolitionists, and had its Democratic institutions tainted by the slave driver's prejudices. She cannot sympathize with Mr. Lincoln's Administration because she had to find fault with Mr. Buchanan's Administration. She must needs sullenly cavil at the present movement of the Northern resurrection, cheer up the Northern sympathizers with the slave trade, branded in the Republican platform, and coquet with the Southern slaveocracy setting up an empire of its own, because she cannot forget that the North of yesterday was not the North of today. The necessity of justifying its attitude by such pettifogging Old Bailey[4] pleas proves more than anything else that the anti-Northern part of the English press is instigated by hidden motives, too mean and dastardly to be openly avowed.

As it is one of its pet maneuvers to taunt the present Republican Administration with the doings of its proslavery predecessors, so it tries hard to persuade the English people that the *New York Herald* ought to be considered the only authentic expositor of Northern opinion. The London *Times* having given out the cue in this direction, the *servum pecus*[5] of the other anti-Northern organs, great and small, persist in beating the same bush. So says the *Economist*: "In the light of the strife, New York papers and New York politicians were not wanting who exhorted the combatants, now that they had

4   Seat of the Central Criminal Court in London.
5   Slavish herd.

large armies in the field, to employ them not against each other but against Great Britain—to compromise the internal quarrel, the slave question included, and invade the British territory without notice and with overwhelming force." The *Economist* knows perfectly well that the *N.Y. Herald*'s efforts, which were eagerly supported by the London *Times*, at embroiling the United States into a war with England only intended securing the success of Secession and thwarting the movement of Northern regeneration.

Still, there is one concession made by the anti-Northern English press. The *Saturday [Review]* snob tells us, "What was at issue in Lincoln's election, and what has precipitated the convulsion, was merely *the limitation of the institution of slavery to states where that institution already exists.*" And the *Economist* remarks:

> It is true enough that it was the aim of the Republican Party which elected Mr. Lincoln to prevent slavery from spreading into the unsettled Territories ... It may be true that the success of the North, if complete and unconditional, would enable them to confine slavery within the fifteen states which have already adopted it, and might thus lead to its eventual extinction—though this is rather probable than certain.

In 1859, on the occasion of John Brown's Harper's Ferry expedition, the very same *Economist* published a series of elaborate articles with a view to prove that by dint of an *economical law,* American slavery was doomed to gradual extinction from the moment it should be deprived of its power of expansion. That "economical law" was perfectly understood by the slaveocracy. "In 15 years more," said Toombs, "without a great increase in Slave territory, either the slaves must be permitted to flee from the whites, or the whites must flee from the slaves." The limitation of slavery to its constitutional area, as proclaimed by the Republicans, was the distinct ground upon which the menace of Secession was first uttered in the House of Representatives, on December 19, 1859. Mr. Singleton (Mississippi) having asked Mr. Curtis (Iowa), "if the Republican Party would never let the South have another foot of slave territory while it remained in the Union," and Mr. Curtis having responded in the affirmative, Mr. Singleton *said this would dissolve the Union.* His advice to Mississippi was the sooner it got out of the Union the better—"gentlemen should recollect that Jefferson Davis led our forces in Mexico, and still he lives, perhaps to lead the Southern army."[6] Quite apart from the *economical law* which makes the diffusion of slavery a vital condition for its maintenance within its constitutional areas, the leaders of the South had never deceived themselves as to its necessity for keeping up their *political* sway over the United States. John Calhoun, in the defense of his propositions to the Senate, stated distinctly on Feb. 19, 1847, "that the Senate was the only balance of power left to the South in the Government," and that the creation of new slave states had become necessary "for the retention of the equipoise of power in the Senate." Moreover, the Oligarchy of the 300,000 slave owners could not even maintain their sway at home save by constantly throwing out to their white plebeians the bait of prospective conquests within and without the frontiers of the United States. If, then, according to the oracles of the English press, the North had arrived at the fixed resolution of circumscribing slavery within its present limits and of thus extinguishing it in a constitutional way, was this not sufficient to enlist the sympathies of antislavery England?

But the English Puritans seem indeed not to be contented save by an explicit Abolitionist war. "This," says the *Economist*, "therefore, not being a war for the emancipation of the Negro race, on what other ground can we be fairly called upon to sympathize so warmly with the Federal cause?" "There was a time," says the *Examiner*, "when our sympathies were with the North, thinking that it was really in earnest in making a stand against the encroachments of the slave states" and in adopting "emancipation as a measure of justice to the black race."

However, in the very same numbers in which these papers tell us that they cannot sympathize with the North because its war is no Abolitionist war, we are informed that "the desperate expedient" of proclaiming Negro emancipation and summoning the slaves to a general insurrection is a thing "the mere conception of which is repulsive and dreadful" and that "a compromise" would be "far preferable to success purchased at such a cost and *stained by such a crime.*"

---

6 For Singleton's speech of December 19, 1859, see the Appendix to the *Congressional Globe, First Session 36ᵗʰ Congress, Part IV* (Washington 1860), pp. 47–54.

Thus the English eagerness for the Abolitionist war is all cant. The cloven foot peeps out in the following sentences: "Lastly," says the *Economist*, "is the Morrill tariff a title to our gratitude and to our sympathy, or is the certainty that, in case of Northern triumph, that tariff should be extended over the whole Republic a reason why we ought to be clamorously anxious for their success?" "The North Americans," says the *Examiner*, "are in earnest about nothing but a selfish protective tariff…The southern states were tired of being robbed of the fruits of their slave labor by the protective tariff of the North."

The *Examiner* and The *Economist* complement each other. The latter is honest enough to confess at last that with him and his followers sympathy is a mere question of tariff, while the former reduces the war between North and South to a tariff war, to a war between Protection and Free Trade. The *Examiner* is perhaps not aware that even the South Carolina Nullifiers of 1832, as General Jackson testifies, used Protection only as a pretext for secession, but even the *Examiner* ought to know that the present rebellion did not wait upon the passing of the Morrill tariff for breaking out. In point of fact, the Southerners could not have been tired of being robbed of the fruits of their slave labor by the Protective tariff of the North, considering that from 1846–1861 a Free Trade tariff had obtained.

The *Spectator* characterizes in its last number the secret thought of some of the anti-Northern organs in the following striking manner:

> What, then, do the anti-Northern organs really profess to think desirable, under the justification of this plea of deferring to the inexorable logic of facts? They argue that disunion is desirable just because, as we have said, it is the only possible step to a conclusion of this "causeless and fratricidal strife," and next, of course—only as an afterthought, and as a humble apology for Providence and "justification of the ways of God to man," now that the inevitable necessity stands revealed—for further reasons discovered as beautiful adaptations to the moral exigencies of the country, when once the issue is discerned. It is discovered that it will be very much for the advantage of the states to be dissolved into rival groups. They will mutually check each other's ambition; they will neutralize each other's power; and if ever England should get into a dispute with

one or more of them, more jealousy will bring the antagonistic groups to our aid. This will be, it is urged, a very wholesome state of things, for it will relieve us from anxiety and it will encourage political "competition," that great safeguard of honesty and purity, among the states themselves.

Such is the case—very gravely urged—of the numerous class of Southern sympathizers now springing up among us. Translated into English—and we grieve that an English argument on such a subject should be of a nature that requires translating—it means that we deplore the present great scale of this "fratricidal" war because it may concentrate in one fearful spasm a series of chronic petty wars and passions and jealousies among groups of rival states in times to come. The real truth is, and this very un-English feeling distinctly discerns this truth, though it cloaks it in decent phrases, that rival groups of American states could not live together in peace or harmony. The chronic condition would be one of malignant hostility rising out of the very causes which have produced the present contest. It is asserted that the different groups of states have different tariff interests. These different tariff interests would be the sources of constant petty wars if the states were once dissolved, and slavery, the root of all the strife, would be the spring of innumerable animosities, discords, and campaigns. No stable equilibrium could ever again be established among the rival states. And yet it is maintained that this long future of incessant strife is the providential solution of the great question now at issue—the only real reason why it is looked upon favorably being this: that whereas the present great-scale conflict may issue in a restored and stronger political unity, the alternative of infinitely multiplied small-scale quarrels will issue in a weak and divided continent that England cannot fear.

Now we do not deny that the Americans themselves sowed the seeds of this petty and contemptible state of feeling by the unfriendly and bullying attitude they have so often manifested to England, but we do say that the state of feeling on our part is petty and contemptible. We see that in a deferred issue there is no hope of a deep and enduring tranquility for America, that it means a decline and fall of the American nation into quarrelsome clans and tribes, and yet we hold up our hands in horror at the present "fratricidal" strife because it holds out hopes of finality. We exhort them to look favorably on the indefinite future of small strifes, equally fratricidal and probably far more demoralizing, because the latter would draw out of our side the thorn of American rivalry.

New York Daily Tribune, October 11, 1861

The Civil War in The United States

"Let him go, he is not worth thine ire!"[1] This advice from Leporello to Don Juan's deserted love is now the repeated call of English statesmanship to the North of the United States—recently voiced anew by Lord John Russell. If the North lets the South go, it will free itself from any complicity in slavery—its historical original sin—and it will create the basis for a new and higher stage of development.

Indeed, if North and South formed two autonomous countries like England and Hanover, for instance, their separation would be no more difficult than was the separation of England and Hanover. "The South," however, is neither geographically clearly separate from the North nor is it a moral entity. It is not a country at all, but a battle cry.

The advice of an amicable separation presupposes that the Southern Confederacy, although it took the offensive in the Civil War, is at least conducting it for defensive purposes. It presupposes that the slaveholders' party is concerned only to unite the areas it has controlled up till now into an autonomous group of states, and to release them from the domination of the Union. Nothing could be more wrong. "*The South needs its entire territory*. It will and must have it." This was the battle cry with which the secessionists fell upon Kentucky. By their "entire territory" they understand primarily all the so-called *border states*: Delaware, Maryland, Virginia, North Carolina, Kentucky, Tennessee, Missouri, and Arkansas. Moreover, they claim the whole territory south of the line which runs from the

---

1 From Byron's *Don Juan*. Leporello's advice was mischievous in its intent.

northwest corner of Missouri to the Pacific Ocean. Thus what the slaveholders call "the South" covers more than three quarters of the present area of the Union. A large part of the territory which they claim is still in the possession of the Union and would first have to be conquered from it. But none of the so-called border states, including those in Confederate possession, was ever *an actual slave state*. The border states form, rather, that area of the United States where the system of slavery and the system of free labor exist side by side and struggle for mastery: the actual battleground between South and North, between slavery and freedom. The war waged by the Southern Confederacy is, therefore, not a war of defense but a war of conquest, aimed at extending and perpetuating slavery.

The chain of mountains which begins in Alabama and stretches North to the Hudson River—in a manner of speaking the spinal column of the United States—cuts the so-called South into three parts. The mountainous country formed by the Allegheny Mountains with their two parallel ranges, the Cumberland Range to the west and the Blue Ridge Mountains to the east, forms a wedgelike division between the lowlands along the western coast of the Atlantic Ocean and the lowlands of the southern valleys of the Mississippi. The two lowland regions separated by this mountain country form, with their vast rice swamps and wide expanses of cotton plantations, the actual area of slavery. The long wedge of mountain country which penetrates into the heart of slavery, with its correspondingly freer atmosphere, invigorating climate, and soil rich in coal, salt, limestone, iron ore, and gold—in short, every raw material necessary for diversified industrial development—is for the most part already a free country. As a result of its physical composition, the soil here can only be successfully cultivated by free small farmers. The slave system vegetates here only as a sporadic growth and has never struck roots. In the largest part of the so-called border states it is the inhabitants of these highland regions who comprise the core of the free population, which out of self-interest, if nothing else, has sided with the Northern party.

Let us consider the contested area in detail.

Delaware, the northeasternmost of the border states, belongs to the Union both morally and in actual fact. Since the beginning of the war all attempts on the part of the secessionists to form even a faction favorable to them have come to grief against the unanimity of the population. The slave element in this state has long been dying out. Between 1850 and 1860 alone the number of slaves declined by a half, so that Delaware now has only 1,798 slaves out of a total population of 112,218. Nevertheless, the Southern Confederacy lays claim to Delaware, and it would in fact be militarily untenable as soon as the South took control of Maryland.

Maryland exhibits the abovementioned conflict between highlands and lowlands. Out of a total population of 687,034 there are in Maryland 87,188 slaves. The recent general elections to the Washington Congress have again forcefully proved that the overwhelming majority of the people sides with the Union. The army of 30,000 Union troops at present occupying Maryland is not only to serve as a reserve for the army on the Potomac, but also to hold the rebellious slaveholders in the interior of the state in check. Here a phenomenon can be seen similar to those in other border states, i.e., that the great mass of the people sides with the North and a numerically insignificant slaveholders' party sides with the South. What the slaveholders' party lacks in numbers it makes up for in the instruments of power, secured by many years' possession of all state offices, hereditary preoccupation with political intrigue, and the concentration of great wealth in a few hands.

Virginia at present forms the great cantonment where the main secessionist army and the main Unionist army confront each other. In the northwest highlands of Virginia the slaves number 15,000, while the free majority, which is twenty times as large, consists for the most part of independent farmers. The eastern lowlands of Virginia, on the other hand, have almost half a million slaves. The raising and selling of Negroes represents its main source of income. As soon as the lowland ringleaders had carried through the secession ordinance in the state legislature at Richmond, by means of intrigue, and had in all haste thrown open the gates of Virginia to the Southern army, northwestern Virginia seceded from the secession and formed a new state; it took up arms under the banner of the Union and is now defending its territory against the Southern invaders.

Tennessee, with 1,109,847 inhabitants, of whom 275,784 are slaves, is in the hands of the Southern Confederacy, which has placed the whole state under martial law and imposed a system of proscription which recalls the days of the Roman triumvirate. In the winter of 1860–61, when the slaveholders suggested a general people's convention to vote on the question of secession, the majority of the people turned down a convention in order to forestall any pretext for the secessionist movement. Later, when Tennessee had been militarily overrun by the Southern Confederacy and had been subjected to a system of terror, a third of the voters in the elections still declared themselves in favor of the Union. As in most of the border states, the actual center of resistance to the slaveholders' party here is to be found in the mountainous country, in east Tennessee. On June 17, 1861, a general convention of the people of east Tennessee assembled in Greenville, declared itself for the Union, delegated the former Governor of the state, Andrew Johnson, one of the most ardent Unionists, to the Senate in Washington, and published a "declaration of grievances" which exposes all the deception, intrigue and terror used to "vote out" Tennessee from the Union. Since then the secessionists have held east Tennessee in check by force of arms.

Similar situations to those in West Virginia and east Tennessee are to be found in the north of Alabama, northwest Georgia, and the north of North Carolina.

Farther west, in the border state of Missouri, whose population of 1,173,317 includes 114,965 slaves—the latter mostly concentrated in the northwestern area of the state—the people's convention of August 1861 decided in favor of the Union. Jackson, the Governor of the state and tool of the slaveholders' party, rebelled against the Missouri legislature and was outlawed; he then put himself at the head of the armed hordes which fell upon Missouri from Texas, Arkansas, and Tennessee in order to bring it to its knees before the Confederacy and to sever its bond with the Union by the sword. Next to Virginia, Missouri represents the main theater of the civil war at the moment.

New Mexico—not a state, but merely a territory, whose twenty-five slaves were imported under Buchanan's presidency so that a slave constitution could be sent after them from Washington—has felt no enthusiasm for the South, as even the South concedes. But the South's enthusiasm for New Mexico caused it to spew a band of armed adventurers over the border from Texas. New Mexico has entreated the Union government for protection against these liberators.

As will have been noticed, we lay particular stress on the numerical proportion of slaves to free citizens in the individual border states. This proportion is in fact of decisive importance. It is the thermometer with which the vitality of the slave system must be measured. The very soul of the whole secessionist movement is to be found in South Carolina. It has 402,541 slaves to 301,271 free men. Second comes Mississippi, which gave the Southern Confederacy its dictator, Jefferson Davis. It has 436,696 slaves to 354,699 free men. Third comes Alabama, with 435,132 slaves to 529,164 free men.

The last of the contested border states which we still have to mention is Kentucky. Its recent history is particularly characteristic of the policy of the Southern Confederacy. Kentucky, with 1,135,713 inhabitants, has 225,490 slaves. In three successive general elections (in winter 1860–61, when delegates were elected for a congress of the border states; in June 1861, when the elections for the Washington Congress were held; and finally in August 1861 in the elections for the Kentucky state legislature), an increasing majority decided in favor of the Union. On the other hand, Magoffin, the Governor of Kentucky, and all the state dignitaries are fanatical supporters of the slaveholders' party, as is Breckinridge, Kentucky's representative in the Senate at Washington, Vice-President of the United States under Buchanan, and presidential candidate of the slaveholders' party in 1860. Although the influence of the slaveholders' party was too weak to win Kentucky for secession, it was powerful enough to tempt it into a declaration of neutrality at the outbreak of war. The Confederacy recognized its neutrality as long as it suited its purpose, as long as it was busy crushing the resistance in east Tennessee. No sooner had this been achieved when it hammered on the gates of Kentucky with the butt-end of a gun: "*The South needs its entire territory*. It will and must have it!"

At the same time, a corps of Confederate freebooters invaded the "neutral" state from the southwest and southeast. Kentucky awoke from its dream of neutrality; its legislature openly sided with the Union, surrounded the treacherous Governor with a committee of public safety, called the people to arms, outlawed Breckinridge, and ordered the secessionists to withdraw immediately from the area which they had invaded. This was the signal for war. A Confederate army is moving in on Louisville while volunteers stream in from Illinois, Indiana, and Ohio to save Kentucky from the armed missionaries of slavery.

The attempts made by the Confederacy to annex Missouri and Kentucky, for example, expose the hollowness of the pretext that it is fighting for the rights of the individual states against the encroachment of the Union. To be sure, it acknowledges the right of the individual states which it counts as belonging to the "South" to break away from the Union, but by no means their right to remain in the Union.

No matter how much slavery, the war without, and military dictatorship within give the actual slave states a temporary semblance of harmony, even they are not without dissident elements. Texas, with 180,388 slaves out of 601,039 inhabitants, is a striking example. The law of 1845, by virtue of which Texas entered the ranks of the United States as a slave state, entitled it to form not just one but five states out of its territory. As a result the South would have won ten instead of two new votes in the American Senate; and an increase in the number of its votes in the Senate was a major political objective at that time. From 1845 to 1860, however, the slaveholders found it impracticable to split up Texas—where the German population plays a great part[2]—into even two states without giving the party of free labor the upper hand over the party of slavery. This is the best proof of how strong the opposition to the slaveholders' oligarchy is in Texas itself.

Georgia is the biggest and most populous of the slave states. With a total of 1,057,327 inhabitants, it has 462,230 slaves; that is, nearly half the population. Nevertheless, the slaveholders' party has not yet succeeded in having the constitution which it imposed on the South at Montgomery sanctioned in Georgia by a general vote of the people.

In the Louisiana state convention, which met on March 21, 1861, at New Orleans, Roselius, the state's political veteran, declared: "The

2 The German Texans, who formed in the 1850s about one fifth of the state's white population, included a large proportion of refugees from the 1848 revolution.

Montgomery constitution is not a constitution, but a conspiracy. It does not inaugurate a government by the people, but *a detestable and unrestricted oligarchy.* The people were not permitted to play any part in this matter. The Convention of Montgomery has dug the grave of political liberty, and now we are summoned to attend its burial."

The oligarchy of 300,000 slaveholders used the Montgomery Congress not only to proclaim the separation of the South from the North; it also exploited the Congress to overturn the internal system of government of the slave states, to completely subjugate that part of the white population which had still maintained some degree of independence under the protection of the democratic Constitution of the Union. Even between 1856 and 1860 the political spokesmen, lawyers, moralists, and theologians of the slaveholders' party had tried to prove not so much that Negro slavery is justified but rather that color is immaterial and that slavery is the lot of the working class everywhere.

It can be seen, then, that the war of the Southern Confederacy is, in the truest sense of the word, a war of conquest for the extension and perpetuation of slavery. The larger part of the border states and territories are still in the possession of the Union, whose side they have taken first by way of the ballot box and then with arms. But for the Confederacy they count as "the South," and it is trying to conquer them from the Union. In the border states which the Confederacy has for the time being occupied it holds the relatively free highland areas in check by means of martial law. Within the actual slave states themselves it is supplanting the democracy which existed hitherto by the unbridled oligarchy of 300,000 slaveholders.

By abandoning its plans for conquest, the Southern Confederacy would abandon its own economic viability and the very purpose of secession. Indeed, secession only took place because it no longer seemed possible to bring about the transformation of the border states and territories within the Union. On the other hand, with a peaceful surrender of the contested area to the Southern Confederacy the North would relinquish more than three quarters of the entire territory of the United States to the slave republic. The North would lose the Gulf of Mexico completely, the Atlantic

Ocean with the exception of the narrow stretch from the Penobscot estuary to Delaware Bay, and would even cut itself off from the Pacific Ocean. Missouri, Kansas, New Mexico, Arkansas, and Texas would be followed by California. Unable to wrest the mouth of the Mississippi from the hands of the strong, hostile slave republic in the South, the great agricultural states in the basin between the Rocky Mountains and the Alleghenies, in the valleys of the Mississippi, Missouri, and Ohio, would be forced by economic interests to secede from the North and to join the Southern Confederacy. These Northwestern states would in turn draw the other Northern states lying further east after them—with the possible exception of New England—into the same vortex of secession.

The Union would thus not in fact be dissolved, but rather *reorganized, a reorganization on the basis of slavery,* under the acknowledged control of the slaveholding oligarchy. The plan for such a reorganization was openly proclaimed by the leading Southern spokesmen at the Montgomery Congress and accounts for the article of the new constitution which leaves open the possibility of each state of the old Union joining the new Confederacy. The slave system would thus infect the whole Union. In the Northern states, where Negro slavery is, in practice, inoperable, the whole working class would be gradually reduced to the level of helotry. This would be in full accord with the loudly proclaimed principle that only certain races are capable of freedom, and as in the South actual labor is the lot of the Negroes, so in the North it is the lot of the Germans and Irish or their direct descendants.

The present struggle between South and North is thus nothing less than a struggle between two social systems: the system of slavery and the system of free labor. The struggle has broken out because the two systems can no longer peacefully coexist on the North American continent. It can only be ended by the victory of one system or the other.

While the border states, the contested areas in which the two systems have so far fought for control, are a thorn in the flesh of the South, it cannot, on the other hand, be overlooked that they have formed the North's main weak point in the course of the war. Some of the slaveholders in these districts feigned loyalty to the North at the bidding of the Southern conspirators; others indeed found that it accorded with their real interests and traditional outlook to side with the Union. Both groups have equally crippled the North. Anxiety to keep the "loyal" slaveholders of the border states in good humor and fear of driving them into the arms of the secession—in a word, a tender regard for the interests, prejudices, and sensibilities of these ambiguous allies—have afflicted the Union government with incurable paralysis since the beginning of the war, driven it to take half measures, forced it to hypocritically disavow the principle at issue in the war and to spare the enemy's most vulnerable spot—the root of the evil—*slavery itself.*

When Lincoln recently was faint-hearted enough to revoke Frémont's Missouri proclamation emancipating Negroes belonging to the rebels,[3] this was only in deference to the loud protest of the "loyal" slaveholders of Kentucky. However, a turning point has already been reached. With Kentucky, the last border state has been pressed into the series of battlefields between South and North. With the real war for the border states being conducted in the border states themselves, the question of winning or losing them has been withdrawn from the sphere of diplomatic and parliamentary negotiations. One section of the slaveholders will cast off its loyalist mask; the other will content itself with the prospect of compensation, such as Great Britain gave the West Indian planters.[4] Events themselves demand that the decisive pronouncement be made: *the emancipation of the slaves.*

Several recent declarations demonstrate that even the most obdurate Northern Democrats and diplomats feel themselves drawn to this point. In an open letter General Cass, War Minister under Buchanan and hitherto one of the South's most ardent allies, declares the emancipation of the slaves to be the *sine qua non* for the salvation of the Union. Dr. Brownson, the spokesman of the Northern Catholic party, and according to his own admission the most energetic opponent of the emancipation movement between

---

3   General Frémont, the first Republican candidate for the presidency in 1856, issued this proclamation in August 1861 and began granting freedom to slaves on his military authority. Lincoln soon ordered Frémont to stop these measures.

4   In 1833 the British government paid West Indian planters £2 for every slave set free.

1836 and 1860, published in his last *Review* for October an article *in favor of* abolition. Among other things he says, "If we have opposed Abolition heretofore because we would preserve the Union, we must *a fortiori* now oppose slavery whenever, in our judgment, its continuance becomes incompatible with the maintenance of the Union, or of the nation as a free republican state."[5]

Finally, the *World*, a New York organ of the Washington Cabinet's diplomats, closes one of its latest tirades against the abolitionists with these words: "On the day when it shall be decided that either slavery or the Union must go down, on that day sentence of death is passed on slavery. If the North cannot triumph *without* emancipation, it will triumph *with* emancipation."

Die Presse, November 7, 1861

---

5   *Brownson's Quarterly Review*, Third New York Series, New York, 1861, Vol. II, 510–46.

The American Civil War

PART I

From whatever standpoint one regards it, the American Civil War presents a spectacle without parallel in the annals of military history. The vast extent of the disputed territory; the far-flung front of the lines of operation; the numerical strength of the hostile armies, the creation of which drew barely any support from a prior organizational basis; the fabulous costs of these armies; the manner of leading them; and the general tactical and strategical principles in accordance with which the war is waged are all new in the eyes of the European onlooker.

The secessionist conspiracy, organized, patronized, and supported long before its outbreak by Buchanan's administration, gave the South an advantage by which alone it could hope to achieve its aim. Endangered by its slave population and by a strong Unionist element among the whites themselves, with a number of free men two-thirds smaller than the North, but readier to attack, thanks to the multitude of adventurous idlers that it harbors—for the South everything depended on a swift, bold, almost foolhardy offensive. If the Southerners succeeded in taking St. Louis, Cincinnati, Washington, Baltimore, and perhaps Philadelphia, they might then count on a panic, during which diplomacy and bribery could secure recognition of the independence of all the slave states. If this first onslaught failed, at least at the decisive points, their position must then become daily worse, simultaneously with the development of the strength of the North. This point was rightly understood by the men who in truly Bonapartist spirit had organized the secessionist conspiracy. They opened the campaign in corresponding manner. Their bands of adventurers overran Missouri and Tennessee, while their more regular troops invaded east Virginia and prepared a *coup de main* against Washington. With the miscarriage of this coup, the Southern campaign was, from the *military standpoint*, lost.

The North came to the theater of war reluctantly, sleepily, as was to be expected with its higher industrial and commercial development. The social machinery was here far more complicated than in the South, and it required far more time to give its motion this unwonted direction. The enlistment of the volunteers for three months was a great but perhaps unavoidable mistake. It was the policy of the North to remain on the defensive in the beginning at all decisive points, to organize its forces, to train them through operations on a small scale and without the risk of decisive battles, and as soon as the organization was sufficiently strengthened and the traitorous element simultaneously more or less removed from the army to pass finally to an energetic, unflagging offensive and, above all, to reconquer Kentucky, Tennessee, Virginia, and North Carolina. The transformation of the civilians into soldiers was bound to take more time in the North than in the South. Once effected, one could count on the individual superiority of the Northern man.

By and large, and allowing for mistakes which sprang more from political than from military sources, the North acted in accordance with those principles. The guerrilla warfare in Missouri and West Virginia, while it protected the Unionist populations, accustomed the troops to field service and to fire without exposing them to decisive defeats. The great disgrace of Bull Run was to some extent the result of the earlier error of enlisting volunteers for three months. It was senseless to allow a strong position, on difficult terrain and in possession of a foe little inferior in numbers, to be attacked by raw recruits in the front ranks. The panic which took possession of the Union army at the decisive moment, the cause of which has still not been clarified, could surprise no one who was in some degree familiar with the history of peoples' wars. Such things happened to the French troops very often from 1792 to 1795; they did not, however, prevent these same troops from winning the battles of Jemappes and Fleurus, Moutenotte, Castiglione, and Rivoli. The jests of the European press over the Bull Run panic had only one excuse for their silliness—the previous bragging of a section of the North American press.

The six months' respite that followed the defeat of Manassas was utilized by the North better than by the South. Not only were the Northern ranks recruited in greater measure than the Southern. Their officers received better instructions; the discipline and training of the troops did not encounter the same obstacles as in the South. Traitors and incompetent interlopers were more and more removed, and the period of the Bull Run panic already belongs to the past. The armies on both sides are naturally not to be measured by the standard of great European armies or even of the former regular army of the United States. Napoleon could in fact drill battalions of raw recruits in the depots during the first month, have them on the march during the second, and during the third lead them against the foe, but then every battalion received a sufficient stiffening of officers and noncommissioned officers, every company some old soldiers, and on the day of the battle the new troops were brigaded together with veterans and, so to speak, framed by the latter. All these conditions were lacking in America. Without the considerable mass of military experience that emigrated to America in consequence of the European revolutionary commotions of 1848–1849, the organization of the Union Army would have required a much longer time still. The very small number of the killed and wounded in proportion to the sum total of the troops engaged (customarily one in twenty) proves that most of the engagements, even the latest in Kentucky and Tennessee, were fought mainly with firearms at fairly long range, and that the incidental bayonet charges either soon halted before the enemy's fire or put the foe to flight before it came to a hand-to-hand encounter. Meanwhile, the new campaign has been opened under more favorable auspices with the advance of Buell and Halleck through Kentucky to Tennessee. After the reconquest of Missouri and West Virginia, the Union opened the campaign with the advance into Kentucky. Here the secessionists held three strong positions, fortified camps: Columbus on the Mississippi to their left, Bowling Green in the center, Mill Spring on the Cumberland River to the right. Their line stretched three hundred miles from west to east. The extension of this line denied the three corps the possibility of affording each other mutual support and offered the Union troops the chance of attacking each individually with superior forces. The great mistake in the disposition of the secessionists sprang from the attempt to hold all they had occupied. A single, fortified, strong central camp, chosen as the battlefield for a decisive engagement and held by the main body of the army, would have defended Kentucky far more effectively. It must either have attracted the main force of the Unionists or put the latter in a dangerous position should they attempt to march on without regard to so strong a concentration of troops.

Under the given circumstances the Unionists resolved to attack those three camps one after another, to maneuver their enemy out of them and force him to accept battle in open country. This plan, which conformed to all the rules of the art of war, was carried out with energy and dispatch. Towards the middle of January a corps of about 15,000 Unionists marched on Mill Spring, which was held by 20,000 secessionists. The Unionists maneuvered in a manner that led the enemy to believe he had to deal only with a weak reconnoitering corps. General Zollicoffer fell forthwith into the trap, sallied from his fortified camp, and attacked the Unionists. He soon convinced himself that a superior force confronted him. He fell, and his troops suffered a complete defeat, like the Unionists at Bull Run. This time, however, the victory was exploited in quite other fashion.

The stricken army was hard pressed until it arrived broken, demoralized, without field artillery or baggage, in its encampment at Mill Spring. This camp was pitched on the northern bank at the Cumberland River, so that in the event of another defeat the troops had no retreat open to them save across the river by way of a few steamers and riverboats. We find in general that almost all the secessionist camps were pitched on the *enemy* side of the stream. To take up such a position is not only according to rule, but also very practical if there is a bridge in the rear. In such case the encampment serves as the bridgehead and gives its holders the chance of throwing their fighting forces at pleasure on both banks of the stream and so maintaining complete command of these banks.

Without a bridge in the rear, on the contrary, a camp on the enemy side of the stream cuts off the retreat after an unlucky engagement and compels the troops to capitulate or exposes them to massacre and drowning, a fate that befell the Unionists at Ball's Bluff on the enemy side of the Potomac, whither the treachery of General Stone had sent them.

When the beaten secessionists had pitched their camp at Mill Spring, they had at once understood that an attack by the enemy on their fortifications must be repulsed or in a very short time capitulation must follow. After the experience of the morning they had lost confidence in their powers of resistance. Accordingly, when next day the Unionists advanced to attack the camp, they found that the foe had taken advantage of the night to put across the stream, leaving the camp, the baggage, the artillery and stores behind him. In this way the extreme right of the secessionist line was pushed back to Tennessee, and east Kentucky, where the mass of the population is hostile to the slaveholders' party, was reconquered for the Union.

At the same time—towards the middle of January—the preparations for dislodging the secessionists from Columbus and Bowling Green commenced. A strong flotilla of mortar vessels and ironclad gunboats was held in readiness, and the news was spread in all directions that it was to serve as a convoy to a large army marching along the Mississippi from Cairo to Memphis and New Orleans. All the demonstrations on the Mississippi, however, were merely mock maneuvers. At the decisive moment the gunboats were brought to the Ohio and thence to the Tennessee, up which they traveled as far as Fort Henry. This place, together with Fort Donelson on the Cumberland River, formed the second line of defense of the secessionists in Tennessee. The position was well chosen, for in case of a retreat behind the Cumberland the latter stream would have covered its front, the Tennessee its left flank, while the narrow strip of land between the two streams was sufficiently covered by the two forts abovementioned. The swift action of the Unionists, however, broke through the line itself before the left wing and the center of the first line were attacked.

In the first week of February the gunboats of the Unionists appeared before Fort Henry, which surrendered after a short bombardment. The garrison escaped to Fort Donelson, since the land forces of the expedition were not strong enough to encircle the place. The gunboats now traveled down the Tennessee again, upstream to the Ohio, and thence up the Cumberland as far as Fort Donelson. A single gunboat sailed boldly up the Tennessee through the very heart of the State of Tennessee, skirting the State of Mississippi and pushing on as far as Florence in north Alabama, where a series of swamps and banks (known by the name of the Muscle Shoals) forbade further navigation. This fact, that a single gunboat made this long voyage of at least 150 miles and then returned, without experiencing any kind of attack, proves that Union sentiment prevails along the river and will be very useful to the Union troops should they push forward so far.

The boat expedition up the Cumberland now combined its movements with those of the land forces under Generals Halleck and Grant. The secessionists at Bowling Green were deceived over the movements of the Unionists. They accordingly remained quietly in their camp while, a week after the fall of Fort Henry, Fort Donelson was surrounded on the land side by 40,000 Unionists and threatened on the river side by a strong flotilla of gunboats. Like the camps at Mill Spring and Fort Henry, Fort Donelson had the river lying in the rear, without a bridge for retreat. It was the strongest place the Unionists had attacked up to the present. The works were carried out with the greatest care; moreover, the place was capacious enough to accommodate the 20,000 men who occupied it. On the first day of the attack the gunboats silenced the fire of the batteries trained towards the river side and bombarded the interior of the defense works, while the land troops drove back the enemy outposts and forced the main body of the secessionists to seek shelter right under the guns of their own defense works. On the second day the gunboats, which had suffered severely the day before, appear to have accomplished but little. The land troops, on the contrary, had to fight a long and, in places, hot encounter with the columns of the garrison, which sought to break through the right wing of the enemy in order to secure their line of retreat to Nashville. However, an energetic attack of the Unionist right wing on the left wing of the secessionists, and considerable reinforcements that the left wing of the Unionists received, decided the victory in favor of the assailants. Divers outworks had been stormed. The garrison, forced into its inner lines of defense, without the chance of retreat and manifestly not in a position to withstand an assault next morning, surrendered unconditionally on the following day.

Die Presse, March 26, 1862

PART II

Conclusion of yesterday's feuilleton.
   With Fort Donelson, the enemy's artillery, baggage, and military stores fell into the hands of the Unionists; 13,000 secessionists surrendered on the day of its capture, 1,000 more the next day; and as soon as the outposts of the victors appeared before Clarksville, a town that lies farther up the Cumberland River, it opened its gates. Here too considerable supplies for the secessionists had been stored.
   The capture of Fort Donelson presents only one riddle: the flight of General Floyd with 5,000 men on the second day of the bombardment. These fugitives were too numerous to be smuggled away in steamboats during the night. With some measures of precaution on the part of the assailants, they could not have got away.
   Seven days after the surrender of Fort Donelson, Nashville was occupied by the Federals. The distance between the two places amounts to about 100 English miles, and a march of 15 miles a day, on very wretched roads and during the most unfavorable season of the year, redounds to the honor of the Unionist troops. On receipt of the news of the fall of Fort Donelson, the secessionists evacuated Bowling Green; a week later, they abandoned Columbus and withdrew to a Mississippi island 45 miles south. Thus Kentucky was completely reconquered for the Union. Tennessee, however, can be held by the secessionists only if they invite and win a big battle. They are said in fact to have concentrated 65,000 men for this purpose. Meanwhile, nothing prevents the Unionists from bringing a superior force against them.
   The leadership of the Kentucky campaign from Somerset to Nashville deserves the highest praise. The reconquest of so extensive a territory, the advance from the Ohio to the Cumberland during

a single month, evidence an energy, resolution, and speed such as have seldom been attained by regular armies in Europe. One may compare, for example, the slow advance of the Allies from Magenta to Solferino in 1859—without pursuit of the retreating foe, without endeavor to cut off his stragglers or in any way to envelop and encircle whole bodies of his troops.

Halleck and Grant, in particular, furnish good examples of resolute military leadership. Without the least regard either for Columbus or Bowling Green, they concentrate their forces on the decisive points, Fort Henry and Fort Donelson, launch a swift and energetic attack on these and precisely thereby render Columbus and Bowling Green untenable. Then they march at once to Clarksville and Nashville, without allowing the retreating secessionists time to take up new positions in north Tennessee. During this rapid pursuit, the corps of secessionist troops in Columbus remains completely cut off from the center and right wing of its army. English papers have criticized this operation unjustly. Even if the attack on Fort Donelson failed, the secessionists kept busy by General Buell at Bowling Green could not dispatch sufficient men to enable the garrison to follow the repulsed Unionists into the open country or to endanger their retreat. Columbus, on the other hand, lay so far off that it could not interfere with Grant's movements at all. In fact, after the Unionists had cleared Missouri of the secessionists, Columbus was for the latter an entirely useless post. The troops that formed its garrison had greatly to hasten their retreat to Memphis or even to Arkansas in order to escape the danger of ingloriously laying down their arms.

In consequence of the clearing of Missouri and the reconquest of Kentucky, the theater of war has so far narrowed that the different armies can cooperate to a certain extent along the whole line of operations and work for the achievement of definite results. In other words, the war now takes on for the first time a *strategic* character, and the geographical configuration of the country acquires a new interest. It is now the task of the Northern generals to find the Achilles heel of the cotton states.

Up to the capture of Nashville no concerted strategy between the army of Kentucky and the army on the Potomac was possible. They were too far apart from one another. They stood in the same front line, but their lines of operation were entirely different. Only with the victorious advance into Tennessee did the movements of the army of Kentucky become important for the entire theater of war.

The American papers influenced by McClellan are going great guns with the "anaconda" envelopment theory. According to this an immense line of armies is to wind round the rebellion, gradually constrict its coils, and finally strangle the enemy. This is sheer childishness. It is a rehash of the so-called *cordon system* devised in Austria about 1770, which was employed against the French from 1792 to 1797 with such great obstinacy and with such constant failure. At Jemappes, Fleurus, and, more especially, at Moutenotte, Millesimo, Dego, Castiglione, and Rivoli, the knockout blow was dealt to this system. The French cut the "anaconda" in two by attacking at a point where they had concentrated superior forces. Then the coils of the "anaconda" were cut to pieces seriatim.

In well-populated and more or less centralized states there is always a center, with the occupation of which by the foe the national resistance would be broken. Paris is a shining example. The slave states, however, possess no such center. They are thinly populated, with few large towns and all these on the seacoast. The question therefore arises: Does a military center of gravity nevertheless exist, with the capture of which the backbone of their resistance breaks, or are they, as Russia still was in 1812, not to be conquered without occupying every village and every plot of land—in a word, the entire periphery? Cast a glance at the geographical formation of *Secessia*, with its long stretch of coast on the Atlantic Ocean and its long stretch of coast on the Gulf of Mexico. So long as the Confederates held Kentucky and Tennessee, the whole formed a great compact mass. The loss of both these states drives an immense wedge into their territory, separating the states on the North Atlantic Ocean from the states on the Gulf of Mexico. The direct route from Virginia and the two Carolinas to Texas, Louisiana, Mississippi, and even, in part, to Alabama leads through Tennessee, which is now occupied by the Unionists. The *sole* route that, after the complete conquest of Tennessee by the Union, connects the two sections of the slave states goes through Georgia. This proves that *Georgia is the key to Secessia*. With the loss of Georgia the Confederacy would be cut into two sections which would have lost all connection with one another. A reconquest of Georgia by the secessionists, how-ever, would be almost unthinkable, for the Unionist fighting forces would be concentrated in a center position, while their adversar-ies, divided into two camps, would have scarcely sufficient forces to summon to a united attack.

Would the conquest of all Georgia, with the seacoast of Florida, be requisite for such an operation? By no means. In a land where communication, particularly between distant points, depends more on railways than on highways, the seizure of the railways is suffi-cient. The southernmost railway line between the states on the Gulf of Mexico and the Atlantic coast goes through Macon and Gordon near Milledgeville.

The occupation of these two points would accordingly cut *Secessia* in two and enable the Unionists to beat one part after another. At the same time, one gathers from the above that no Southern republic is capable of living without the possession of Tennessee. Without Tennessee, Georgia's vital spot lies only eight or ten days' march from the frontier; the North would constantly have its hand at the throat of the South, and on the slightest pressure the South would have to yield or fight for its life anew, under circumstances in which a single defeat would cut off every prospect of success.

From the foregoing considerations it follows:

The Potomac is *not* the most important position of the war the-ater. The taking of Richmond and the advance of the Potomac army further South—difficult on account of the many streams that cut across the line of march—could produce a tremendous moral effect. From a purely military standpoint, they would decide *nothing*.

The decision of the campaign belongs to the Kentucky army, now in Tennessee. On the one hand, this army is nearest the decisive points; on the other hand, it occupies a territory without which Secession is incapable of living. This army would accordingly have to be strengthened at the expense of all the rest and the sacrifice of all minor operations. Its next points of attack would be Chattanooga and Dalton on the upper Tennessee, the most important railway centers of the entire South. After their occupation the connection between the eastern and western states of *Secessia* would be limited to the connecting lines in Georgia. The further question would then arise of cutting off another railway line with Atlanta and Georgia, and finally of destroying the last connection between the two sections by the capture of Macon and Gordon.

On the contrary, should the "anaconda" plan be followed, then despite all successes in particular cases and even on the Potomac, the war may be prolonged indefinitely, while the financial difficulties together with diplomatic complications acquire fresh scope.

Die Presse, March 27, 1862

A Criticism of American Affairs

The crisis which at the moment dominates conditions in the United States has been brought about by twofold causes: military and political.

Had the last campaign been conducted according to a *single* strategic plan, the main army of the West must then, as previously explained in these columns, have availed itself of its successes in Kentucky and Tennessee to penetrate through north Alabama to Georgia and to seize there the railroad centers at Decatur, Milledgeville, etc. The connection between the Eastern and the Western army of the Secessionists would thereby have been broken and their mutual support rendered impossible. Instead of this, the Kentucky army marched south down the Mississippi in the direction of New Orleans and its victory near Memphis had no other result than to dispatch the greater part of Beauregard's troops to Richmond, so that the Confederates here now suddenly confronted McClellan, who had not exploited the defeat of the enemy's troops at Yorktown and Williamsburg, and on the other hand had from the first split up his own fighting forces, with a superior army in a superior position. McClellan's generalship, already described by us previously, was in itself sufficient to secure the downfall of the strongest and best-disciplined army. Finally, War Secretary Stanton made an unpardonable mistake. To make an impression abroad, he suspended recruiting after the conquest of Tennessee and so condemned the army to constant attenuation, just when it stood most in need of reinforcements for a rapid, decisive offensive. Despite the strategic blunders and despite McClellan's generalship, with a steady influx of recruits the war, if not decided by now, would nevertheless have been rapidly nearing a victorious decision. Stanton's step was so much the more unfortunate as the South was then enlisting every man from 18 to 35 years old, to a man, and was therefore staking everything on a *single* card. It is those people who have been trained in the meantime that almost everywhere give the Confederates the upper hand and secure the initiative to them. They held Halleck fast, dislodged Curtis from Arkansas, beat McClellan, and under Stonewall Jackson gave the signal for the guerrilla raids that now reach as far as the Ohio.

In part, the military causes of the crisis are connected with the political. It was the influence of the Democratic Party that elevated an incompetent like McClellan, because he was formerly a supporter of Breckinridge, to the position of commander in chief of all the military forces of the North. It was anxious regard for the wishes, advantages, and interests of the spokesmen of the *border slave states* that hitherto broke off the Civil War's point of principle and, so to speak, deprived it of its soul. The "loyal" slaveholders of these border states saw to it that the fugitive-slave laws dictated by the South were maintained and the sympathies of the Negroes for the North forcibly suppressed; that no general could venture to put a company of Negroes in the field; and that slavery was finally transformed from the Achilles' heel of the South into its invulnerable hide of horn. Thanks to the slaves, who perform all productive labors, the entire manhood of the South that is fit to fight can be led into the field!

At the present moment, when secession's stocks are rising, the spokesmen of the border states increase their claims. However, Lincoln's appeal to them shows, where it threatens them with inundation by the Abolition party, that things are taking a revolutionary turn. Lincoln knows what Europe does not know, that it is by no means apathy or giving way under pressure of defeat that causes his demand for 300,000 recruits to meet with such a cold response. New England and the Northwest, which have provided the main body of the army, are determined to enforce a revolutionary waging of war on the government and to inscribe the battle slogan of "Abolition of Slavery!" on the star-spangled banner. Lincoln yields only hesitantly and uneasily to this pressure from without, but knows that he is incapable of offering resistance to it for long. Hence his fervent appeal to the border states to renounce the institution of slavery voluntarily and under the conditions of a favorable contract. He knows that it is only the continuance of slavery in the border states that has so far left slavery untouched in the South and prohibited the North from applying its great radical remedy. He errs only if he imagines that the "loyal" slaveholders are to be moved by benevolent speeches and rational arguments. They will yield only to force.

So far we have only witnessed the first act of the Civil War—the *constitutional* waging of war. The second act, the revolutionary waging of war, is at hand.

Meanwhile, during its first session, the Congress—which has now adjourned—has decreed a series of important measures that we will briefly summarize here:

Apart from its financial legislation, it has passed the Homestead Bill that the Northern popular masses had long striven for in vain; by this, a part of the state lands is given gratis for cultivation to the colonists, whether American-born or immigrants. It has abolished slavery in [the District of] Columbia and the national capital, with monetary compensation for the former slaveholders. Slavery has been declared "forever impossible" in all the *Territories* of the United States. The Act under which the new State of West Virginia is taken into the Union prescribes abolition of slavery by stages and declares all Negro children born after July 4, 1863, to be born free. The conditions of this emancipation by stages are on the whole borrowed from the law that was enacted 70 years ago in Pennsylvania for the same purpose. By a fourth Act, all slaves of rebels are to be emancipated as soon as they fall into the hands of the republican army. Another law, which is now being put into effect *for the first time*, provides that these emancipated Negroes may be militarily organized and sent into the field against the South. The independence of the Negro republics of Liberia and Haiti has been recognized, and, finally, a treaty for the abolition of the slave trade has been concluded with England.

Thus, however the dice may fall in the fortunes of battle, it can now safely be said that Negro slavery will not long outlive the Civil War.

Die Presse, August 9, 1862

Abolitionist Demonstrations in America

It was previously observed in these columns that President Lincoln, legally cautious, constitutionally conciliatory, by birth a citizen of the border slave state of Kentucky, escapes only with difficulty from the control of the "loyal" slaveholders, seeks to avoid any open breach with them, and precisely thereby calls forth a conflict with the parties of the North which are consistent in point of principle and are pushed more and more into the foreground by events. The speech that Wendell Phillips delivered at Abington, Massachusetts, on the occasion of the anniversary of the slaves' emancipation in the British West Indies, may be regarded as a prologue to this conflict.

Together with Garrison[1] and G. Smith, Wendell Phillips is the leader of the Abolitionists in New England. For 30 years he has without intermission and at the risk of his life proclaimed the emancipation of the slaves as his battle cry, regardless alike of the persiflage of the press, the enraged howls of paid rowdies, and the conciliatory representations of solicitous friends. Even by his opponents he is acknowledged as one of the greatest orators of the North, as combining iron character with forceful energy and purest conviction. The London *Times*—and what could characterize this magnanimous paper more strikingly—today *denounces* Wendell Phillips's speech at Abington to the government at Washington. It is an "abuse" of freedom of speech. Anything more violent it is scarcely possible to image—says the *Times*—and anything more daring in time of Civil War was never perpetrated in any country by any sane man who valued his life and liberty. In reading the

---

1 William Lloyd Garrison.

speech…it is scarcely possible to avoid the conclusion that the speaker's object was to force the government to prosecute him.[2]

And the *Times*, in spite of, or perhaps because of its hatred of, the Union government, appears not at all disinclined to assume the role of public prosecutor!

In the present state of affairs, Wendell Phillips's speech is of greater importance than a battle bulletin. We therefore epitomize its most striking passages.[3]

The government, he says among other things, fights for the maintenance of slavery, and therefore it fights in vain. Lincoln wages a political war. Even at the present time he is more afraid of Kentucky than of the entire North. He believes in the South. The Negroes on the Southern battlefields, when asked whether the rain of cannon-balls and bombs that tore up the earth all round and split the trees asunder did not terrify them, answered, "No, massa; we know that they are not meant for us!" The rebels could speak of McClellan's bombs in the same way. They know that they are not meant for them, to do them harm. I do not say that McClellan is a traitor, but I say that if he were a traitor, he must have acted exactly as he has done. Have no fear for Richmond; McClellan will not take it. If the war is continued in this fashion, without a rational aim, then it is a useless squandering of blood and gold. It would be better were the South independent today than to hazard one more human life for a war based on the present execrable policy. To continue the war in the fashion prevailing hitherto requires 125,000 men a year and a million dollars a day.

But you cannot get rid of the South. As Jefferson said of slavery, "The Southern states have the wolf by the ears, but they can neither hold him nor let him go." In the same way we have the South by the ears and can neither hold it nor let it go. Recognize it tomorrow and you will have no peace. For eighty years it has lived with us, in fear of us the whole time, with hatred for us half the time, ever troubling and abusing us. Made presumptuous by conceding its present claims, it would not keep within an imaginary borderline a year—nay, the moment that we speak of conditions of peace, it will cry

2   The London *Times*, August 22, 1862.
3   For the complete speech see W. Phillips, *Speeches, Lectures and Letters, Series 1* Boston 1864, 448–463. The address is entitled "The Cabinet."

victory! We shall never have peace until slavery is uprooted. So long as you retain the present tortoise at the head of our government, you make a hole with one hand in order to fill it with the other. Let the entire nation endorse the resolutions of the New York Chamber of Commerce and then the army will have something for which it is worthwhile fighting. Had Jefferson Davis the power, he would not capture Washington. He knows that the bomb that fell in this Sodom would rouse the whole nation.

The entire North would thunder with one voice: "Down with slavery, down with everything that stands in the way of saving the republic!" Jefferson Davis is quite satisfied with his successes. They are greater than he anticipated, far greater! If he can continue to swim on them till March 4, 1863, England will then, and this is in order, recognize the Southern Confederacy...The President has not put the Confiscation Act into operation. He may be honest, but what has his honesty to do with the matter? He has neither insight nor foresight. When I was in Washington, I ascertained that three months ago Lincoln had written the proclamation for a general emancipation of the slaves and that McClellan blustered him out of his decision and that the representatives of Kentucky blustered him into the retention of McClellan, in whom he places no confidence. It will take years for Lincoln to learn to combine his legal scruples as an attorney with the demands of the Civil War. This is the appalling condition of a democratic government and its greatest evil.

In France a hundred men, convinced for good reasons, would carry the nation with them, but in order that our government may take a step, nineteen millions must previously put themselves in motion. And to how many of these millions has it been preached for years that slavery is an institution ordained by God! With these prejudices, with paralyzed hands and hearts, you entreat the President to save you from the Negro! If this theory is correct, then only slaveholding despotism can bring a temporary peace...I know Lincoln. I have taken his measure in Washington. He is a first-rate *second-rate* man. He waits honestly, like another Vesenius, for the nation to take him in hand and sweep away slavery through him...In past years, not far from the platform from which I now speak, the Whigs fired off small mortars in order to stifle my voice. And what is the result?

The sons of these Whigs now fill their own graves in the marshes of Chickahominy! Dissolve this Union in God's name and put another in its place, on the cornerstone of which is written: "Political equality for all the citizens of the world…" During my stay in Chicago I asked lawyers of Illinois, among whom Lincoln had practiced, what sort of man he was. Whether he could say No. The answer was: "He lacks backbone. If the Americans wanted to elect a man absolutely incapable of leadership, of initiative, then they were bound to elect Abraham Lincoln…Never has a man heard him say No!…" I asked, "Is McClellan a man who can say No?" The manager of the Chicago Central Railroad, on which McClellan was employed, answered, "He is incapable of making a decision. Put a question to him and it takes an hour for him to think of the answer. During the time that he was connected with the administration of the Central Railroad, he never decided a single important controversial question."

And these are the two men who, above all others, now hold the fate of the Northern republic in their hands! Those best acquainted with the state of the army assure us that Richmond could have been taken five times, had the do-nothing at the head of the army of the Potomac allowed it, but he preferred to dig up dirt in the Chickahominy swamps, in order ignominiously to abandon the locality and his dirt ramparts. Lincoln, out of cowardly fear of the border slave states, keeps this man in his present position, but the day will come when Lincoln will confess that he has never believed in McClellan…Let us hope that the war lasts long enough to transform us into men, and then we shall quickly triumph. God has put the thunderbolt of emancipation into our hands in order to crush this rebellion…

Die Presse, August 30, 1862

Letters

Letter from Marx to Pavel Vasilyevich Annenkov

... Thus, M. Proudhon, mainly because he lacks the historical knowledge, has not perceived that as men develop their productive forces, that is, as they live, they develop certain relations with one another and that the nature of these relations is bound to change with the change and growth of these productive forces. He has not perceived that *economic categories* are only *abstract expressions* of these actually existing relations and only remain true while these relations exist. He therefore falls into the error of the bourgeois economists, who regard these economic categories as eternal laws and not as historical laws which are valid only for a particular historical development, for a definite development of the productive forces. Instead, therefore, of regarding the politico-economic categories as abstract expressions of the real, transitory, historic social relations, M. Proudhon, by a mystic inversion, regards real relations merely as reifications of these abstractions. These abstractions themselves are formulas which have been slumbering in the bosom of God the Father since the beginning of the world.

But here our good M. Proudhon falls into severe intellectual convulsions. If all these economic categories are emanations from the bosom of God, if they constitute the hidden and eternal life of man, how does it come about, first, that there is such a thing as development, and secondly, that M. Proudhon is not a conservative? He explains these evident contradictions by a whole system of antagonisms ...

Now I will give you an example of M. Proudhon's dialectics.

Freedom and *slavery* constitute an antagonism. I need not speak either of the good or of the bad sides of freedom. As to slavery, I need not speak of its bad sides. The only thing that has to be explained is the good side of slavery. We are not dealing with indirect slavery, the slavery of the proletariat, but with direct slavery, the slavery of the black people in Surinam, in Brazil, and in the Southern States of North America.

Direct slavery is as much the pivot of our industrialism today as machinery, credit, etc. Without slavery, no cotton; without cotton, no modern industry. It is slavery which has given value to the colonies; the colonies have created world trade; world trade is the necessary condition of large-scale machine industry. Thus, before the traffic in Negroes began, the colonies supplied the Old World with only very few products and did not visibly change the face of the earth. Slavery is therefore an economic category of the utmost importance. Without slavery, North America, the most progressive country, would be turned into a patriarchal land. If North America were wiped off the map of the world the result would be anarchy, the total decay of trade and of modern civilization. But to make slavery disappear would mean to wipe America off the map of the world. Since slavery is an economic category, it has existed in every nation since the world began. Modern nations have merely known how to disguise slavery in their own countries while they openly imported it into the New World. After these observations on slavery, how will our worthy M. Proudhon proceed? He will look for the synthesis between freedom and slavery, the true *juste-milieu*, in other words, equilibrium between slavery and freedom...

Indeed, he does what all good bourgeois do. They all assert that in principle—that is, considered as abstract ideas—competition, monopoly, etc. are the only basis of life, but that in practice they leave much to be desired. They all want competition without the pernicious effects of competition. They all want the impossible, namely, the conditions of bourgeois existence without the necessary consequences of those conditions. None of them understands that the bourgeois form of production is historical and transitory, just as the feudal form was. This mistake arises from the fact that the bourgeois man is to them the only possible basis of every society; they cannot imagine a society in which men have ceased to be bourgeois...

You will now understand why M. Proudhon is the declared enemy of every political movement. The solution of actual problems does not lie for him in public action but in the dialectical rotations of his own head. Since to him the categories are the motive force, it is not necessary to change practical life in order to change the categories. Quite the contrary. One must change the categories and the consequence will be a change in the existing society.

In his desire to reconcile the contradictions, M. Proudhon does not even ask whether it is not the basis of those contradictions that must really be overthrown. He is exactly like the political doctrinaire who chooses to regard the king, the chamber of deputies, and the chamber of peers as integral parts of social life, as eternal categories. All he is looking for is a new formula by which to establish an equilibrium between these powers whose equilibrium consists precisely in the actually existing movement in which one power is now the conqueror and now the slave of the other. Thus in the eighteenth century a number of mediocre minds were busy finding the true formula which would bring the social estates, nobility, king, parliament, etc., into equilibrium, and they woke up one morning to find that all this—king, parliament and nobility—had disappeared. The true equilibrium in this antagonism was the overthrow of all the social relations which served as a basis for these feudal institutions and for the antagonisms of these feudal institutions.

Because M. Proudhon places eternal ideas, the categories of pure reason, on the one side and human beings and their practical life, which, according to him, is the application of these categories, on the other, one finds with him from the beginning a *dualism* between life and ideas, between soul and body, a dualism which recurs in many forms. You can see now that this antagonism is nothing but the incapacity of M. Proudhon to understand the profane origin and the profane history of the categories which he deifies...

December 28, 1846

Letters between Karl Marx and
Frederick Engels (1860–1866)

MARX TO ENGELS, JANUARY 11, 1860[1]

In my opinion, the biggest things that are happening in the world today are on the one hand the movement of the slaves in America started by the death of John Brown, and on the other the movement of the serfs in Russia...

I have just seen in the *Tribune* that there has been a fresh rising of slaves in Missouri, naturally suppressed. But the signal has now been given. If things get serious by and by, what will then become of Manchester?

ENGELS TO MARX, JANUARY 26, 1860

Your opinion of the significance of the slave movement in America and Russia is now confirmed. The Harper's Ferry affair with its aftermath in Missouri bears its fruit: the free Negroes in the South

---

1   This and the extracts which follow relating to the American Civil War have been taken from the complete German edition of the works of Karl Marx and Frederick Engels: *Gesamtausgabe, Dritte Abteilung* ("*Der Briefwechsel zwischen Marx und Engels*"), *Band* 2 (1854–1860) and *Band* 3 (1861–1867) [*Collected Works*, Third Division ("The Correspondence Between Marx and Engels"), Vols. 2 and 3], Berlin 1930. A number of the letters are contained in K. Marx and F. Engels, *Correspondence, A Selection with Commentary and Notes*, London and New York 1934.

are everywhere hunted out of the states, and I have just read in the first New York cotton report (W. P. Wright and Co., January 10, 1860) that the planters have hurried their cotton on to the ports in order to guard against any probable consequences arising out of the Harper's Ferry affair.

ENGELS TO MARX, JANUARY 7, 1861

Things in North America are also becoming exciting. Matters must be going very badly for them with the slaves if the Southerners play so risky a game. The least volunteer *putsch* from the North could set everything ablaze. In any case, it seems that one way or another slavery is rapidly going to come to an end, and then it will be the same with cotton production. But how this will react on England will then soon become manifest. And with such mighty movements an ass like Bonaparte believes he can permanently fish in troubled waters.

MARX TO ENGELS, JUNE 9, 1861

Many thanks for the letter about America. Should anything important (militarily) occur, then always write me your opinion about it. According to the picture that I have formed of General Scott—now, moreover, 76 years old—from the Mexican War (see Ripley), I expect the greatest blunders from him unless the old donkey is controlled by others. Slowness and indecision, above all. For the rest, I see by the facts reported in the *Tribune* that the North now speaks openly of a slave war and the destruction of slavery.

ENGELS TO MARX, NOVEMBER 27, 1861

Have these Yankees then gone completely crazy to carry out the mad coup with the Confederate Commissioners? The fact that here in the Channel too a warship was waiting for the mail steamer proves that general instructions must have been issued from Washington.

To take political prisoners by force on a foreign ship is the clearest *casus belli* there can be. The fellows must be sheer fools to land themselves in for a war with England. If war should actually break out, you can send your letters to New York via Germany or the Havre addressed to an intermediary, but you will have to take care that you don't give any assistance to the enemies of the Queen.

MARX TO ENGELS, DECEMBER 9, 1861

War, as I have declared in the *Presse* from the first day, will not break out with America, and I only regret that I had not the means to exploit the asininity of the Reuter and Times–swayed Stock Exchange during this fool period.

MARX TO ENGELS, MARCH 3, 1862

I should be glad if you supplied me *this week* (by Friday morning) with an *English* article on the American War. You can write *entirely without constraint*. The *Tribune* will print it as the letter of a foreign officer. *Nota bene:* The *Tribune* hates McClellan, who is in league with the Democratic Party and who, *so long as* he was commander in chief of all the armies, prevented any action not only on the Potomac (where this was perhaps justified) but in *all* theaters of war, particularly in the West, by *direct intervention*. (He was also the soul of the extremely disgraceful intrigue against Frémont.) This Mc, moreover, out of *esprit de corps* and hatred of the civilians, protected all the traitors in the army, e.g., Colonel Maynard and General Stone. The arrest of the latter ensued a day or two after [Mc]Clellan had been deposed as commander-in-chief of the whole army. In the same way, the shameless Washington "representative" of the *New York Herald* was arrested as a spy contrary to M'Clellan's wishes and after he had entertained the entire staff of M'C[lellan] the day before at a champagne breakfast.

MARX TO ENGELS, MAY 6, 1862

I shall write to Dana once more. I miss the sending of the *Tribune* sadly. This is a mean trick of Greeley and McElrath. From the last numbers of the *Tribune* for March I have learned two things. Firstly, that McClellan had been *accurately* informed eight days beforehand of the Confederates' retreat. Secondly, that the *Times*'s Russell availed himself of his nosing in Washington during the *Trent* affair to gamble on the Stock Exchange in New York…

Bonaparte's present maneuvers in Mexico (the affair originally emanated from Pam²) are explained by the fact that Juarez only recognizes the official debt to France of £46,000. But Miramon and his gang, per medium of the Swiss banker Jecker *et* Co., had issued state bonds to the amount of $52,000,000 (on which about $4,000,000 have been paid). These state bonds—Jecker *et* Co. being only the *hommes de pailles³*—have fallen almost for *zéro* into the hands of Morny *et* Co. They demand recognition of them by Juarez. *Hinc illae lacrimae.*⁴

Schurz is—a brigadier general with Frémont! ! !

MARX TO ENGELS, MAY 27, 1862

The blowing up of the *Merrimac* seems to me an evident act of cowardice on the part of the dirty dogs of Confederacy. The hounds could still risk something. It is wonderfully fine how the *Times* (which supported all the Coercion Bills against Ireland with so much fiery zeal) wails that "liberty" must be lost in the event of the North tyrannizing the South. The *Economist* is also good. In its last number it declares that the Yankees' financial prosperity—the nondepreciation of their paper money—is *incomprehensible* to it (although the matter is perfectly simple). It had hitherto consoled its readers from week to week with this depreciation. Although it now admits that it does not understand what is its business and has misled its readers concerning this, it is at present solacing

---

2   Lord Palmerston, prime minister 1855–58 and 1859–65.
3   Straw men [original editor's note].
4   Hence these tears [original editor's note].

them with dark doubts about the "military operations," of which it officially knows nothing.

What extraordinarily facilitated the paper operations of the Yankees (the main point being the confidence placed in their cause and therewith in their government) was without question the circumstance that in consequence of secession the West was almost denuded of paper money and therefore of a circulating medium generally. All the banks whose principal securities consisted of the bonds of slave states were bankrupted. Moreover, currency for millions, which circulated in the West in the form of direct banknotes of the Southern banks, was swept away. Then, partly in consequence of the Morrill tariff, partly in consequence of the war itself, which largely put an end to the import of luxuries, the Yankees had a balance of trade and therefore a rate of exchange favorable to themselves and against Europe the whole time. An unfavorable rate of exchange might have badly affected the patriotic confidence in their paper on the part of the philistines.

For the rest—this comical concern of John Bull for the interest on the national debt that Uncle Sam will have to pay! As if it were not a mere bagatelle in comparison with Bull's national debt; moreover, the United States are unquestionably richer today than were the Bulls with their debt of a billion in 1815.

Has Pam not got Bonaparte into a pretty pickle in Mexico?

ENGELS TO MARX, MAY 29, 1862

Anneke is with Buell's army and from today is writing in the *Augsburger*. I am rather anxious about Halleck's troops; the affair drags on so long, and yet he does not appear to receive any reinforcements, though Spence's lies in the *Times* have surely no significance. Willich is a colonel (the eternal colonel!) and commands the 32nd Indiana regiment...

A certain amount of guerrilla warfare does now seem after all to be beginning, but it is certainly not of great importance, and if only a victory ensues, the reserve forces following in its wake, together with some cavalry, will soon put an end to the business. In case of a defeat, it would of course be vexatious.

ENGELS TO MARX, JULY 30, 1862[5]

Things go wrong in America, and it is after all Mr. Stanton who is chiefly to blame, for the reason that after the conquest of Tennessee he suspended recruiting out of sheer vainglory and so condemned the army to constant weakening just when it stood most in need of reinforcements for a rapid, decisive offensive. With a steady influx of recruits, even if the war were not decided by now, its success would nevertheless have been beyond doubt. With continual victories recruits would also have come freely. This step was all the sillier as the South was then enlisting all men from 18 to 35 years of age, and was therefore staking everything on a *single* card. It is those people who have joined up in the meantime who now give the Confederates the upper hand everywhere and secure the initiative to them. They held Halleck fast, dislodged Curtis from Arkansas, smote McClellan, and under Jackson in the Shenandoah valley gave the signal for the guerrilla raids that now reach as far as the Ohio. No one could have acted more stupidly than Stanton.

Further. When Stanton saw that he could not dislodge McClellan from the command of the Potomac army, he perpetrated the stupidity of weakening him by conferring special commands on Frémont, Banks, and McDowell *and of splitting up the forces to the end of removing McClellan*. The consequence of this is not only that McC[lellan] has been beaten, but also that public opinion now maintains that it is not McC[lellan] but Stanton who is to blame for the defeat. Serves Mr. Stant[on] right.

All that would be of no consequence; it might even be of service, in that the war would at last be waged in a revolutionary way. But there's the trouble. The defeats do not stir these Yankees up; they make them slack. If, merely to obtain recruits, they have already come to the point of declaring themselves prepared to take them *for nine months only*, what is meant is nothing other than this: we are in a bad way, and all we want is the semblance of an army as a means of making a demonstration during the peace negotiations. Those 300,000 volunteers were the criterion, and by refusing to provide

---

5   Part of this letter is included by Marx in his article "A Criticism of American Affairs," *Die Presse*, August 9, 1862, 198–201.

them the North declares that to it, its whole cause is *au fond* muck. Furthermore, what cowardice in government and Congress. They are afraid of conscription, of resolute financial steps, of attacks on slavery, of everything that is urgently necessary; they let everything loaf along as it will, and if the semblance of some measure finally gets through Congress, the honorable Lincoln so qualifies it that nothing at all is left of it any longer. This slackness, this collapse like a punctured pig's bladder, under the pressure of defeats that have annihilated one army, the strongest and best, and actually left Washington exposed, this total absence of any elasticity in the whole mass of the people—this proves to me that it is all up. The few mass meetings, etc., do not mean anything; they don't attain even the stir of a presidential election.

In addition, the total lack of talent. One general more stupid than the other. Not one that would be capable of the least initiative or of independent decision. For three months the initiative once more wholly with the adversary. Then, one financial measure more lunatic than the other. Helplessness and cowardice everywhere, save among the common soldiers. The politicians in like case—just as absurd and devoid of counsel. And the populace is more helpless than if it had lingered three thousand years under the Austrian scepter.

For the South, on the contrary—it's no use shutting one's eyes to the fact—it's a matter of bloody earnest. That we get no cotton is already one proof. The guerrillas in the border states are a second. But that after being thus shut off from the world, an agricultural people can sustain such a war and after severe defeats and losses in resources, men, and territory can nevertheless now stand forth as the victor and threaten to carry its offensive right into the North, this is in my opinion decisive. Besides, they fight quite famously, and with the second occupation of Kentucky and Tennessee, what Union feeling still existed there outside the highlands is now surely lost.

If they get Missouri, they get the Territories too, and then the North can pack up.

As said, if the North does not proceed forthwith in revolutionary fashion, it will get an ungodly hiding and deserve it—and it looks like it.

MARX TO ENGELS, JULY 30, 1862

As to America, that, says he [Lassalle], is quite interesting. The Yankees have no "ideas." "Individual liberty" is merely a "negative idea," etc., and more of this old, decayed, speculative rubbish.

MARX TO ENGELS, AUGUST 7, 1862

I do not altogether share your views on the American Civil War. I do not think that all is up. The Northerners have been dominated from the first by the representatives of the border slave states, who also pushed McClellan, that old partisan of Breckinridge, to the top. The Southerners, on the other hand, acted as one man from the beginning. The North itself has turned the slaves into a military force on the side of the Southerners, instead of turning it against them. The South leaves productive labor to the slaves and could therefore put its whole fighting strength in the field without disturbance. The South had unified military leadership, the North had not. That no strategic plan existed was already obvious from all the maneuvers of the Kentucky army after the conquest of Tennessee. In my opinion all this will take another turn. In the end the North will make war seriously, adopt revolutionary methods, and throw over the domination of the border slave statesmen. A single Negro regiment would have a remarkable effect on Southern nerves.

The difficulty of getting the 300,000 men seems to me purely political. The Northwest and New England wish to, and will, force the government to give up the diplomatic method of conducting war which it has used hitherto, and they are now making terms on which the 300,000 men shall come forth. If Lincoln does not give way (which he will do, however), there will be a revolution.

As to the lack of military talent, the method which has prevailed up till now of selecting generals purely from considerations of diplomacy and party intrigue is scarcely designed to bring talent to the front. General Pope seems to me to be a man of energy, however.

With regard to the financial measures, they are clumsy, as they are bound to be in a country where up to now no taxes (for the whole state) have in fact existed; but they are not nearly so idiotic as the measures taken by Pitt and Co. The present depreciation of money is due, I think, not to economic but to purely political reasons—distrust. It will therefore change with a different policy.

The long and short of the business seems to me to be that a war of this kind must be conducted on revolutionary lines, while the Yankees have so far been trying to conduct it constitutionally.

MARX TO ENGELS, SEPTEMBER 10, 1862

As regards the Yankees, I am assuredly still of my previous opinion that the North will finally prevail; certainly the Civil War may go through all sorts of episodes, even armistices, perhaps, and be long drawn out. The South would and could only conclude peace on condition that it received the border slave states. In this event California would also fall to it; the Northwest would follow, and the entire Federation, with perhaps the exception of the New England states, would form a single country once more, this time under the acknowledged supremacy of the slaveholders. It would be the reconstruction of the United States on the basis demanded by the South. This, however, is impossible and will not happen.

The North can, for its part, only conclude peace if the Confederacy limits itself to the old slave states and those confined between the Mississippi River and the Atlantic. In this case the Confederacy would soon come to its blessed end. Intervening armistices, etc., on the basis of a *status quo*, could at most entail pauses in the prosecution of the war.

The manner in which the North wages war is only to be expected from a *bourgeois* republic, where fraud has so long reigned supreme. The South, an oligarchy, is better adapted thereto, particularly as it is an oligarchy where the whole of the productive labor falls on the Negroes and the four millions of "white trash" are filibusters by profession. All the same, I would wager my head that these boys come off second best, despite "Stonewall Jackson." To be sure, it is possible that it will come to a sort of revolution in the North itself first.

Willich is a brigadier general and, as Kapp has related in Cologne, Steffen is now to take the field also.

It seems to me that you let yourself be swayed a little too much by the military aspect of things.

MARX TO ENGELS, OCTOBER 29, 1862

As for America, I believe that the Maryland campaign was decisive insofar as it showed that even in this section of the border states most sympathetic to the South, support for the Confederates is weak. But the whole struggle turns on the border states. Whoever gets them dominates the Union. At the same time, the fact that Lincoln issued the forthcoming Emancipation Act at a moment when the Confederates were pushing forward in Kentucky shows that all consideration for the loyal slaveholders in the border states has ceased. The emigration of the slave owners from Missouri, Kentucky, and Tennessee to the South, with their black chattels, is already enormous, and if the war is prolonged for a while, as it is certain to be, the Southerners will have lost all hold there. The South began the war for these territories. The war itself was the means of destroying its power in the border states, where apart from this the ties with the South were becoming weaker every day, because a market can no longer be found for the breeding of slaves and the internal slave trade. In my opinion, therefore, for the South it will only be a matter now of the defensive. But their sole possibility of success lay in an offensive. If the report is confirmed that Hooker is getting the active command of the Potomac army, that McClellan is being "retired" to the "theoretical" post of commander in chief, and that Halleck is taking over the chief command in the West, then the conduct of the war in Virginia may also take on a more energetic character. Moreover, the most favorable time of year for the Confederates is now past.

There is no doubt at all that morally the collapse of the Maryland campaign was of the most tremendous importance.

As to finance, the United States know from the time of the War of Independence, and we know from the Austrian experience, how far one can go with depreciated paper money. It is a fact that the Yankees never exported more corn to England than they have this year, that the present harvest is again far above the average, and that the trade balance was never more favorable for them than it has been for the last two years. As soon as the new system of taxation (a very hackneyed one, it is true, exactly in Pitt's style) comes into operation, the paper money which up to now has only been continually *emitted* will also at last begin to *flow back again*. An extension of the paper issue on the present scale will therefore became superfluous and further depreciation will thus be checked. What had made even the present depreciation less dangerous than it was in France, and even in England, in similar circumstances has been the fact that the Yankees never prohibited *two prices*, a gold price and a paper price. The actual damage done resolves itself into a state debt, for which the proper equivalent has never been received, and a premium on jobbing and speculation.

When the English boast that their depreciation was never more than 11½ percent (other people believe that it amounted to more than double this during some time), they conveniently forget that they not only continued to pay their old taxes but every year paid new ones as well, so that the return flow of the banknotes was assured from the beginning, while the Yankees have actually carried on the war for a year and a half *without taxes* (except the greatly diminished import duties), simply by repeating the issue of paper. For a process of this kind, which has now reached the turning point, the actual depreciation is still comparatively small.

The fury with which the Southerners have received Lincoln's Acts proves their importance. All Lincoln's Acts appear like the mean pettifogging conditions which one lawyer puts to his opposing lawyer. But this does not alter their historic content, and indeed it amuses me when I compare them with the drapery in which the Frenchman envelops even the most unimportant point.

Of course, like other people, I see the repulsive side of the form the movement takes among the Yankees, but I find the explanation of it in the nature of "bourgeois" democracy. The events over there are a world upheaval, nevertheless, and there is nothing more disgusting in the whole business than the English attitude towards them.

ENGELS TO MARX, NOVEMBER 5, 1862

As regards America I also think, of course, that the Confederates in Maryland have received an unexpected moral blow of great significance. I am also convinced that the *definite* possession of the border states will decide the result of the war. But I am by no means certain that the affair is going to proceed along such classic lines as you appear to believe. Despite all the screams of the Yankees, there is still no sign whatever available that the people regard this business as a real question of national existence. On the contrary, these election victories of the Democrats go to prove rather that the party which has had enough of the war is growing. If there were only some proof or some indication that the masses in the North were beginning to rise as they did in France in 1792 and 1793, then it would all be very fine. But the only revolution to be expected seems rather to be a Democratic counterrevolution and a rotten peace, including the partition of the border states. That this would not be the end of the affair by a long way—granted. But for the present moment I must say I cannot work up any enthusiasm for a people which on such a colossal issue allows itself to be continually beaten by a fourth of its own population and which after eighteen months of war has achieved nothing more than the discovery that all its generals are idiots and all its officials rascals and traitors. After all, the thing must happen differently, even in a bourgeois republic, if it is not to end in utter failure. I entirely agree with what you say about the meanness of the English way of looking at the business.

ENGELS TO MARX, NOVEMBER 15, 1862

I impatiently await the steamer that is bringing news of the New York elections. If the Democrats triumph in the State of New York, then I no longer know what I am to think of the Yankees. That a people placed in a great historical dilemma, which is at the same time a matter of its own existence, can after eighteen months' struggle become reactionary in its mass and vote for climbing down is a bit beyond my understanding. Good as it is from one aspect that even in America the bourgeois republic exposes itself in thoroughgoing fashion, so that in future it can never again be preached on its own merits, but solely as a means, and a form of transition, to the social revolution, still it is mortifying that a lousy oligarchy with only half the number of inhabitants proves itself just as strong as the unwieldy, great, helpless democracy. For the rest, if the Democrats triumph, the worthy McClellan and the West Pointers have the better of it most beautifully, and its glory will soon be at an end. The fellows are capable of concluding peace, if the South returns to the Union on condition that the President shall always be a Southerner and the Congress shall always consist of Southerners and Northerners in equal numbers. They are even capable of proclaiming Jeff Davis President of the United States forthwith and to surrender even the whole of the border states, if there is no other way to peace. Then, good-bye America.

Of Lincoln's emancipation, likewise, one still sees no effect up to the present, save that from fear of a Negro inundation the Northwest has voted Democratic.

MARX TO ENGELS, NOVEMBER 17, 1862

It seems to me that you are looking too much at only one side of the American quarrel. I have looked at a mass of Southern papers in the American coffeehouse and have seen from these that the Confederacy is in a tight corner. The English newspapers have suppressed the battle of "Corinth." The Southern papers describe it as the most extraordinarily bad luck that has befallen them since the armed rising. The State of *Georgia* has declared the Confederate "Conscription Acts" to be null and void. In the person of Floyd the thief, *Virginia* has disputed the right of the "*creatures* (literally) of Jefferson Davis" further to levy troops in his state. Oldham, representative of *Texas* in the Congress of Richmond, has lodged a protest against the transportation of the "picked troops" of the Southwest to the East, that is, Virginia. From all these disputes two things emerge quite incontestably:

That the Confederate government has overreached itself in its violent efforts to fill the ranks of the army;

That the states are asserting their "state rights" against the separatist Confederacy, just as the latter made them its pretext against the Union.

I regard the victories of the Democrats in the North as a reaction, which was made easy for this conservative and blackleg element by the Federal government's bad direction of the war and financial blunders. It is for the rest a species of reaction met with in every revolutionary movement, and at the time of the Convention, for instance, was so strong that it was considered counterrevolutionary to want to submit the death of the King to *suffrage universel*[6] and under the Directory so strong that Mr. Bonaparte I had to bombard Paris.

On the other hand, the elections have no bearing on the composition of the Congress prior to December 4, 1863; they serve, therefore, merely as a spur to the Republican government, over whose head the sword hangs. And in any case the Republican House of Representatives will put the term of life allotted to it to better use, if only from hatred of the opposing party.

As to McClellan, he has in his own army Hooker and other Republicans, who will any day arrest him on the order of the government.

In addition, there is the French attempt at intervention, which will call forth a reaction against the reaction.

I do not therefore regard things as so bad. What might be much more injurious in my view is the sheep's attitude of the workers in Lancashire. Such a thing has never been heard of in the world. All the more is this the case as the manufacturing rabble do not even pretend "to make sacrifices" themselves, but leave to the rest of England the honor of keeping their army going for them; that is, impose on the rest of England the costs of maintenance of their variable capital.

During this recent period England has disgraced herself more than any other country, the workers by their christian slave nature, the bourgeois and aristocrats by their enthusiasm for slavery in its most direct form. But the two manifestations supplement one another.

---

6   Universal suffrage; that is, a general vote.

MARX TO ENGELS, JANUARY 2, 1863

Burnside seems to have committed great tactical blunders in the battle of Fredericksburg. He was obviously nervous in the employment of such great military forces. As far, however, as the fundamental asininity is concerned: 1. In connection with the wait of 26 days, there is unquestionably direct treason at work in the war administration at Washington. Even the New York correspondent of the *Times* admitted that only after weeks did Burnside obtain resources which had been promised him immediately. 2. That nevertheless he then made this attack shows the moral weakness of the man. The worthy *Tribune* began to cast suspicion on him and threatened him with dismissal. This paper, with its enthusiasm and its ignorance, does great harm.

The Democrats and M'Clellanists naturally cried out in unison, in order to exaggerate the unfortunate position. For the "rumor" that M'Clellan, the "Monk" of the *Times*, had been summoned to Washington, we are indebted to Mr. Reuter.

"Politically," the defeat was good. They ought not to have had good luck before January 1, 1863. Anything of the sort could have caused the "Proclamation" to be revoked.

The *Times* and Co. are utterly furious over the workers' meetings in Manchester, Sheffield, and *London*. It is very good that the eyes of the Yankees are opened in this way. For the rest, Opdyke (Mayor of New York and political economist) has already said at a meeting in New York: "We know that the English working class are with us, and that the governing classes of England are against us."

I greatly regret that Germany does not hold similar demonstrations. They cost nothing and "internationally" bring in large returns. Germany would have all the more warrant for these, as in this war she has done more for the Yankees than France in the eighteenth century. It is the old German stupidity of not making herself felt in the world theater and stressing what she actually accomplishes.

ENGELS TO MARX, FEBRUARY 17, 1863

Things look rotten in Yankeeland. It is true that with the customary irony of world history the Democrats, as against the philistine, have now become the war party, and the bankrupt poetaster Ch. Mackay has again made himself thoroughly ridiculous. I also hear from private sources in New York that the preparations of the North are being continued on a hitherto unheard-of scale. But, on the other hand, the signs of moral slackening are increasing daily, and the inability to conquer is daily becoming greater. Where is the party whose victory and *avènement*[7] would be synonymous with prosecution of the war *à outrance*[8] and by every means? The *people* has been bamboozled, that is the trouble, and it is lucky that a peace is a physical impossibility, otherwise they would have made one long ago, merely to be able to live for the almighty dollar again.

A Confederate major, who participated in the engagements near Richmond on Lee's staff, told me during the last few days that according to papers which Lee himself had shown him, the rebels had no less than 40,000 stragglers at the end of these actions! He referred specifically to the Western regiments of the Federals with great respect; for the rest, however, he is an ass. [*The conclusion of this letter is missing—Ed.*]

ENGELS TO MARX, JUNE 11, 1863

There are nice goings-on in America. Fighting Joe has made an awful fool of himself with his boasts,[9] Rosecrans is asleep, and only Grant operates well. His movement against Vicksburg from southwest to northeast, cutting off the relief army, repulsing it; then

---

7   Advent; appearance on the scene.
8   To the finish.
9   Refers to General Hooker. Toward the close of March 1863, Hooker announced to his officers that his plans were perfect and that he would have no mercy upon Lee. At the battle of Chancellorsville (May 1863), the Confederate army, though outnumbered two to one, forced Hooker to retreat. Despite this reverse, the Union commander issued an order in which he congratulated his army for its "achievements." (For his General Orders, No. 49, see *War of the Rebellion: Official Records, Army*, 1 ser., xxv, pt. 1, p. 171).

rapid advance against Vicksburg; and even the impetuous, unavailing assaults are all very good. I do not believe in the possibility of assembling sufficient relief troops in time. On the other hand, we have so often seen the American generals suddenly operate well for a fortnight and then perpetrate the greatest asininities once more, that one can say nothing whatever about their future movements.

MARX TO ENGELS, MAY 26, 1864

What do you say of Grant's operations? The *Times*, of course, has admiration only for Lee's strategy, concealed behind retreats. "It," said Tussy[10] this morning, "considers this very canny, I dare say." I wish for nothing more fervently than that Butler may have success. It would be priceless, if he marched into Richmond first. It would be bad if Grant had to retreat, but I think that fellow knows what he is about. At any rate, the first Kentucky campaign, Vicksburg, and the beating that Bragg got in Tennessee are due to him.

MARX TO ENGELS, JUNE 7, 1864

The American news seems to me to be very good, and I was particularly delighted with today's leader in the *Times*, in which it proves that Grant is being beaten continuously and will possibly be punished for his defeats—by the capture of Richmond.

MARX TO ENGELS, SEPTEMBER 7, 1864

As regards America, I consider the present moment, *entre nous*, to be very critical. If it brings Grant a great defeat or Sherman a great victory, then it's all right. A chronic series of small checks, precisely at the present election time, would be dangerous. I am entirely of your opinion that thus far Lincoln's reelection is pretty certain,

---

10   Refers to Eleanor Marx, Karl Marx's youngest daughter. She became the wife of the English socialist, Edward Aveling, and took an active part in the British labor movement.

still a hundred to one. But in the model country of the democratic swindle this election time is full of contingencies that may give the logic of events (an expression that Magnus Urquhartus[11] considers to be just as senseless as "the justice of a locomotive") a quite unexpected smack in the face. An armistice seems to be very necessary for the South, to save it from complete exhaustion. It has been the first to bring up this cry not only in its Northern organs, but directly in the Richmond organs, though now, when it has found an echo in New York, the *Richmond Examiner* throws it back to the Yankees with scorn. That Mr. Davis has decided to treat the Negro soldiers as "prisoners of war"—latest official instruction of his War Secretary—is very characteristic.

Lincoln has in his hands great resources with which to carry this election. (Peace proposals on his part are naturally mere humbug!) The election of an opposition candidate would probably lead to a real *revolution.* But all the same one cannot fail to recognize that for the coming eight weeks, in which the issue will in the first instance be decided, much depends on military accident. This is absolutely the most critical point since the beginning of the war. If this is shifted, old Lincoln can then blunder on to his heart's content. For the rest, the old man cannot possibly "make" generals. He could already choose his ministers better. The Confederate papers, however, attack their ministers quite as much as the Yankees do those at Washington. If Lincoln gets through this time—as is very probable—it will be on a much more radical platform and under wholly changed circumstances. In conformity with his legal manner, the old man will then find more radical methods compatible with his conscience.

MARX TO ENGELS, DECEMBER 2, 1864

The worst of such an agitation is that one is much bothered as soon as one participates in it. For example, it was again a matter of an

---

11 The "Great Urquhart," or David Urquhart, who was a British diplomat, writer and publisher of *The Free Press*, to which Marx contributed from 1856–7.

Address, this time to Lincoln,[12] and again I had to compose the stuff (which was much harder than a substantial work), in order that the phraseology to which this sort of scribbling is restricted should at least be distinguished from the democratic, vulgar phraseology...

As the Address to Lincoln was to be handed to Adams, *part* of the Englishmen on the Committee wanted to have the deputation introduced by a member of Parliament, since it was customary. This hankering was defeated by the majority of the English and the unanimity of the Continentals, and it was declared, on the contrary, that such old English customs ought to be abolished. On the other hand, M. Le Lubez[13], like a real *crapaud*, wanted to have the Address made out not to Lincoln, but to the American people. I have made him duly ridiculous and explained to the Englishmen that the French democratic etiquette is not worth a farthing more than the monarchical etiquette.

MARX TO ENGELS, FEBRUARY 6, 1865

... Lincoln's answer[14] to us is in today's *Times*.

MARX TO ENGELS, FEBRUARY 10, 1865

The fact that Lincoln has replied to us so courteously and to the "Bourgeois Emancipation Society" so rudely and purely formally has made the *Daily News* so angry that it did *not* print the reply to us. When, however, it saw to its sorrow that the *Times* did so, it had to publish it *belatedly* in the *stop press*. *Levy*, too, has had to swallow the bitter pill. The difference between L[incoln]'s reply to us and to the bourgeois has made such a stir here that the "Clubs" in the West

---

12   For the Address of the First International to Lincoln, see pp. 211–2.

13   Lubez was a French democrat who lived in London. He taught music and French and acted as secretary-correspondent for France in the general council of the First International. On account of intrigue and slander, Lubez was expelled from the International in 1866.

14   For Lincoln's answer to the Address of the First International, as transmitted by Adams, the American ambassador, see pp. 213–4.

End are shaking their heads over it. You can understand how much good this does our people.

MARX TO ENGELS, MARCH 4, 1865

The Confederacy seems to be at an end.

MARX TO ENGELS, JUNE 24, 1865

Johnson's policy disquiets me.[15] Ridiculous affectation of severity against single persons, up to the present extremely vacillating and weak in substance. The reaction has already begun in America and will soon be greatly strengthened, if the hitherto prevailing slackness does not quickly cease.

---

15   The elevation of Johnson to the presidency following the assassination of Lincoln was enthusiastically hailed by the leaders of the Radical wing of the Republican Party. They saw in the new president a mn after their own heart, a vigorous opponent of "the bloated slaveocracy" of the South. As such, they expected him to punish the ex-Confederate leaders, to break up their large landed estates and to guarantee Negro suffrage. Their expectations, however, were not realized, as Johnson, wedged between a falling oligarchy (slave planters) and a rising plutocracy (industrial and financial bourgeoisie), decided to fight the latter by capitulating to the former. The result was a "reactionary holiday" the beginnings of which became apparent in May 1865, when Johnson issued a proclamation providing for the reconstruction of seven Southern states along the lines laid down by Lincoln. During the summer and fall of 1865, all of these states, except Texas, complied with the President's request, elected state officials and sent representatives to Congress. However, in December 1865, both houses declined to permit the newly elected members to take their seats. Under these circumstances, the battle was on with Stevens, the leader of the parliamentary Left, gradually winning over a majority of congressmen to the formulation of a Radical reconstruction program. See J.S. Allen, *Reconstruction: The Battle for Democracy*, New York 1937. For the Address of the First International to Johnson, see pp. 214–5.

ENGELS TO MARX, JULY 15, 1865

I, too, like Mr. Johnson's policy less and less. His hatred of Negroes comes out more and more violently, while as against the old lords of the South he lets all power go out of his hands. If things go on like this, in six months all the old villains of secession will be sitting in Congress at Washington. Without colored suffrage nothing whatever can be done there, and J[ohnson] leaves it to the vanquished, the ex-slaveholders, to decide upon this matter. It is too absurd. However, one must certainly reckon with things developing differently from what Messrs. the Barons imagine. The majority of them are surely totally ruined and will be glad to sell land to migrants and speculators from the North. These will come soon enough and change many things. The mean whites, I think, will gradually die out. With this stock there is nothing more to be done; what is left after two generations will merge with the migrants into a stock entirely different. The Negroes will probably become small squatters, as in Jamaica. So that finally, indeed, the oligarchy goes down, but the process could now be brought to a speedy conclusion on the spot at one time, whilst, as it is, it becomes long-drawn-out.

MARX TO ENGELS, APRIL 23, 1866

After the Civil War phase the United States are really only now entering the revolutionary phase, and the European wiseacres, who believe in the omnipotence of Mr. Johnson, will soon be disillusioned.

INSTRUCTIONS FOR THE LONDON DELEGATES TO THE PROVISIONAL GENERAL COUNCIL OF THE IWA DRAFTED BY MARX IN AUGUST 1866

Limitation of the Working Day—A preliminary condition, without which all further attempts at improvement and emancipation must prove abortive, is the *limitation of the working day*. It is needed to restore the health and physical energies of the working class, that is the great body of every nation, as well as to secure them the possibility of intellectual development, social intercourse, social and political action. We propose eight hours' work as the *legal limit* of the working day, this limitation being generally agreed by the workmen of the United States of America, the Congress [of the IWA] will raise it to [become] the common platform of the working classes all over the world. [Adopted by the IWA and published in *Der Verbote*, 10 and 11, October–November 1866.]

MARX TO ENGELS, JULY 25, 1877

What do you think of the workers of the United States? This eruption against the oligarchy of associated capital which has arisen since the Civil War will of course be put down, but it could quite well form the starting point for the establishment of a serious workers party in the United States. There are, moreover, favorable circumstances. The policy of the new President will turn the Negroes into allies of the workers, and the large expropriations of the land (especially fertile land) in favor of the railway, mining, etc., companies will convert the farmers of the West, who are already very disenchanted, into allies of the workers. Thus a fine mess is in the offing there, and transferring the center of the International to the United States might, *post festum*, turn out to have been a peculiarly opportune move.

Letters between Marx and Lincoln

ADDRESS OF THE INTERNATIONAL WORKINGMEN'S ASSOCIATION TO ABRAHAM LINCOLN

To Abraham Lincoln,
President of the United States of America.

Sir,

We congratulate the American people upon your reelection by a large majority.

If resistance to the Slave Power was the reserved watchword of your first election, the triumphant war cry of your reelection is Death to Slavery.

From the commencement of the titanic American strife the workingmen of Europe felt instinctively that the star-spangled banner carried the destiny of their class. The contest for the territories which opened the dire *epopée*,[1] was it not to decide whether the virgin soil of immense tracts should be wedded to the labor of the immigrant or prostituted by the tramp of the slave driver?

When an oligarchy of 300,000 slaveholders dared to inscribe, for the first time in the annals of the world, "slavery" on the banner of armed revolt; when on the very spots where hardly a century ago the idea of one great democratic republic had first sprung up, whence the first Declaration of the Rights of Man was issued, and

---

1   Epic.

the first impulse given to the European revolution of the eighteenth century; when on those very spots counterrevolution, with systematic thoroughness, gloried in rescinding "the ideas entertained at the time of the formation of the old Constitution" and maintained "slavery to be a beneficent institution, indeed the only solution of the great problem of the relation of labor to capital," and cynically proclaimed property in man "the cornerstone of the new edifice," then the working classes of Europe understood at once, even before the fanatic partisanship of the upper classes for the Confederate gentry had given its dismal warning, that the slaveholders' rebellion was to sound the tocsin for a general holy crusade of property against labor, and that for the men of labor, with their hopes for the future, even their past conquests were at stake in that tremendous conflict on the other side of the Atlantic. Everywhere they bore therefore patiently the hardships imposed upon them by the cotton crisis, opposed enthusiastically the proslavery intervention, importunities of their "betters," and from most parts of Europe contributed their quota of blood to the good cause.

While the workingmen, the true political power of the North, allowed slavery to defile their own republic, while before the Negro, mastered and sold without his concurrence, they boasted it the highest prerogative of the white-skinned laborer to sell himself and choose his own master, they were unable to attain the true freedom of labor or to support their European brethren in their struggle for emancipation, but this barrier to progress has been swept off by the red sea of civil war.

The workingmen of Europe feel sure that as the American War of Independence initiated a new era of ascendancy for the middle class, so the American antislavery war will do for the working classes. They consider it an earnest of the epoch to come, that it fell to the lot of Abraham Lincoln, the single-minded son of the working class, to lead his country through the matchless struggle for the rescue of an enchained race and the reconstruction of a social world.

Signed on behalf of the International Workingmen's Association, the Central Council...

Bee-Hive (London), January 7, 1865

THE AMERICAN AMBASSADOR'S REPLY TO THE ADDRESS OF THE INTERNATIONAL WORKINGMEN'S ASSOCIATION

To the Editor of the Times.

Sir,

   Some few weeks since a congratulatory address was sent from the Central Council of the above Association to Mr. Lincoln. The address was transmitted through the United States' Legation and the following reply has been received. Its publication will oblige,

   Respectfully yours,

W. R. Cremer.
Legation of the United States,
London, Jan. 31.

Sir,

   I am directed to inform you that the address of the Central Council of your association, which was duly transmitted through this legation to the President of the United States, has been received by him. So far as the sentiments expressed by it are personal, they are accepted by him with a sincere and anxious desire that he may be able to prove himself not unworthy of the confidence which has been recently extended to him by his fellow citizens and by so many of the friends of humanity and progress throughout the world. The government of the United States has a clear consciousness that its policy neither is nor could be reactionary, but at the same time it adheres to the course which it adopted at the beginning, of abstaining everywhere from propagandism and unlawful intervention. It strives to do equal and exact justice to all states and to all men, and it relies upon the beneficial results of that effort for support at home and for respect and goodwill throughout the world. Nations do not exist for themselves alone, but to promote the welfare and happiness of mankind by benevolent intercourse and example. It is in this relation that the United States regard their cause in the present conflict with slavery-maintaining insurgents as the cause of human nature, and they derive new encouragement to persevere from the testimony of the workingmen of Europe that the national attitude is favored with their enlightened approval and earnest sympathies.

I have the honor to be, Sir, your obedient servant,

Charles Francis Adams.

The Times, February 6, 1865.

ADDRESS OF THE INTERNATIONAL WORKINGMEN'S ASSOCIATION TO PRESIDENT JOHNSON

To Andrew Johnson,
President of the United States.

Sir,

The demon of the "peculiar institution," for the supremacy of which the South rose in arms, would not allow his worshipers to honorably succumb on the open field. What he had begun in treason, he must needs end in infamy. As Philip II's war for the Inquisition bred a Gerard, thus Jefferson Davis's proslavery war a Booth.

It is not our part to call words of sorrow and horror, while the heart of two worlds heaves with emotion. Even the sycophants who, year after year and day by day, stuck to their Sisyphus work of morally assassinating Abraham Lincoln and the great republic he headed stand now aghast at this universal outburst of popular feeling, and rival with each other to strew rhetorical flowers on his open grave. They have now at last found out that he was a man neither to be browbeaten by adversity nor intoxicated by success; inflexibly pressing on to his great goal, never compromising it by blind haste; slowly maturing his steps, never retracing them; carried away by no surge of popular favor, disheartened by no slackening of the popular pulse; tempering stern acts by the gleams of a kind heart; illuminating scenes dark with passion by the smile of humor; doing his titanic work as humbly and homely as heaven-born rulers do little things with the grandiloquence of pomp and state; in one word, one of the rare men who succeed in becoming great, without ceasing to be good. Such, indeed, was the modesty of this great and good man, that the world only discovered him a hero after he had fallen a martyr.

To be singled out by the side of such a chief, the second victim to the infernal gods of slavery, was an honor due to Mr. Seward. Had he not, at a time of general hesitation, the sagacity to foresee and the manliness to foretell "the irrepressible conflict"? Did he not, in the darkest hours of that conflict, prove true to the Roman duty to never despair of the republic and its stars? We earnestly hope that he and his son will be restored to health, public activity, and well-deserved honors within much less than "90 days."

After a tremendous war, but [one] which, if we consider its vast dimensions, and its broad scope, and compare it to the Old World's 100 years' wars, and 30 years' wars, and 23 years' wars, can hardly be said to have lasted 90 days, yours, Sir, has become the task to uproot by the law what has been felled by the sword, to preside over the arduous work of political reconstruction and social regeneration. A profound sense of your great mission will save you from any compromise with stern duties. You will never forget that to initiate the new era of the emancipation of labor, the American people devolved the responsibilities of leadership upon two men of labor—the one Abraham Lincoln, the other Andrew Johnson.

Signed on behalf of the International Workingmen's Association, London, May 13, 1865, by the Central Council...

Bee-Hive, May 20, 1865

Articles

Woodhull & Clafin's Weekly

INDEPENDENCE VS. DEPENDENCE! WHICH?

Though not attributed, this article was likely written by Victoria Woodhull.

In this age of progress, wherein rapid strides are being made in all branches of civilization, woman seems to be about the only constituent feature devoid of the general spirit that controls. All the elements of society are becoming more distinctly individualized with increasing heterogeneity. Its lines of demarcation, while increasing numerically, become more distinct. The whole tendency is to individual independence and mutual dependence. It is most true that in the aid progress receives from peoples, the female element is but poorly represented, but its effects are sufficiently obvious and diffusive to demonstrate, even to her, that there must be a forward movement made by the sex, else it will be left entirely too far in the rear to perform even an unimportant part in the great wants that the immediate future will develop.

The wife was formerly the housekeeper; she is becoming less and less so every day. Many of the duties that once devolved upon her are now performed by special trades. Each branch of housewifery is coming to be the basis of a separate branch of business. Schools perform all the duties of education that once devolved upon the mother, and tailors and dressmakers absorb the labor of the ward-

Victoria Woodhull, 1872

robe. The grocer and the baker pretty nearly supply the table, while the idea of furnishing meals complete is rapidly gaining acceptance. Thus, one by one, the duties of the housewife are being taken from her by the better understanding and adaptation of principles of general economy.

While this revolution is in progress, the preparatory steps to cooperative housekeeping are being taken. Thousands live at one place and eat at another, when once such practice was unknown. Dining saloons are increasing more rapidly than any other branch of business, and more transient meals are eaten every day. The result of this will be a division of living under the two systems represented by the two classes of hotels—the table d'hôte and the à la carte. The residence portions of our cities will be converted into vast hotels, which will be arranged and divided for the accommodation of families of all sizes. A thousand people can live in one hotel, under one general system of superintendence, at much less expense than two hundred and fifty families of four members each can in as many houses and under as many systems. As a system of economy this practice is sure to prevail, for progress in this respect is as equally marked as in attainment, and, if we mistake not, is of a higher order. To obtain more effect from a given amount of power is a higher branch of science than to obtain the same by increasing the power. To lessen resistance is better than to increase power, and on this principle progress in the principles of living is being made toward cooperation. Allowing that the practice will become general, what will become of the "special sphere" of woman that is painted in such vivid colors by the opponents of the extension of female privileges? Are the powers of woman to be wasted upon vain frivolities so widely practiced now, when this principle is already operating, or are they to be cast in some useful channel—some honorable calling? Is fashion to consume the entire time of women of the immediate future, or shall they become active members of the social body, not only forming a portion of its numbers but contributing their share to the amount of results to be gained? True, the beginning of this practice is forcing woman into wider fields of usefulness; forcing them without preparation into competition with man, who has been trained to industry from youth—a vast disparity over which the complaint of unequal pay is sometimes raised without real cause.

Does woman foresee what these things are to lead to, or does she prefer to remain blind to the tendencies of progress in this regard? It is evident to every mind not willfully blind that woman is gradually merging into all the employments of life. [She is] being driven to it by the force of circumstances coming from new developments. It is a necessity. Occupation they must have, for not all women even will be content to lead useless lives. This condition is gradually increasing both in volume and extent, and with a persistency which overcomes all opposition custom offers, it proclaims its intentions. Why cannot its drift be recognized as a matter of course and all provisions made to help the cause along? Women who do not perceive these things, from habitual blindness to all that usefulness indicates, may be excused for their supineness; but men, who are habitually provident, stand condemned of inconsistency for all the opposition manifested to the course events will pursue.

In consideration of the fact that woman is entering the active sphere of life and is every day widening this sphere, can she sit in utter quiescence saying she has no desire to establish herself as an element of power politically? In this she voluntarily acknowledges her inferiority and her willingness to remain the political slave, which is but a shade removed from the slavery that cost the country so much life to extinguish.

However much man may at present resist the bold demands of the few now calling for political equality, were the sex as a whole to rouse itself into a comprehension of the situation and its prophecies, with the determination to assert equality of privilege in the control of that in which they have an equality of interest, he would not dare to refuse. Let the question be put home to yourselves in the light of rising events and considered with calmness and wisdom. Are you willing to remain a political nonentity, a dependent upon the consideration of those who do possess political rights, and be subservient to masters of others' making? Shall you not the rather demand political equality, basing it on an equality of interest in the results to be obtained through the exercise of political rights? The first means continued dependence; the last means the beginning of independence. These are the questions. Consider them.

June 25, 1870

THE RIGHTS OF CHILDREN

We clip the following sensible remarks from an article in the Philadelphia *Daily Chronicle*, and commend them to the consideration of our readers:

This is the age when, for the first time in human history, the rights of all living things are, in some way, recognized as existing. We are far enough yet from according to all their rights, but we talk about them; we see them, and thought is busy to determine how they should be best secured.

Even the dumb animals have their advocates. The bird flies, and the horse labors, exempt from many a former abuse, danger, or ill. Man, with his superior muscle and pluck, has secured for himself a recognition that forbids others to trample upon privileges which he calls his own. And woman, too, is rising with her demand that whatever is man's right should also be conceded as her right as well. It is an age of rights; we wish to give all their due; and those who cannot speak for themselves must be spoken for.

In regard to women, our idea is that their present condition is neither as bad as it has been nor as good as it will be. There has already been so much thought and said about their rights as to receive some modification and a fairer degree of common justice. But in regard to the rights of children very little has been thought, or said, or done. They cannot speak for themselves. There are few to speak for them. They are still looked upon very much as property. It is still conceded that their parents have an exclusive right to them. If those parents wish to send them to beg day after day, it is thought that they have an undoubted right to do so. If they desire to send their children forth as bootblacks at six or eight years of age, there are few interested, or disposed, to dispute their right to do so. Or, if they will that their children must stand all day at the loom, or by the spindles, or do some kind of manual work, instead of going to school, it is usually regarded as right that they should do even this. Nobody, perhaps, regards it as wisdom for them to do any of these things, but there are enough who regard it as an undoubted parental prerogative.

Now it is just this which we wish to stoutly and emphatically deny. The children have rights of their own, rights in which society ought to protect them in all cases where parental wisdom fails to do it. Children are not property. They are not the born servants and slaves of their parents. They belong to themselves, and it is their inalienable right to be, in an age like this, fitted for taking some useful and self-supporting place in the world's works. It is their right to receive an education according to their capacity, just as good as our public schools can provide. No parental authority has any right to intervene between them and those advantages which shall make their experience and influence in life the best possible. It is really of less consequence that the home of today be uncomfortable, than that both it and the homes of its children should be without promise. And parents should not be allowed to sacrifice the future of their children to their own desire to get on a little further in the world. Children ought to be protected against this shortsighted avarice of their fathers and mothers. Children are not to blame for the ignorance in which they are growing up. The fault is first parental, then social. If parents are poor and ignorant, general laws ought to provide that every child should not suffer unnecessarily from neglect, and humane individuals ought to see to it that in every neighborhood those laws take effect.

These poor parents plead that they need the work of their children to help in the maintenance of the family, to buy the clothing and the daily bread. In some cases this plea is just. In a larger number of cases it is groundless. Where it is just, it would be a better public economy to keep the family and pay for the children's schooling than to allow the parents to deprive the children of their early advantages, their right to the privilege of education. The better citizens they would then become would more than repay the community in dollars and cents for its forethought and justice.

It ought to be a recognized first principle that every child born into the bosom of society has a right to the very best we can do for it. The welfare of the whole community is more or less involved in its welfare. If it is so cared for as to be useful and productive, society is the gainer. But if it be left in neglect, becomes a vagrant, a criminal, or a sot, society is continually taxed for its support and has constantly a heavy bill of expenses to defend itself from its vicious depredations. If we do not secure to children their inalienable rights, we suffer grievously for our neglect. We make the public expense greater, the public safety less, the public morality lower, and allow the whole public tone to fall far below the demands of a nominally Christian and enlightened age.

There are many other considerations touching the rights of children which are applicable to their treatment in the home. But today we had in view their treatment by society—its duty to secure them protection against the enslaving desire of poor and ignorant parents. We have abundant occasion to consider the matter. Here stand these twenty thousand children who have no schooling, no wise provisions made for them, who are beggars, vagrants, little bootblacks, newsboys, and who are maturing every day. What are their prospects? What are they likely to become? What are all the Christians, all the philanthropists, all the wealthy and the wise doing to secure them their higher rights?

December 5, 1870

INTERVIEW WITH KARL MARX, THE HEAD OF L'INTERNATIONALE

R. Landor

You have asked me to find out something about the International Association, and I have tried to do so. The enterprise is a difficult one just now. London is indisputably the headquarters of the association, but the English people have got a scare, and smell International in everything as King James smelled gunpowder after the famous plot. The consciousness of the society has naturally increased with the suspiciousness of the public, and if those who guide it have a secret to keep, they are of the stamp of men who keep a secret well. I have called on two of their leading members, have talked with one freely, and I here give you the substance of my conversation. I have satisfied myself of one thing: that it is a society of genuine workingmen, but that these workmen are directed by social and political theories of another class. One man whom I saw, a leading member of the council, was sitting at his workman's bench during our interview, and left off talking to me from time to time to receive a complaint, delivered in no courteous tone, from one of the many little masters in the neighborhood who employed him. I have heard this same man make eloquent speeches in public, inspired in every passage with the energy of hate toward the classes that call themselves his rulers. I understood the speeches after this glimpse at the domestic life of the orator. He must have felt that he had brains enough to have organized a working government, and yet here he was obliged to devote his life to the most revolting task work of a mechanical profession. He was proud and sensitive, and yet at every turn he had to return a bow for a grunt and a smile for a command that stood on about the same level in the scale of civility with a huntsman's

call to his dog. This man helped me to a glimpse of one side of the
nature of the International, the result of LABOR AGAINST CAPITAL
of the workman who produces against the middleman who enjoys.
Here was the hand that would smile hard when the time came, and
as to the head that plans, I think I saw that too, in my interview
with Dr. Karl Marx.

Dr. Karl Marx is a German doctor of philosophy, with a German
breadth of knowledge derived both from observation of the living
world and from books. I should conclude that he has never been
a worker in the ordinary sense of the term. His surroundings and
appearance are those of a well-to-do man of the middle class. The
drawing room into which I was ushered on the night of the interview would have formed very comfortable quarters for a thriving
stockbroker who had made his competence and was now beginning
to make his fortune. It was comfort personified, the apartment of
a man of taste and of easy means, but with nothing in it peculiarly
characteristic of its owner. A fine album of Rhine views on the table,
however, gave a clue to his nationality. I peered cautiously into the
vase on the side table for a bomb. I sniffed for petroleum, but the
smell was the smell of roses. I crept back stealthily to my seat, and
moodily awaited the worst.

He has entered and greeted me cordially, and we are sitting face-
to-face. Yes, I am tête-à-tête with the revolution incarnate, with the
real founder and guiding spirit of the International Society, with
the author of the address in which capital was told that if it warred
on labor it must expect to have its house burned down about its
ears—in a word, with the APOLOGIST FOR THE COMMUNE of Paris.
Do you remember the bust of Socrates? the man who died rather
than protest his belief in the Gods of the time—the man with the
fine sweep of profile for the forehead running meanly at the end
into a little snub, curled-up feature, like a bisected pothook, that
formed the nose. Take this bust in your mind's eye, color the beard
black, dashing it here and there with puffs of gray; clap the head
thus made on a portly body of the middle height, and the Doctor
is before you. Throw a veil over the upper part of the face and you
might be in the company of a born vestryman. Reveal the essential
feature, the immense brow, and you know at once that you have to

deal with that most formidable of all composite individual forces—
a dreamer who thinks, a thinker who dreams.

I went straight to my business. The world, I said, seemed to be
in the dark about the International, hating it very much but not
able to say clearly what thing it hated. Some, who professed to
have peered further into the gloom than their neighbors, declared
that they had made out a sort of Janus figure, with a fair, honest
workman's smile on one of its faces, and on the other a murderous
conspirator's scowl. Would he light up the case of mystery in which
the theory dwelt?

The professor laughed—chuckled a little, I fancied, at the thought
that we were so frightened of him. "There is no mystery to clear up,
dear sir," he began, in a very polished form of the Hans Breitmann
dialect, "except perhaps the mystery of human stupidity in those
who perpetually ignore the fact that our association is a public one,
and that the fullest reports of its proceedings are published for all
who care to read them. You may buy our rules for a penny, and a
shilling laid out in pamphlets will teach you almost as much about
us as we know ourselves."

R. L.: Almost—yes, perhaps so, but will not the something I shall
not know constitute the all-important reservation? To be quite
frank with you, and to put the case as it strikes an outside observer,
this general claim of depreciation of you must mean something
more than the ignorant ill-will of the multitude. And it is still
pertinent to ask, even after what you have told me, What is the
International Society?

Dr. M.: You have only to look at the individuals of which it is
composed—workmen.

R. L.: Yes, but the soldier need be no exponent of the statecraft
that sets him in motion. I know some of your members, and I can
believe that they are not of the stuff of which conspirators are made.
Besides, a secret shared by a million men would be no secret at all.
But what if these were only the instruments in the hands of a bold
and—I hope you will forgive me for adding—not overscrupulous
conclave.

Dr. M.: There is nothing to prove it.

R. L.: The last Paris insurrection?

Dr. M.: I demand firstly the proof that there was any plot at all—that anything happened that was not the legitimate effect of the circumstances of the moment; or, the plot granted, I demand the proofs of the participation in it of the International Association.

R. L.: The presence in the communal body of so many members of the association.

Dr. M.: Then it was a plot of the Freemasons too, for their share in the work as individuals was by no means a slight one. I should not be surprised, indeed, to find the Pope setting down the whole insurrection to their account. But try another explanation. The insurrection in Paris was made by the workmen of Paris. The ablest of the workmen must necessarily have been its leaders and administrators, but the ablest of the workmen happen also to be members of the International Association. Yet the association, as such, may be in no way responsible for their action.

R. L.: It will seem otherwise to the world. People talk of secret instructions from London, and even grants of money. Can it be affirmed that the alleged openness of the association's proceedings precludes all secrecy of communication?

Dr. M.: What association ever formed carried on its work without private as well as public agencies? But to talk of secret instruction from London, as of decrees in the matter of faith and morals from some center of Papal domination and intrigue, is wholly to misconceive the nature of the International. This would imply a centralized form of government for the International, whereas the real form is designedly that which gives the greatest play to local energy and independence. In fact, the International is not properly a government for the working class at all. It is a bond of union rather than a controlling force.

R. L.: And of union to what end?

Dr. M.: The economical emancipation of the working class by the conquest of political power. The use of that political power to the attainment of social ends. It is necessary that our aims should be thus comprehensive to include every form of working-class activity. To have made them of a special character would have been to adapt them to the needs of one section—one nation of workmen alone. But how could all men be asked to unite to further the objects of a few? To have done that, the association must have forfeited its title of International. The association does not dictate the form of political movements; it only requires a pledge as to their end. It is a network of affiliated societies spreading all over the world of labor. In each part of the world some special aspect of the problem presents itself, and the workmen there address themselves to its consideration in their own way. Combinations among workmen cannot be absolutely identical in detail in Newcastle and in Barcelona, in London and in Berlin. In England, for instance, the way to show political power lies open to the working class. Insurrection would be madness where peaceful agitation would more swiftly and surely do the work. In France, a hundred laws of repression and a mortal antagonism between classes seem to necessitate the violent solution of social war. The choice of that solution is the affair of the working classes of that country. The International does not presume to dictate in the matter, and hardly to advise. But to every movement it accords its sympathy and its aid within the limits assigned by its own laws.

R. L.: And what is the nature of that aid?

Dr. M.: To give an example, one of the commonest forms of the movement for emancipation is that of strikes. Formerly, when a strike took place in one country, it was defeated by the importation of workmen from another. The International has nearly stopped all that. It receives information of the intended strike; it spreads that information among its members, who at once see that for them the seat of the struggle must be forbidden ground. The masters are thus left alone to reckon with their men. In most cases the men require no other aid than that. Their own subscriptions or those of the societies to which they are more immediately affiliated supply them with funds, but should the pressure upon them become too heavy and the strike be one of which the association approves, their necessities are supplied out of the common purse. By these means a strike of the cigar makers of Barcelona was brought to a victorious issue the other day. But the society has no interest in strikes, though it supports them under certain conditions. It cannot possibly gain by them in a pecuniary point of view, but it may easily lose. Let us sum it all up in a word. The working classes remain poor amid the increase of wealth, wretched amid the increase of luxury. Their material privation dwarfs their moral as well as their physical stature. They cannot rely on others for a remedy. It has become then with them an imperative necessity to take their own case in hand. They must revise the relations between themselves and the capitalists and landlords, and that means they must transform society. This is the general end of every known workmen's organization—land and labor leagues, trade and friendly societies, cooperative stores and cooperative production are but means toward it. To establish a perfect solidarity between these organizations is the business of the International Association. Its influence is beginning to be felt everywhere. Two papers spread its views in Spain, three in Germany, the same number in Austria and in Holland, six in Belgium, and six in Switzerland. And now that I have told you what the International is, you may, perhaps, be in a position to form your own opinion as to its pretended plots.

R. L.: And Mazzini, is he member of your body?

Dr. M. (laughing): Ah, no. We should have made but little progress if we had not got beyond the range of his ideas.

R. L.: You surprise me. I should certainly have thought that he represented most advanced views.

Dr. M.: He represents nothing better than the old idea of a middle-class republic. We seek no part with the middle class. He has fallen as far to the rear of the modern movement as the German professors, who, nevertheless, are still considered in Europe as the apostles of the cultured democratism of the future. They were so at one time—before '48, perhaps, when the German middle class, in the English sense, had scarcely attained its proper development. But now they have gone over bodily to the reaction, and the proletariat knows them no more.

R. L.: Some people have thought they saw signs of a positivist element in your organization.

Dr. M.: No such thing. We have positivists among us, and others not of our body who work as well. But this is not by virtue of their philosophy, which will have nothing to do with popular government as we understand it, and which seeks only to put a new hierarchy in place of the old one.

R. L.: It seems to me, then, that the leaders of the new international movement have had to form a philosophy as well as an association for themselves.

Dr. M.: Precisely. It is hardly likely, for instance, that we could hope to prosper in our war against capital if we derived our tactics, say, from the political economy of Mill. He has traced one kind of relationship between labor and capital. We hope to show that it is possible to establish another.

R. L.: And the United States?

Dr. M.: The chief centers of our activity are for the present among the old societies of Europe. Many circumstances have hitherto tended to prevent the labor problem from assuming an all-absorbing importance in the United States. But they are rapidly disappearing, and it is rapidly coming to the front there with the growth, as in Europe, of a laboring class distinct from the rest of the community and divorced from capital.

R. L.: It would seem that in this country the hoped-for solution, whatever it may be, will be attained without the violent means of revolution. The English system of agitating by platform and press until minorities become converted into majorities is a hopeful sign.

Dr. M.: I am not so sanguine on that point as you. The English middle class has always shown itself willing enough to accept the verdict of the majority, so long as it enjoyed the monopoly of the voting power. But mark me: as soon as it finds itself outvoted on what it considers vital questions, we shall see here a new slave-owner's war.

I have here given you as well as I can remember them the heads of my conversation with this remarkable man. I shall leave you to form your own conclusions. Whatever may be said for or against the probability of its complicity with the movement of the Commune, we may be assured that in the International Association the civilized world has a new power in its midst with which it must soon come to a reckoning for good or ill.

August 12, 1871

Conclusion to *Black and White*

Thomas Fortune

I know it is not fashionable for writers on economic questions to tell the truth, but the truth should be told, though it kill. When the wail of distress encircles the world, the man who is linked by "the touch of nature" which "makes the whole world kin" to the common destiny of the race universal, who hates injustice wherever it lifts up its head, who sympathizes with the distressed, the weak, and the friendless in every corner of the globe, such a man is morally bound to tell the truth as he conceives it to be the truth.

In these times, when the lawmaking and enforcing authority is leagued against the people, when great periodicals—monthly, weekly, and daily—echo the mandates or anticipate the wishes of the powerful men who produce our social demoralization, it becomes necessary for the few men who do not agree to the arguments advanced or the interests sought to be bolstered up to "cry aloud and spare not." The man who with the truth in his possession flatters with lies, that "thrift may follow fawning," is too vile to merit the contempt of honest men.

The government of the United States confiscated as "contraband of war" the slave population of the South, but it left to the portion of the unrepentant rebel a far more valuable species of property. The slave, the perishable wealth, was confiscated to the government and then manumitted, but property in land, the wealth which perishes not nor can fly away, and which had made the institution of slavery possible, was left as the heritage of the robber who had not hesitated to lift his iconoclastic hand against the liberties of his country.

Thomas Fortune, 1887

The baron of feudal Europe would have been paralyzed with astonishment at the leniency of the conquering invader who should take from him his slave, subject to mutation, and leave him his landed possessions, which are as fixed as the Universe of Nature. He would ask no more advantageous concession. But the United States took the slave and left the thing which gave birth to *chattel slavery* and which is now fast giving birth to *industrial slavery*, a slavery more excruciating in its exactions, more irresponsible in its machinations than that other slavery, which I once endured. The chattel slave–holder must, to preserve the value of his property, feed, clothe, and house his property and give it proper medical attention when disease or accident threaten its life. But industrial slavery requires no such care. The new slaveholder is only solicitous of obtaining the maximum of labor for the minimum of cost. He does not regard the man as of any consequence when he can no longer produce. Having worked him to death, or ruined his constitution and robbed him of his labor, he turns him out upon the world to live upon the charity of mankind or to die of inattention and starvation. He knows that it profits him nothing to waste time and money upon a disabled industrial slave. The multitude of laborers from which he can recruit his necessary laboring force is so enormous that solicitude on his part for one that falls by the wayside would be a gratuitous expenditure of humanity and charity which the world is too intensely selfish and materialistic to expect of him. Here he forges wealth and death at one and the same time. He could not do this if our social system did not confer upon him a monopoly of the soil from which subsistence must be derived, because the industrial slave, given an equal opportunity to produce for himself, would not produce for another. On the other hand, the large industrial operations, with the multitude of laborers from which Adam Smith declares employers grow rich, as far as this applies to the soil would not be possible, since the vast volume of increased production brought about by the industry of the multitude of coequal small farmers would so reduce the cost price of food products as to destroy the incentive to speculation in them, and at the same time utterly destroy the necessity or the possibility of famines, such as those which have from time to time come upon the Irish people. There could be no famine, in the natural course of things, where all had an opportunity to cultivate as much land as they could wherever they found any not already under cultivation by someone else. It needs no stretch of the imagination to see what a startling tendency the announcement that all vacant land was free to settlement upon condition of cultivation would have to the depopulation of overcrowded cities like New York, Baltimore, and Savannah, where the so-called pressure of population upon subsistence has produced a hand-to-hand fight for existence by the wage workers in every avenue of industry.

This is no fancy picture. It is a plain, logical deduction of what would result from the restoration to the people of that equal chance in the race of life which every man has a right to expect, to demand, and to exact as a condition of his membership of organized society.

The wag who started the "forty acres and a mule" idea among the black people of the South was a wise fool; wise in that he enunciated a principle which every argument of sound policy should have dictated, *upon the condition that the forty acres could in no wise be alienated*, and that it could be regarded *only as property as long as it was cultivated;* and a fool because he designed simply to impose upon the credulity and ignorance of his victims. But the justness of the "forty acre" donation cannot be controverted. In the first place, the slave had earned this miserable stipend from the government by two hundred years of unrequited toil, and, secondly, as a free man, he was inherently entitled to so much of the soil of his country as would suffice to maintain him in the freedom thrust upon him. To tell him he was a free man, and at the same time shut him off from free access to the soil upon which he had been reared, without a penny in his pocket, and with an army of children at his coattail— some of his reputed wife's children being the illegitimate offspring of a former inhuman master—was to add insult to injury, to mix syrup and hyssop, to aggravate into curses the pretended conference of blessings.

When I think of the absolutely destitute condition of the colored people of the South at the close of the Rebellion, when I remember the moral and intellectual enervation which slavery had produced in them, when I remember that not only were they thus bankrupt but that they were absolutely and unconditionally cut off from the soil, with absolutely no right or title in it, I am surprised—not that they have already got a respectable slice of landed interests, not that they have taken hold eagerly of the advantages of moral and intellectual opportunities of development placed in their reach by the charitable philanthropy of good men and women, not that they have bought homes and supplied them with articles of convenience and comfort, often of luxury—but I am surprised that the race did not turn robbers and highwaymen, and in turn terrorize and rob society as society had for so long terrorized and robbed them. The thing is strange, marvelous, phenomenal in the extreme. Instead of becoming outlaws, as the critical condition would seem to have indicated, the black men of the South *went manfully to work* to better their own condition and the crippled condition of the country which had been produced by the ravages of internecine rebellion; *while the white men of the South, the capitalists, the land-sharks, the poor white trash, and the nondescripts, with a thousand years of Christian civilization and culture behind them, with "the boast of chivalry, the pomp of power," these white scamps, who had imposed upon the world the idea that they were paragons of virtue and the heaven-sent vicegerents of civil power, organized themselves into a band of outlaws whose concatenative chain of auxiliaries ran through the entire South, and deliberately proceeded to murder innocent men and women for* POLITICAL REASONS *and to systematically rob them of their honest labor, because they were too accursedly lazy to labor themselves.*

But this highly abnormal, unnatural condition of things is fast passing away. The white man, having asserted his superiority in the matters of assassination and robbery, has settled down upon a barrel of dynamite, as he did in the days of slavery, and will await the explosion with the same fatuity and self-satisfaction true of him in other days. But as convulsions from within are more violent and destructive than convulsions from without, being more deep-seated and therefore more difficult to reach, the next explosion will be more disastrous, more far-reaching in its havoc than the one which metamorphosed social conditions in the South and from the dreadful reactions of which we are just now recovering.

As I have said elsewhere, the future struggle in the South will be not between white men and black men but between capital and labor, landlord and tenant. Already the cohorts are marshalling to the fray; already the forces are mustering to the field at the sound of the slogan.

The same battle will be fought upon Southern soil that is in preparation in other states, where the conditions are older in development, but no more deep-seated, no more pernicious, no more blighting upon the industries of the country and the growth of the people.

It is not my purpose here to enter into an extended analysis of the foundations upon which our land system rests, nor to give my views as to how matters might be remedied. I may take up the question at some future time. It is sufficient for my purpose to have indicated that the social problems in the South, as they exfoliate more and more as resultant upon the war, will be found to be the same as those found in every other section of our country, and to have pointed out that the questions of "race," "condition," "politics," etc. will all properly adjust themselves with the advancement of the people in wealth, education, and forgetfulness of the unhappy past.

The hour is approaching when the laboring classes of our country, North, East, West and South, will recognize that they have a *common cause*, a *common humanity*, and a *common enemy*, and that therefore, if they would triumph over wrong and place the laurel wreath upon triumphant justice, without distinction of race or of previous condition *they must unite!* And unite they will, for "a fellow feeling makes us wond'rous kind." When the issue is properly joined, the rich, be they black or be they white, will be found upon the same side, and the poor, be they black or be they white, will be found on the same side.

Necessity knows no law and discriminates in favor of no man or race.

Preface to the American Edition of *The Condition of the Working-Class in England*

Frederick Engels[1]

Ten months have elapsed since, at the translator's wish, I wrote the Appendix[2] to this book, and during these ten months, a revolution has been accomplished in American society such as in any other country would have taken at least ten years. In February 1885, American public opinion was almost unanimous on this one point: that there was no working class, in the European sense of the word, in America; that consequently no class struggle between workmen and capitalists such as tore European society to pieces was possible in the American Republic; and that, therefore, Socialism was a thing of foreign importation which could never take root on American soil. And yet at that moment the coming class struggle was casting its gigantic shadow before it in the strikes of the Pennsylvania coal miners, and of many other trades, and especially in the preparations all over the country for the great Eight Hours' movement, which was to come off, and did come off, in the May following. That I then duly appreciated these symptoms, that I anticipated a

---

1 Published in the American edition of *The Condition of the Working-Class in England*, New York 1887. Printed according to the text of the book.
2 The Appendix to the American edition of *The Condition of the Working-Class in England* was, except for the paragraph quoted in the next footnote, used by Engels as the basis of his preface to the English edition of 1892.

working-class movement on a national scale, my Appendix shows,[3] but no one could then foresee that in such a short time the movement would burst out with such irresistible force, would spread with the rapidity of a prairie fire, would shake American society to its very foundations.

The fact is there, stubborn and indisputable. To what an extent it had struck with terror the American ruling classes was revealed to me, in an amusing way, by American journalists who did me the honor of calling on me last summer; the "new departure" had put them into a state of helpless fright and perplexity. But at that time the movement was only just on the start; there was but a series of confused and apparently disconnected upheavals of that class which, by the suppression of negro slavery and the rapid development of manufactures, had become the lowest stratum of American society.

---

3   In this appendix Engels wrote: "There were two circumstances which for a long time prevented the unavoidable consequences of the Capitalist system from showing themselves in the full glare of day in America. These were the easy access to the ownership of cheap land, and the influx of immigration. They allowed, for many years, the great mass of the native American population to "retire" in early manhood from wage labor and to become farmers, dealers, or employers of labor, while the hard work for wages, the position of a proletarian for life, mostly fell to the lot of immigrants. But America has outgrown this early stage. The boundless backwoods have disappeared, and the still more boundless prairies are faster and faster passing from the hands of the Nation and the States into those of private owners. The great safety valve against the formation of a permanent proletarian class has practically ceased to act. A class of lifelong and even hereditary proletarians exists at this hour in America. A nation of sixty millions striving hard to become, and with every chance of success, too, the leading manufacturing nation of the world—such a nation cannot permanently import its own wage-working class, not even if immigrants pour in at the rate of half a million a year. The tendency of the Capitalist system towards the ultimate splitting-up of society into two classes, a few millionaires on the one hand, and a great mass of mere wageworkers on the other, this tendency, though constantly crossed and counteracted by other social agencies, works nowhere with greater force than in America; and the result has been the production of a class of native American wageworkers, who form, indeed, the aristocracy of the wage-working class as compared with the immigrants, but who become conscious more and more every day of their solidarity with the latter and who feel all the more acutely their present condemnation to lifelong wage toil, because they still remember the bygone days, when it was comparatively easy to rise to a higher social level."—*Ed.*

Frederick Engels, 1879

Before the year closed, these bewildering social convulsions began to take a definite direction. The spontaneous, instinctive movements of these vast masses of working people, over a vast extent of country, the simultaneous outburst of their common discontent with a miserable social condition, the same everywhere and due to the same causes, made them conscious of the fact that they formed a new and distinct class of American society, a class of—practically speaking—more or less hereditary wageworkers, proletarians. And with true American instinct this consciousness led them at once to take the next step towards their deliverance: the formation of a political workingmen's party, with a platform of its own, and with the conquest of the Capitol and the White House for its goal. In May, the struggle for the Eight Hours' working day, the troubles in Chicago, Milwaukee, etc., the attempts of the ruling class to crush the nascent uprising of Labor by brute force and brutal class justice; in November, the new Labor Party organized in all great centers, and the New York, Chicago, and Milwaukee elections. May and November have hitherto reminded the American bourgeoisie only of the payment of coupons of U.S. bonds; henceforth May and November will remind them, too, of the dates on which the American working class presented *their* coupons for payment.

In European countries, it took the working class years and years before they fully realized the fact that they formed a distinct and, under the existing social conditions, a permanent class of modern society, and it took years again until this class consciousness led them to form themselves into a distinct political party, independent of, and opposed to, all the old political parties formed by the various sections of the ruling classes. On the more favored soil of America, where no medieval ruins bar the way, where history begins with the elements of modern bourgeois society as evolved in the seventeenth century, the working class passed through these two stages of its development within ten months.

Still, all this is but a beginning. That the laboring masses should feel their community of grievances and of interests, their solidarity as a class in opposition to all other classes; that in order to give expression and effect to this feeling, they should set in motion the political machinery provided for that purpose in every free country—that is the first step only. The next step is to find the common remedy for these common grievances, and to embody it in the platform of the new Labor Party. And this—the most important and the most difficult step in the movement—has yet to be taken in America.

A new party must have a distinct positive platform, a platform which may vary in details as circumstances vary and as the party itself develops, but still one upon which the party, for the time being, is agreed. So long as such a platform has not been worked out, or exists but in a rudimentary form, so long the new party, too, will have but a rudimentary existence; it may exist locally but not yet nationally; it will be a party potentially but not actually.

That platform, whatever may be its first initial shape, must develop in a direction which may be determined beforehand. The causes that brought into existence the abyss between the working class and the capitalist class are the same in America as in Europe; the means of filling up that abyss are equally the same everywhere. Consequently, the platform of the American proletariat will in the long run coincide, as to the ultimate end to be attained, with the one which, after sixty years of dissensions and discussions, has become the adopted platform of the great mass of the European militant proletariat. It will proclaim, as the ultimate end, the conquest of political supremacy by the working class, in order to effect the direct appropriation of all means of production—land, railways, mines, machinery, etc.—by society at large, to be worked in common by all for the account and benefit of all.

But if the new American party, like all political parties everywhere, by the very fact of its formation aspires to the conquest of political power, it is as yet far from agreed upon what to do with that power when once attained. In New York and the other great cities of the East, the organization of the working class has proceeded upon the lines of Trades' Societies, forming in each city a powerful Central Labor Union. In New York the Central Labor Union, last November, chose for its standard-bearer Henry George, and consequently its temporary electoral platform has been largely imbued with his principles. In the great cities of the Northwest, the electoral battle was fought upon a rather indefinite labor platform, and the influence of Henry George's theories was scarcely, if at all, visible. And while in these great centers of population and of industry the new class movement came to a political head, we find all over the country two widespread labor organizations: the Knights of Labor[4] and the Socialist Labor Party,[5] of which only the latter

---

4 The Noble Order of the Knights of Labor was a working-class organization founded in Philadelphia in 1869. Existing illegally until 1878, it observed a semi-mysterial ritual. That year the organization emerged from the underground, retaining some of its secret features. The Knights of Labor aimed to liberate workers by setting up cooperatives. They took in all skilled and even unskilled trades, without discrimination on account of sex, race, nationality, or religion. The organization reached the highest point of its activity during the 1880s, when, under pressure from the masses, the leaders of the order were compelled to consent to an extensive strike movement. Its membership at that time was over 700,000, including 60,000 Negroes. However, on account of the opportunistic tactics of the leaders, who were opposed to revolutionary class struggle, the order forfeited its prestige among the masses. Its activity came to an end in the next decade.

5 The Socialist Labor Party came into existence in 1876 as a result of the union of the American sections of the First International with other working-class

has a platform in harmony with the modern European standpoint as summarized above.

Of the three more or less definite forms under which the American labor movement thus presents itself, the first, the Henry George movement in New York, is for the moment of a chiefly local significance. No doubt New York is by far the most important city of the States, but New York is not Paris and the United States are not France. And it seems to me that the Henry George platform, in its present shape, is too narrow to form the basis for anything but a local movement, or at best for a short-lived phase of the general movement. To Henry George, the expropriation of the mass of the people from the land is the great and universal cause of the splitting up of the people into Rich and Poor. Now this is not quite correct historically. In Asiatic and classical antiquity, the predominant form of class oppression was slavery; that is to say, not so much the expropriation of the masses from the land as the appropriation of their persons. When, in the decline of the Roman Republic, the free Italian peasants were expropriated from their farms, they formed a class of "poor whites" similar to that of the Southern Slave States before 1861, and between slaves and poor whites, two classes equally unfit for self-emancipation, the old world went to pieces. In the Middle Ages, it was not the expropriation of the people *from*, but on the contrary their appropriation *to* the land which became the source of feudal oppression. The peasant retained his land, but was attached to it as a serf or villein, and made liable to tribute to the lord in labor and in produce. It was only at the dawn of modern times, towards the end of the fifteenth century, that the expropriation of the peasantry on a large scale laid the foundation for the modern class of wageworkers who possess nothing but their labor power and can live only by the selling of that labor power to others. But if the expropriation from the land brought this class into existence, it was the development of capitalist production, of modern industry and agriculture on a large scale, which perpetuated it, increased it, and shaped it

---

socialist organizations in the United States. This party consisted mainly of immigrants, particularly Germans. Its activities were sectarian, and its leaders, because they refused to work in the trade unions, were incapable of heading the mass movement of the American workers.

into a distinct class with distinct interests and a distinct historical mission. All this has been fully expounded by Marx (*Capital*,
Part VIII: "The So-Called Primitive Accumulation"). According
to Marx, the cause of the present antagonism of the classes and
of the social degradation of the working class is their expropriation from *all* means of production, in which the land is of course
included.

If Henry George declares land monopolization to be the sole
cause of poverty and misery, he naturally finds the remedy in the
resumption of the land by society at large. Now, the Socialists of
the school of Marx, too, demand the resumption, by society, of the
land, and not only of the land but of all other means of production likewise. But even if we leave these out of the question, there
is another difference. What is to be done with the land? Modern
Socialists, as represented by Marx, demand that it should be held
and worked in common and for common account, and the same
with all other means of social production, mines, railways, factories,
etc.; Henry George would confine himself to letting it out to individuals as at present, merely regulating its distribution and applying
the rents for public, instead of, as at present, for private purposes.
What the Socialists demand implies a total revolution of the whole
system of social production; what Henry George demands leaves
the present mode of social production untouched, and has, in fact,
been anticipated by the extreme section of Ricardian bourgeois
economists who, too, demanded the confiscation of the rent of land
by the State.

It would of course be unfair to suppose that Henry George has
said his last word once for all. But I am bound to take his theory
as I find it.

The second great section of the American movement is formed by
the Knights of Labor. And that seems to be the section most typical
of the present state of the movement, as it is undoubtedly by far the
strongest. An immense association, spread over an immense extent
of country in innumerable "assemblies," representing all shades of
individual and local opinion within the working class, the whole of
them sheltered under a platform of corresponding indistinctness
and held together much less by their impracticable constitution
than by the instinctive feeling that the very fact of their clubbing

together for their common aspiration makes them a great power in the country: a truly American paradox, clothing the most modern tendencies in the most medieval mummeries and hiding the most democratic and even rebellious spirit behind an apparent, but really powerless, despotism—such is the picture the Knights of Labor offer to a European observer. But if we are not arrested by mere outside whimsicalities, we cannot help seeing in this vast agglomeration an immense amount of potential energy evolving slowly but surely into actual force. The Knights of Labor are the first national organization created by the American working class as a whole; whatever be their origin and history, whatever their shortcomings and little absurdities, whatever their platform and their constitution, here they are, the work of practically the whole class of American wageworkers: the only national bond that holds them together, that makes their strength felt to themselves not less than to their enemies, and that fills them with the proud hope of future victories. For it would not be exact to say that the Knights of Labor are liable to development. They are constantly in full process of development and revolution, a heaving, fermenting mass of plastic material seeking the shape and form appropriate to its inherent nature. That form will be attained as surely as historical evolution has, like natural evolution, its own immanent laws. Whether the Knights of Labor will then retain their present name or not makes no difference, but to an outsider it appears evident that here is the raw material out of which the future of the American working-class movement, and along with it the future of American society at large, has to be shaped.

The third section consists of the Socialist Labor Party. This section is a party but in name, for nowhere in America has it, up to now, been able actually to take its stand as a political party. It is, moreover, to a certain extent foreign to America, having until lately been made up almost exclusively by German immigrants, using their own language and for the most part little conversant with the common language of the country. But if it came from a foreign stock, it came, at the same time, armed with the experience earned during long years of class struggle in Europe, and with an insight into the general conditions of working-class emancipation far superior to that hitherto gained by American workingmen. This is a fortunate circumstance for the American proletarians, who thus are enabled to appropriate, and to take advantage of, the intellectual and moral fruits of the forty years' struggle of their European class-mates, and thus to hasten on the time of their own victory. For, as I said before, there cannot be any doubt that the ultimate platform of the American working class must and will be essentially the same as that now adopted by the whole militant working class of Europe, the same as that of the German-American Socialist Labor Party. So far, this party is called upon to play a very important part in the movement. But in order to do so, they will have to doff every remnant of their foreign garb. They will have to become out-and-out American. They cannot expect the Americans to come to them; they, the minority and the immigrants, must go to the Americans, who are the vast majority and the natives. And to do that, they must above all things learn English.

The process of fusing together these various elements of the vast moving mass—elements not really discordant, but indeed mutually isolated by their various starting points—will take some time and will not come off without a deal of friction, such as is visible at different points even now. The Knights of Labor, for instance, are here and there, in the Eastern cities, locally at war with the organized Trades Unions. But then, this same friction exists within the Knights of Labor themselves, where there is anything but peace and harmony. These are not symptoms of decay for capitalists to crow over. They are merely signs that the innumerable hosts of workers, for the first time set in motion in a common direction, have as yet found out neither the adequate expression for their common interests, nor the form of organization best adapted to the struggle, nor the discipline required to insure victory. They are as yet the first levies *en masse* of the great revolutionary war, raised and equipped locally and independently, all converging to form one common army, but as yet without regular organization and common plan of campaign. The converging columns cross each other here and there; confusion, angry disputes, even threats of conflict arise. But the community of ultimate purpose in the end overcomes all minor troubles; ere long, the straggling and squabbling battalions will be formed in a long line of battle array, presenting to the enemy a well-ordered front, ominously silent under their glittering arms, supported by bold skirmishers in front and by unshakable reserves in the rear.

To bring about this result, the unification of the various independent bodies into one national Labor Army, with no matter how inadequate a provisional platform, provided it be a truly working-class platform—that is the next great step to be accomplished in America. To effect this, and to make that platform worthy of the cause, the Socialist Labor Party can contribute a great deal, if they will only act in the same way as the European Socialists acted at the time when they were but a small minority of the working class. That line of action was first laid down in the *Communist Manifesto* of 1847 in the following words:

> The Communists [that was the name we took at the time and which even now we are far from repudiating] do not form a separate party opposed to other working-class parties.
>
> They have no interests separate and apart from the interests of the whole working class.
>
> They do not set up any sectarian principles of their own, by which to shape and model the proletarian movement.
>
> The Communists are distinguished from the other working-class parties by this only: 1. In the national struggles of the proletarians of the different countries, they point out, and bring to the front, the common interests of the whole proletariat, interests independent of all nationality; 2. In the various stages of development which the struggle of the working class against the capitalist class has to pass through, they always and everywhere represent the interests of the movement as a whole.
>
> The Communists, therefore, are on the one hand practically the most advanced and resolute section of the working-class parties of all countries, that section which ever pushes forward all others; on the other hand, theoretically, they have over the great mass of the proletarians the advantage of clearly understanding the line of march, the conditions, and the ultimate general results of the proletarian movement.
>
> Thus they fight for the attainment of the immediate ends, for the enforcement of the momentary interests of the working class, but in the movement of the present, they represent and take care of the future of the movement.

That is the line of action which the great founder of Modern Socialism, Karl Marx, and with him I and the Socialists of all nations, who worked along with us, have followed for more than forty years, with the result that it has led to victory everywhere, and that at this moment the mass of European Socialists in Germany and in France; in Belgium, Holland, and Switzerland; in Denmark and Sweden as well as in Spain and Portugal are fighting as one common army under one and the same flag.

Frederick Engels
London, January 26, 1887

Speeches at the Founding of the Industrial Workers of the World

Lucy Parsons

I can assure you that after the intellectual feast that I have enjoyed immensely this afternoon, I feel fortunate to appear before you now in response to your call. I do not wish you to think that I am here to play upon words when I tell you that I stand before you and feel much like a pygmy before intellectual giants, but that is only the fact.

I wish to state to you that I have taken the floor because no other woman has responded and I feel that it would not be out of place for me to say in my poor way a few words about this movement. We, the women of this country, have no ballot even if we wished to use it, and the only way that we can be represented is to take a man to represent us. You men have made such a mess of it in representing us that we have not much confidence in asking you, and I for one feel very backward in asking the men to represent me. We have no ballot, but we have our labor. I think it is August Bebel, in his *Woman in the Past, Present and Future*—a book that should be read by every woman that works for wages—Bebel says that men have been slaves throughout all the ages, but that woman's condition has been worse, for she has been the slave of a slave.

There was never a greater truth uttered. We are the slaves of the slaves. We are exploited more ruthlessly than men. Wherever wages are to be reduced, the capitalist class use women to reduce them, and if there is anything that you men should do in the future it is to

Lucy Parsons, c. 1886

organize the women. And I say that if the women had inaugurated a boycott of the State Street stores since the teamsters' strike, the stores would have surrendered long ago. I do not stand before you to brag. I had no man connected with that strike to make it of interest to me to boycott the stores, but I have not bought one penny's worth there since that strike was inaugurated. I intended to boycott all of them as one individual at least, so it is important to educate the women.

Now, I wish to show my sisters here that we fasten the chains of slavery upon our sisters, sometimes unwittingly, when we go down to the department store and look around so cheap. When we come to reflect, it simply means the robbery of our sisters, for we know that the things cannot be made for such prices and give women who made them fair wages. I wish to say that I have attended many conventions in the twenty-seven years since I came here to Chicago a young girl, so full of life and animation and hope. It is to youth that hope comes; it is to age that reflection comes. I have attended conventions from that day to this, of one kind and another, and taken part in them. I have taken part in some in which our Comrade Debs had a part. I was at the organization that he organized in this city some eight or ten years ago. Now, the point I want to make is that these conventions are full of enthusiasm. And that is right: we should sometimes mix sentiment with soberness; it is a part of life.

But when you go out of this hall, when you have laid aside your enthusiasm, then comes the solid work. Are you going out of here with your minds made up that the class which we call ourselves, revolutionary Socialists so-called—that class is organized to meet organized capital with the millions at its command? It has many weapons to fight us. First, it has money. Then, it has legislative tools. Then, it has armories, and last, it has the gallows. We call ourselves revolutionists. Do you know what the capitalists mean to do to you revolutionists? I simply throw these hints out that you young people may become reflective and know what you have to face at the first, and then it will give you strength. I am not here to cause any discouragement, but simply to encourage you to go on in your grand work.

Now, that is the solid foundation that I hope this organization will be built on—that it may be built not like a house upon the sand, that when the waves of adversity come it may go over into the ocean of oblivion, but that it shall be built upon a strong, granite-hard foundation, a foundation made up of the hearts and aspirations of the men and women of this twentieth century, who have set their minds, their hands, their hearts, and their heads against the past with all its miserable poverty, with its wage slaves, with its children ground into dividends, with its miners away down under the earth and with never the light of sunshine, and with its women selling the holy name of womanhood for a day's board. I hope we understand that this organization has set its face against that iniquity, and that it has set its eyes to the rising star of liberty that means fraternity, solidarity, the universal brotherhood of man. I hope that while politics have been mentioned here—I am not one of those who, because a man or woman disagrees with me, cannot act with them—I am glad and proud to say I am too broad-minded to say they are a faker or fool or a fraud because they disagree with me.

My view may be narrow and theirs may be broad, but I do say to those who have intimated politics here as being necessary or a part of this organization, that I do not impute to them dishonesty or impure motives. But as I understand the call for this convention, politics had no place here; it was simply to be an economic organization, and I hope for the good of this organization that when we go away from this hall, and our comrades go some to the west, some to the east, some to the north, and some to the south, while some remain in Chicago, and all spread this light over this broad land and carry the message of what this convention has done, that there will be no room for politics at all.

There may be room for politics—I have nothing to say about that—but it is a bread-and-butter question, an economic issue, upon which the fight must be made. Now, what do we mean when we say revolutionary Socialist? We mean that the land shall belong to the landless, the tools to the toiler, and the products to the producers. Now, let us analyze that for just a moment, before you applaud me. First, the land belongs to the landless. Is there a single landowner in this country, who owns his land by the constitutional rights given by the constitution of the United States, who will allow you to vote it away from him? I am not such a fool as to believe it. We say, "The tools belong to the toiler." They are owned by the capitalist class. Do you believe they will allow you to go into the halls of the legislature and simply say, "Be it enacted that on and after a certain day the capitalist shall no longer own the tools and the factories and the places of industry, the ships that plow the ocean and our lakes?"

Do you believe that they will submit? I do not. We say, "The product belongs to the producers." It belongs to the capitalist class as their legal property. Do you think that they will allow you to vote them away from them by passing a law and saying, "Be it enacted that on and after a certain day Mr. Capitalist shall be dispossessed?" You may, but I do not believe it. Hence, when you roll under your tongue the expression that you are revolutionists, remember what that word means. It means a revolution that shall turn all these things over where they belong—to the wealth producers.

Now, how shall the wealth producers come into possession of them? I believe that if every man and every woman who works, or who toils in the mines, the mills, the workshops, the fields, the factories, and the farms in our broad America should decide in their minds that they shall have that which of right belongs to them, and that no idler shall live upon their toil, and when your new organization, your economic organization, shall declare as man to man and woman to woman, as brothers and sisters, that you are determined that you will possess these things, then there is no army that is large enough to overcome you, for you yourselves constitute the army. Now, when you have decided that you will take possession of these things, there will not need to be one gun fired or one scaffold erected.

You will simply come into your own, by your own independence and your own manhood, and by asserting your own individuality, and not sending any man to any legislature in any State of the American Union to enact a law that you shall have what is your own—yours by nature and by your manhood and by your very presence upon this Earth. Nature has been lavish to her children. She has placed in this Earth all the material of wealth that is necessary to make men and women happy. She has given us brains to go into her storehouse and bring from its recesses all that is necessary. She has given us these two hands and these brains to manufacture them on a parallel with all other civilizations.

There is just one thing we lack, and we have only ourselves to blame if we do not become free. We simply lack the intelligence to take possession of that hope, and I feel that the men and women who constitute a convention like this can come together and organize that intelligence. I feel that you will at least listen to me, and maybe you will disagree with it.

I wish to say that my conception of the future method of taking possession of this Earth is that of the general strike; that is my conception of it. The trouble with all the strikes in the past has been this: the workingmen, like the teamsters of our cities, these hardworking teamsters, strike and go out and starve. Their children starve. Their wives get discouraged. Some feel that they have to go out and beg for relief, and to get a little coal to keep the children warm, or a little bread to keep the wife from starving, or a little something to keep the spark of life in them so that they can remain wage slaves. That is the way with the strikes in the past.

My conception of the strike of the future is not to strike and go out and starve, but to strike and remain in and take possession of the necessary property of production. If anyone is to starve—I do not say it is necessary—let it be the capitalist class. They have starved us long enough, while they have had wealth and luxury and all that is necessary. You men and women should be imbued with the spirit that is now displayed in far-off Russia and far-off Siberia, where we thought the spark of manhood and womanhood had been crushed out of them. Let us take example from them.

We see the capitalist class fortifying themselves today behind their Citizens' Associations and Employers' Associations in order that they may crush the American labor movement. Let us cast our eyes over to far-off Russia and take heart and courage from those who are fighting the battle there, and from the further fact shown in the dispatches that appear this morning in the news that carries the greatest terror to the capitalist class throughout the world—the emblem that has been the terror of all tyrants through all the ages, and there you will see that the red flag has been raised.

According to the *Tribune*, the greatest terror is evinced in Odessa and all through Russia because the red flag has been raised. They know that where the red flag has been raised, whoever enroll themselves beneath that flag recognize the universal brotherhood of man; they recognize that the red current that flows through the veins of all humanity is identical, that the ideas of all humanity are identical, that those who raise the red flag, it matters not where, whether on the sunny plains of China or on the sun-beaten hills of Africa or on the far-off snowcapped shores of the north, or in Russia or America, that they all belong to the human family and have an identity of interest. That is what they know.

So when we come to decide, let us sink such differences as nationality, religion, politics, and set our eyes eternally and forever towards the rising star of the industrial republic of labor, remembering that we have left the old behind and have set our faces toward the future. There is no power on Earth that can stop men and women who are determined to be free at all hazards. There is no power on Earth so great as the power of intellect. It moves the world and it moves the Earth.

Now, in conclusion, I wish to say to you—and you will excuse me because of what I am going to say and only attribute it to my interest in humanity. I wish to say that nineteen years ago on the fourth of May of this year, I was one of those at a meeting at the Haymarket in this city to protest against eleven workingmen being shot to pieces at a factory in the southeastern part of this city because they had dared to strike for the eight-hour movement that was to be inaugurated in America in 1886.

The Haymarket meeting was called primarily and entirely to protest against the murder of comrades at the McCormick factory. When that meeting was nearing its close someone threw a bomb. No one knows to this day who threw it except the man who threw it. Possibly he has rendered his account with nature and has passed away. But no human being alive knows who threw it. And yet in the soil of Illinois, the soil that gave a Lincoln to America, the soil in which the great, magnificent Lincoln was buried, in the State that was supposed to be the most liberal in the union, five men sleep the last sleep in Waldheim under a monument that has been raised there because they dared to raise their voices for humanity. I say to any of you who are here and can do so, it is well worth your time to go out there and draw some inspiration around the graves of the first martyrs who fell in the great industrial struggle for liberty on American soil.

I say to you that even within the sound of my voice, only two short blocks from where we meet today, the scaffold was erected on which those five men paid the penalty for daring to raise their voices against the iniquities of the age in which we live.

We are assembled here for the same purpose. And do any of you older men remember the telegrams that were sent out from Chicago while our comrades were not yet even cut down from the cruel gallows?

"Anarchy is dead, and these miscreants have been put out of the way."

Oh, friends, I am sorry that I even had to use that word, *anarchy*, just now in your presence, which was not in my mind at the outset.

So if any of you wish to go out there and look at this monument that has been raised by those who believed in their comrades' innocence and sincerity, I will ask you, when you have gone out and looked at the monument, that you will go to the reverse side of the monument and [read] there on the reverse side the words of a man, himself the purest and the noblest man who ever sat in the gubernatorial chair of the State of Illinois, John P. Altgeld. On that monument you will read the clause of his message in which he pardoned the men who were lingering then in [prison in] Joliet.

I have nothing more to say. I ask you to read the words of Altgeld, who was at that time the governor, and had been a lawyer and a judge, and knew whereof he spoke, and then take out your copybooks and copy the words of Altgeld when he released those who had not been slaughtered at the capitalists' behest, and then take them home and change your minds about what those men were put to death for.

Now, I have taken up your time in this because I simply feel that I have a right as a mother, and as the wife of one of those sacrificed men, to say whatever I can to bring the light to bear upon this conspiracy and to show you the way it was. Now, I thank you for the time that I have taken up of yours. I hope that we will meet again some time, you and I, in some hall where we can meet and organize the wageworkers of America, the men and women, so that the children may not go into the factories, nor the women into the factories, unless they go under proper conditions.

I hope even now to live to see the day when the first dawn of the new era will have arisen, when capitalism will be a thing of the past, and the new industrial republic, the commonwealth of labor, shall be in operation. I thank you.

June 29, 1905

Acknowledgments

Thanks to Audrea Lim for assembling and presenting the texts by Marx, Lincoln and others. The writings of both Karl Marx and Abraham Lincoln are voluminous and available in many forms. Those reprinted here are just a small sample to explain the onset and course of the Civil War in the United States. To these we have added a few writings by others who contributed to America's postwar social radicalization, but without attempting to duplicate the extensive and important documentation of the black experience of the war or of Reconstruction.

All the Lincoln speeches can be found on the US Library of Congress website, www.loc.gov.

Marx's "The North American Civil War" and "The Civil War in the United States" were taken from Marx's Political Writings, Volume 2, Surveys From Exile (Verso, 2010). The remaining articles in the "Karl Marx" section were taken from Karl Marx & Frederick Engels' The Civil War in the United States (International Publishers, 1861).

The "Letter from Marx to Annenkov" was taken from Marx Engels Collected Works, Volume 38 (International Publishers, 1975). The remaining letters were taken from Karl Marx & Frederick Engels' The Civil War in the United States (International Publishers, 1969).

"Independence vs. Dependence! Which?" is from Woodhull & Clafin's Weekly, June 25, 1870; "The Rights of Children" is from Woodhull & Clafin's Weekly, December 6, 1870; and "Interview with Karl Marx" is from Woodhull & Clafin's Weekly, August 12, 1871, all on microfiche.

Thomas Fortune's "Conclusion" to Black and White was taken from Thomas Fortune, Black and White (Washington Square Press, 2007).

Engels' "Preface to the US Edition" was taken from Fredriech Engels, The Condition of the Working Class in England (Oxford University Press, 1999).

Lucy Parson's "Speeches at the Founding Convention of the Industrial Workers of the World" was taken from Lucy Parsons, Freedom, Equality & Solidarity (Charles H. Kerr, 2004).